AGAINST THE WIND

AGAINST THE WIND

Reflections on a Self-Determined Life

REINHOLD MESSNER

Translation by James Heath

MOUNTAINEERS BOOKS

MOUNTAINEERS BOOKS is dedicated to the exploration, preservation, and enjoyment of outdoor and wilderness areas.

1001 SW Klickitat Way, Suite 201, Seattle, WA 98134
800-553-4453, www.mountaineersbooks.org

Printed in Canada
Distributed in the United Kingdom by Cordee, www.cordee.co.uk
28 27 26 25 1 2 3 4 5

Design and layout: Ellis Failor-Rich
The translator wishes to thank proofreader Sally Maßmann.
Excerpt on pp. 147–148 © by *Frankfurter Allgemeine Zeitung.* All rights reserved.
Provided by Frankfurter Allgemeine Archive.
Excerpts on pp. 120 and 284 © *Süddeutsche Zeitung.*

Cover photograph: Reinhold Messner in Antarctica (courtesy of Diane Messner)
Photographs and illustrations are from the archive of Reinhold Messner, except the following: pages 10 and 259, Patrick Hürlimann; pages 16, 104, and 273, Diane Messner; page 143, Reini Buchacher, www.buhaha.com; page 179, Georg Tappeiner; page 217, Peppi Tischler; page 218, Staschitz; page 275, courtesy of Florian Jänicke

Library of Congress Cataloging-in-Publication Data is on file for this title.

Mountaineers Books titles may be purchased for corporate, educational, or other promotional sales, and our authors are available for a wide range of events. For information on special discounts or booking an author, contact our customer service at 800-553-4453 or mbooks@mountaineersbooks.org.

Printed on 100% recycled paper and FSC-certified materials®

ISBN (hardcover): 978-1-68051-817-7
ISBN (paperback): 978-1-68051-818-4
ISBN (ebook): 978-1-68051-819-1

An independent nonprofit publisher since 1960

An air walker is someone who follows their heart. They belong to nobody. Air walkers do what they want, and aren't afraid of anything or anyone. Themselves least of all. And because they're not fearful and listen to their heart, they're able to walk through air.

—Robert Schneider, from *Die Luftgängerin*

You force many to relearn about you;
they charge it bitterly against you.
You came close to them and yet passed by;
that they will never forgive.
You pass over and beyond them:
but the higher you ascend,
the smaller you appear to
the eye of envy.

—Friedrich Nietzsche, *Thus Spoke Zarathustra*

CONTENTS

The Thirteen Winds

Headwind
Tailwind
Storm wind
Summit wind
Valley wind
Whirlwind
Fall wind
Windless
Glacier wind
Icy wind
Crosswind
Upwind
Tornado

—Reinhold Messner

HEADWIND

Battling headwinds has been a constant theme if not *the* constant theme of my life. The way I was brought up made me rebellious. Kicking against and overcoming barriers were formative experiences. Each barrier encountered that was unjust, unwelcome or pointless, I challenged and ultimately overcame. During our expedition to the South Pole in 1989, Arved Fuchs and I fought a strong headwind. It often magnified to become a storm that seemed to blow right at us from the Pole itself. Day after day. We had sails with us and attempted to tack into the wind. We were able to ski faster as a result, but it didn't get us one single meter closer to the South Pole. Hoping for a tailwind, we were forced to drag the sleds through heavy snow and torturous sastrugi. We hoped in vain—all the way to the South Pole. On the other side, during the descent from the polar cap to the McMurdo Station, we experienced our first real tailwind. Our heavy sleds, holding us back for more than a thousand kilometers, were now much lighter. We had consumed a significant amount of our provisions and fuel. With the wind from the Pole at our backs, we were finally able to gain ground.

Many years later, in Greenland my brother Hubert and I managed to pull our heavy sleds east to west over the Greenland Ice Sheet thanks to side winds. Then we used our sails to help us proceed northward.

In 1986, with Hans Kammerlander, in the ice couloir on the Lhotse normal route, a serendipitous jet stream from behind helped us ascend. Apart from these instances though, the wind has mostly been against me—on narrow ridges, summit faces, or while pitching tents. And especially back in civilization when it came to coping with criticism.

My mountaineering is more of an art than a sport. It's all about the lines of my routes, telling the story, coping with the danger and the vastness. We mountaineers grow in the face of resistance. Or we fail and stay in the valley. If you want to climb a rock face or a mountain, you have to overcome barriers.

Doing so requires strength and skill, and above all endurance. In 1911, when Paul Preuss climbed alone and unroped through the steep east summit face of Guglia di Brenta in the Dolomites, he made his mark. His climb is a work of art that you can't see or hear, yet it exists all the same. For

High over Sulden on the Ortler

eternity. The same applies to Hermann Buhl, when he climbed Nanga Parbat in 1953 via the Silver Saddle to the summit. He did more than just show what endurance we are capable of. He left us a permanent reminder of his creativity, willpower, and courage in the face of extreme hardship. When Alexander Huber free climbed the great roof via *Pan Aroma* up the north face of the Westliche Zinne/Cima Ovest in the Dolomites in 2007, it was a creative achievement. His wild, spider-like line was a unique act closer to art than sport. He made a mark too—in terms of his spirit. Not all of these extraordinary activities were applauded. Many of our achievements, and more importantly our attitudes, were criticized, called into question, and even demonized, which is how they started to become part of the great legend.

Mountaineers seldom express themselves via paintbrushes, chisels, words, or music. They do it their way by climbing the biggest walls, in huge arenas and between the Earth's gaps and rifts. Their art evolves at the crossroads between mountain nature and human nature. Between the familiar and unfamiliar, self-injury and potential self-destruction, which they seek to avoid step by step, hold by hold. Artists take a similar approach. Giving their all to their work, they are inspired by the same spirit as mountaineers—explorers of limits who leave their mark in unexplored terrain. Their mark-making can be seen in the mountains too. Sometimes they are carved in tree trunks. You hear them when the winds play with the ropes securing their sculptures. You see their colors blending in with the natural surroundings. Perhaps they also have an aerial perspective and see the bigger picture, as climbers do.

When we come down from the mountains, we all go back to our normal lives, carrying the echoes, the silence, the big skies, and the slow pace of altitude with us. This gives us plenty of cause for internal reflection. It seems that it is my destiny to confront my inner skeptic.

Why does this strange, seemingly pointless yet useful, mountaineering game straddle the worlds of art and sport? Is it because traditional mountaineers follow anarchic patterns in an archaic world? Mountaineers don't fight against each other, but alongside each other. Mountaineering is about surviving—not following rules. It's about making it or dying and then, back home, how outsiders perceive this seemingly absurd dichotomy.

It's crucial to protect what's left of wilderness from the so-called civilized world, to prioritize taking action before consumption and to put up with any resistance from the world at large.

I have endured many strong headwinds and have often failed—over and over again—but I've remained undeterred. Critics come and go. Some have dogged me all my life. While others still refuse to recognize that it's in part thanks to their efforts that I have survived. Enduring strong winds means you have to grow wings.

I've talked openly about my wounds, misfortune, and hardships, and I have endured reproaches of the worst kind. I have been subjected to trials far beyond me—including character assassination. A legend about Messner has been woven from all these elements. A legend that I never wanted to be. My part in the great story of alpinism doesn't come down just to me. It has a lot to do with my many opponents too.

The traditional mountaineering narrative is based on anecdotes but also on imagination and legend. We are shaped by the storytelling ability of the mountaineering pioneers and the power of their images created over 200 years of climbing history. My generation embraced these old stories and added our own new experiences. Now we continue to tell the legend. When my wife Diane and I founded Messner Mountain Heritage on my seventy-fifth birthday, we wanted to preserve and champion everything that inspires millions of mountain enthusiasts around the world. We're a silent partnership without hard-and-fast rules, united by our love of the mountains. We're part of a magnificent story, but aren't bothered about belonging to any particular category.

My legacy isn't material. It's the spirit that inspired traditional alpinism—it's grounded in respect.

1

LEARNING TO TAKE RESPONSIBILITY

Human nature and mountain nature can only be understood when the two meet.

—physicist Werner Heisenberg

Growing up as village kids, my siblings and I learned to take responsibility from an early age. We looked after our younger siblings, did our chores, saw to the chickens, collected firewood, and helped out in the garden. When I recall my childhood, I see no idyllic pictures, no church towers, no green hills, no sheep in the meadows. I see only mountains—the forests and distant rocky towers beyond. Living in the countryside has since become part of the Zeitgeist. People admire rural life, nature's magnificence, and the fact that everyone says hello to each other. But such things were simply part of our everyday life.

We had a very pragmatic relationship with our village and its immediate vicinity. The forests were adventure playgrounds, the barns places to hide, the gravel road the meeting point for a horde of children, girls and boys between ages four and twelve.

I never wanted to live like the city kids. I only wanted to be in the village and experience this feeling of sticking together. And I never missed a chance to join in the games we played.

Being outdoors involved a lot of responsibility, which is what made it so exciting. As a boy, I hated being ill, alone in my bedroom, listening to the birds and the children playing outside. Time seemed to move backward. I remember feeling scared of being left out.

In summer, a few of us older kids were allowed to go up to the Gschnagenhardt Alm—a seasonal alpine meadow where the cows grazed. Everything was different there. In contrast to down in the village, there were no priests, no teachers, and no elders to tell us what to do or what not to do. After a trial period of a few weeks, our parents even let us stay up there on our own. We explored the surrounding area, observed wildlife, and went out on our first easy climbing trips. We were really proud, because we had to take responsibility for ourselves. We felt our way around the rock faces and cirques; no one explained them to us. We learned to give danger a wide berth and overcome stumbling blocks.

Overcoming obstacles is part of our DNA. In wild natural environments, day-to-day life was and still is all about survival. The instincts we develop in the process force us to react to danger, despite the circumstances. The same goes for situations where bad people want to hurt other people. My experiences taught me that manmade obstacles can be more destructive than natural ones. Nature has no intentions, and where it has been allowed to remain wild, it can prove a wise teacher.

My introduction to nature wasn't the result of some romantic idea. At the beginning, I didn't see it as an alternative to the industrialized world, and it had little to do with conservation. I was right there in its midst, exposed to it, and had to deal with my fears and doubts.

Back then, I had no idea that these early experiences in the wilderness would enable me to develop important survival skills. They would stand me in good stead on the highest mountains and the widest deserts of this planet. And they support me even more now in a civilization at the mercy of conspiracy theories, hatred, and deliberately orchestrated disinformation. My problem is that I get lost in cyberspace.

2

OVERCOMING RESISTANCE

I've never let schooling interfere with my education.

—writer Grant Allen

Mountains defy every headwind; they represent resistance in its purest form, as we learned on the Geisler/Odle Peaks in the Dolomites, which rise between Villnöss Valley and Gardena Valley. My older brother Helmut has plenty to say on the subject in his account of our climbing trip together during a summer holiday up at the Gschnagenhardt Alm:

> As kids and teenagers, we spent many summers on Gschnagenhardt. After the alpine meadows were mown in mid-August, our parents rented an alpine hut and hay barn from an old farmer from Ranui, where we slept in the scratchy hay. We would buy milk and butter from the neighboring farm on Profanter Alm. Up there, we lived a carefree existence with lots of freedom. The Alm was the perfect base to explore the surrounding area and the Geisler/Odle mountains. We built a raft for the marshy pond, played hide and seek, collected wild chanterelles, raspberries, and mountain cranberries. We romped everywhere with our catapults, aiming at squirrels and birds, without any success.
>
> When we were a bit older, we regularly hiked via the Panascharte over to the Seceda Alm, a high flowery alpine meadow on the southern side of the Geisler/Odle. The Alm looked down over the Gardena Valley, the Sella massif and the Langkofel Group. We felt like explorers discovering a new world. There were tiny fish in the mountain lakes on the meadows. We spent ages trying to work out how to catch and transport them back in our water bottles to Gschnagenhardt via the steep, narrow Mittagsscharte pass. Few of them survived the journey.

During those summer holidays, we often went climbing. I can remember one adventure in particular. While looking for a shorter, more direct route to the southern side of the Odle peaks, Reinhold had seen a narrow notch between the Grosse Fermeda and Kleine Fermeda. He wanted to tackle this exploratory tour just with me, so without our younger siblings. We were 13 and 15 at the time. We took our father's rope and a few slings so that we could belay or abseil. Heading over brittle, but not difficult, rocky terrain, we climbed over the northern side of the notch and down the southern side toward Seceda. Suddenly, we reached the edge of a large cliff. It was too high to abseil down. And down-climbing wasn't possible either, there was too much of an overhang. As the older brother, I argued that we should turn around and head back. Back to the north face.

Gschnagenhardt and the Geisler/Odle Peaks in the Dolomites

However, Reinhold had spotted another option. There was a sloping rocky outcrop that led to the southeastern ridge of the Kleine Fermeda. Our dad had told us impressive tales about it. We had both climbed the Kleine Fermeda several times with him via the easier normal route. Reinhold didn't waste any time. Instead, he traversed the exposed ramp to the southeast ridge and asked me to climb over and join him. As he had seen our dad do, he belayed me the same way, securing the rope behind a rock spike and then over his right shoulder. Back then, we didn't know any better way. I lacked confidence and was really scared. After some exposed climbing, we reached the southeast ridge and continued to climb a large number of pitches to the south summit of the Kleine Fermeda. I hardly dared to look down, our route led up over an overhanging cliff that concealed the huge drop. From there, we made our way to the main summit and took the descent down the normal route on the west ridge that we had previously climbed with our dad.

This spontaneous, independent climb of the Kleine Fermeda southeast ridge was a formative experience. Although he was my younger brother, Reinhold was clearly stronger mentally and better technically. He was confident enough to be assertive, take the lead, and keep track of what we were doing. He led the way, and I followed him—willingly, but somewhat self-consciously. These characteristics have remained with him. He has put them to good use in other areas of life, as his biography shows. From this day on, our mountaineering ambitions and journey through life veered in different directions. I was happy to stick to simpler challenges and well-known mountain climbs. He increasingly sought out tricky, unknown routes in the Geisler/Odle Group and in the Dolomite cliffs of the neighboring valleys, together with our younger brother Günther or experienced climbing partners. From this time on, we trod different paths but are both content with what we have achieved.

The events and experiences of these summer holidays in Gschnagenhardt had, without doubt, a big impact on how we developed as people. Our parents gave us the freedom to put our own capabilities to the test, and to explore the social and geographical restraints that bound us. Each new phase in life presented new possibilities, but also restraints that had to be accepted. This still applies today.

Helmut went away to university and became a university lecturer in education. He was the first to leave home and move from Villnöss where we grew up, first to student accommodation in Merano then on to Innsbruck and finally to Constance in Switzerland. When he left, I missed him a lot. I would even go as far as to say that separation from him was painful. For a long time afterward, I felt wistful when recalling our childhood together. Helmut's skill sets came from going to university, teaching, and a lot of dedication. My own empowerment was a result of overcoming all the many obstacles put before me.

3

LESSONS FROM MY MOTHER

They all know that they're special in their own way.

—Maria Messner-Troi, talking about her nine children

In 1993, on my mother's eightieth birthday, a magazine called the *ff* (*ff—Das Südtiroler Wochenmagazin*) in South Tyrol printed an article by Florian Kronbichler. I am now eighty myself, and my admiration for my mother has continued to grow. Without her foresight, the many obstacles in my path would have broken me. She understood me and comforted me time and time again—and she encouraged me to go my own way.

The magazine sent us an advance copy, as an apology for what was to follow. It's reproduced here with some extra information indicated in parentheses:

> Reinhold Messner held a talk in his local culture center in Villnöss, where he comes from, about his hike around South Tyrol's borders. During the event, he got involved—as he often does—in an argument with members of the audience. It didn't help that his mother was sitting in the front row and called out to him to keep quiet. But once he'd started, he couldn't stop. His mother said that the whole family's problem is that "We like the sound of our own voices."
>
> It's a pleasure to listen to anyone who is prepared not to take themselves too seriously in this respect. On Monday, August 30, Maria Messner-Troi, widow and mother of eight sons and one daughter, will be eighty. The party is planned for the day before. Maria is still so fit and well that she organized the party herself. She's booked a whole room at Kabis, the best restaurant in the village. All the children were invited (including their families, but no one else) and she arranged all the details with the owners. The only thing that hasn't gone to plan is that the children want to pay this time. "In return, they've promised me that there will be no presents," she says.

Messner's mother, Maria Messner-Troi

You can't always have everything your own way. The way she tells it, you can believe her too. Her father was Franz Troi, a tanner from Buchenstein, and her mother came from a family named Wiedenhof in Ritten. In 1942, Maria married teacher Josef Messner, one of the Messners in Villnöss. As she says, "There are far too many of them." She married at just under thirty years old: "Soon enough!" she is fond of saying. "Don't get married too early" was her advice to her own children. Some of them listened. Others didn't, and some have learned afterward that she might have been right.

While her marriage could be summed up as traditional for the countryside, rooted in religion, Maria was clever and cunning and a quiet manipulator in terms of women's rights. It depends on how you see things. "The father's the head of the family," she explains. "And the mother's the neck—it has to turn the head."

This definition is self-explanatory. Josef was the strict father. She was the kind mother. If (or because) he was known to take everything very seriously (from the children's education to village gossip), she was the one who had to play everything down. Who had the final say will never really be clear. "Our father was strict, and this no doubt prevented us from becoming failures. However, our mother's personality shaped what we have become," says her son Reinhold.

Between the time she was thirty and forty-four years old, Maria Messner had nine children. Eight boys and one girl. "Four with fair hair, four with dark hair, and Waltraud is somewhere in the middle, both in terms of hair color and age." Naturally, they were all very fond of their mother. Werner, her youngest, is a mathematician and computer expert. He also studied psychology and once tried to explain to his mother that it was "not possible to really love more than one child." Her answer to her green-about-the-ears son was: "But Werner, how do you know?"

She enjoyed summing up her children for us—all nine of them. Helmut, born 1943, was the "best behaved." He became director of the Pedagogical Institute in Bolzano, "For the child of a teacher, that's probably true fulfilment." It's hard to know if she's being serious or sarcastic. However, she says that Helmut, her oldest son, is the only one of her children that she could have imagined becoming a priest. This would have been "unthinkable" with the others. She doesn't comment on whether she's happy that Helmut rejected religion too.

A year later, in 1944, Reinhold was born. "He wasn't a bad boy, just a bit wild." When he was around seven or eight, he always used to say: "I'm not doing that!" when it was his turn to clean out the chicken shed (the Messner family bred chickens).

Despite this, there were comparatively few clips around the ear from his strict father, as Reinhold's second most common comment was "I'll be off then!"

Wild boy Reinhold was followed by another model son—Günther. He rejected the extra lessons in Italian that his prudent mother wanted to give him (saying: "I don't need 'em"), went to college, and became a bank clerk. Not that it made him happy. His mother says the happiest she saw him was when he was given a place on the 1970 Nanga Parbat Expedition with Reinhold. "That made him happy." However, it was during the expedition that he lost his life.

We come to 1947 and Erich the fourth boy. "Another wild one." He worked hard in the chicken shed, but quickly realized that farming wasn't for him (the family didn't have a farm; they had chickens), so he decided to go to university to become a vet.

He always was good with animals. During military service in Innichen, he grew to like mules (calling them: "the finest of animals, if only they weren't so stubborn") and later he worked with horses. Today, Erich is a big name in South Tyrolean equestrian society. His brother Reinhold also wanted to try his luck with horses and riding. But his mother reports that Erich thought Reinhold had no aptitude for riding, saying "He doesn't like horses!"

In 1949, a girl came along, finally. The neighbors said: "She'll have it easy!" Waltraud says that she remembers it differently. Her father might have referred to her as the "rose bush among eight dung heaps," but brought her up quite strictly, as girls living in rural areas back then were. Ponytails, trousers and miniskirts, and going out at night were no-gos. She was required to be at her brothers' beck and call and help her mother around the house. When the young Waltraud complained about the obvious unfairness when it came to freedoms and chores, her mother would say: "Don't argue, Waltraud. Just get it over and done with." What she really meant was, do it now, because you'll have to do it at some point anyway.

Not exactly a case of solidarity among women—nor encouraging emancipation. For her mother, it was important to teach her daughter to accept the way things were as best you could. She viewed challenging the status quo as impossible and a waste of time.

When Waltraud was about sixteen or seventeen years old and was training to become a preschool teacher in Bolzano, her father did allow her to go dancing one evening. Reinhold was appointed as her chaperone. As a young teacher, Waltraud had made herself look pretty. However, as the two of them walked down the stairs, Reinhold suddenly turned and said: "I don't want to go—you go on your own!" and left.

His younger sister had no choice but to stay at home. Crying bitter tears of humiliation, she explained to her mother what had happened. But her mother told her not to take it to heart. Hardly much consolation.

Waltraud suffered the fate of most sisters with a lot of brothers. She was made to do everything and was also ultimately responsible for looking after their mother.

The next son, Siegfried, was expected to be a "fine chap," as family history seemed to dictate—and he was. As a child, he was never a problem. Maria remembered one occasion when she forgot to give him his bottle of milk. She jumped up and ran to check on the poor little starving boy. And what did she find? "Little Siegfried chuckling contentedly in his cradle." Siegfried went on to become a landscape conservationist and head of the South Tyrol Mountain and Ski Guides.

The next son was Hubert: "Naughty, but wild." Hubert, who is now a pediatrician, must have struck a good balance between wild and conscientious in his mother's eyes. Maybe this explains why she says that she doesn't recall "anything out of the ordinary."

When the director of Vinzentinum boarding school in Brixen expelled him and told his mother that he wouldn't get a place anywhere else, she responded: "Let that be our problem. The boy will find a new school." She wasn't wrong: he became the provincial medical councillor for South Tyrol.

All these success stories are almost becoming boring. Son number seven, Hansjörg, was "wild, but a bit difficult." He dropped out of school. His father forced him to leave home and he was secretly supported financially by his mother. He followed the hippie trail to India and disappeared for three quarters of a year.

Reinhold's ex-partner Uschi bumped into Hansjörg in Kathmandu. He returned home before leaving again, to work and travel through America. But there was a happy ending. After going back to college, he became a psychotherapist with a practice in London. His professional opinion of his mother: "I would like to age as well as her."

In 1957, Werner, the youngest Messner, was born. As an adult he first worked as a mechanic, but Werner didn't want to spend his life "lying under cars." He became a bank employee, but the "constant bean counting" got on his nerves. In the end, he went to study maths and founded a computer company.

And now the 64,000-dollar question for Maria Messner: Is she proud of her children? "Proud? Yes, I'm proud that they do what they do well."

That must have required a lot of tolerance. Maria adopts a somewhat animated tone as she empathizes that she never told her children what to do.

Her motto was "Let the children learn something! They need to do what they know they're good at." This was one of the few parenting principles that she and her husband could agree on.

They would have spent literally a lifetime arguing about how and what, if Maria had been in the mood to argue. "You always give in!" was her husband's repeated reproach.

"I always thought, leave them be," she says.

Her husband has been dead for six years. He died of lung cancer in 1985. Any of the children who smoked soon stopped when they saw the X-rays of their father's lungs. Their mother wasn't able to make Josef kick the habit. However, she was creative about rationing his cigarettes. The former teacher would insist to the end that filter-tipped cigarettes weren't harmful.

Maria's maxim was pretty much to let her children go their own ways. It was a mixture of tolerance, nonchalance, and wise resignation. Her daughter Waltraud heard it often. Reinhold, the rebel, saw it as the secret of his mother's maternal might. Helmut, the "good" son, now sees it from an educational perspective: "A little more willingness to argue wouldn't have hurt."

Maria, like most mothers, took the approach that both parents had their own roles. It was up to the father to do the complaining and disciplining of the children. She didn't compete with him in this respect, but focused on straightening things out afterward instead. On one occasion, when Reinhold and Erich were still at school, they stood up in church in the middle of the sermon and stomped off down the aisle in their nailed boots and out through the door. They were protesting against the sermon. "Those lies he tells from the pulpit!" was how they described their first act of rebellion. Their father was horrified and ashamed; their mother said she "was glad when the boys were finally out the church door."

The Messner boys didn't go back to church much after that. However, their mother is deeply religious. She says this in the same matter-of-fact tone with which she says that she's South Tyrolean and a grandmother. She doesn't deny that she would have been delighted if the children would accompany her to church, on her birthday at least. But they immediately said: "Mama, please can we do without the church!"

Maria doesn't complain despite the fact that, when she considers how many of the children would come to a birthday mass for her, it is clear that most of them would stay away.

She's pleased that "they do come to remember their father and their brothers once a year—even if this has also become a little more relaxed over the years."

Maria says she doesn't mind. She's religious, but without trying to convert anyone. In fact, Maria says she can't remember feeling sad that the children didn't go to church. "The Lord God will find them all," she says.

And though Reinhold doesn't think much of the sacraments, she says, "Even Reinhold believes that there is a God."

She doesn't expect much more from her son. She prays for her children every day, saying "it's only natural," but that she wouldn't dream of praying for their conversion: "it has never occurred to me." When it comes to the Pope, who Reinhold recently wanted to invite to Juval Castle (to discuss the proximity of the mountains to God), Maria says she doesn't like him. "Just his very appearance," she says. Although she felt that "Pope John XXIII was completely different." Mother Teresa is someone she would beatify on the spot.

Reinhold, although she's reluctant to admit it, inspires her defensiveness. She might be proud of him, but she does her best to hide it. Is Reinhold egotistic? Her reply is no—well, yes—at least a little anyway. And the same goes for his eccentricity. But her overall opinion is that "Reinhold is a good lad."

She agrees that Reinhold has been harshly treated, and she realizes that others see Reinhold Messner as either neurotic or self-promotional and that he is always making enemies. "They don't like him," she comments.

Who doesn't like Reinhold? Maria says she doesn't even want to begin to start counting. It's easier to look at it the other way: "Apart from his brothers and sister and his wife, there are only a few people in Vinschgau who really like him." That's as far as she goes. Within the family, her famous son's actions were not always met with undivided approval. They made fun of him, and often openly complained about him. When this happened, she invariably sided with Reinhold and told them to stop.

It was really his father who got upset about his famous son's extreme mountaineering exploits. Each time Reinhold disrespected a South Tyrolean figure of authority or situation, Josef Messner, the former teacher, said Maria, no longer felt comfortable even going out for a drink. When Reinhold openly criticized German-speaking South Tyroleans who, under Nazi rule, were given the "option" of emigrating to Germany or remaining in Italy, he put his father in a difficult position. Josef Messner had been one of the Optants who voted for emigration himself and a local Hitler Youth group leader. Now his own son was talking about "traitors to the homeland."

His mother defended her husband, saying, "it's true," but she also downplayed the story: "Back then it was the Hitler Youth, and today it's the Communist Youth." Her rather free use of comparisons is a trait her son seems to have inherited.

Maria Messner often mediated between the children and their father. In 1970, Reinhold returned from the tragic Nanga Parbat expedition but his younger brother Günther did not. Visiting Reinhold in hospital in Innsbruck where he was recovering from serious frostbite, his father reproached him for not looking after his brother better. In situations like this, his mother said more than just "leave them be." She pulled her husband out of the hospital room and told him to stop moralizing, reminding him that Günther had gone of his own free will, and that if he hadn't: "He might have been unhappy for the rest of his life."

She only confronted her husband this vociferously on one other occasion. When he was about to throw one of the younger boys out, she said: "You can't throw a child out," adding, "Did the children ask if they wanted to be born?"

Maria Messner takes a forbearing view of the deaths of her two sons Günther and Siegfried in the mountains. She says that death in the mountains or on the roads is preferable to suicide. "With suicide you blame yourself that you did something wrong," and adds: "At least I know where they ended up."

She didn't always know where all her children were. There was no sign or sound of Hansjörg for his first nine months in Kathmandu. At least once she found herself thinking, "He might have died." But apart from this, she never lost faith in her children. "If they have a bit of Troi in them," jokes Maria Messner-Troi, alluding to her family's trait of diligence, "and a bit of Messner (in other words, brains), none of them is likely to give up the ghost easily."

Her trust in her boys knows no limits. Although when she first heard that her son Hubert would be setting off on a Greenland expedition with Reinhold, she didn't believe it.

"He's not going. He doesn't have the time," she told herself. But when it was confirmed, she was fine with that too: "He should go. Otherwise, he'll work too much."

She takes life as it comes. "Trusting that things will work out," says Werner. "Children will return if you let them go," adds Waltraud, remembering one of her mother's favorite sayings. "A little bit of giving way, a little bit of standing by your word, a little bit of luck," says Helmut.

Reinhold just says: "She's a strong woman."

When it came to her sons' wives, Maria Messner says that she: "warned all of them about my boys." And when separations happened, she never blamed them: "When things don't work out, it's better if they split up." She has never held a grudge against any of her daughters-in-law.

Reinhold Messner suggested that *ff* ask his mother why "none of her children became a good-for-nothing." Maria didn't even understand the question. "Good-for-nothing? The thought never crossed my mind." Then she realizes that someone might be fishing for a compliment and concludes: "My lads all know their worth."

The self-perception and self-confidence that my mother gave me helped me to brave even the worst headwinds. In 1970, when I staggered half-dead through the upper Diamir Valley, lost without any bearings, I didn't pray to God—I thought of my mother. Thinking of her kept me going. I had to make it back home alive to tell her about our odyssey.

The trust that our parents give us in our childhood years lasts a lifetime. Trust given like that grows if we are allowed to learn to take responsibility at an early age. Fledglings only leave a safe nest. They soar upward on the thermals, learning to love the winds and cherish a headwind. The same goes for human beings, if what we do, we do with dedication.

I have my mother to thank for the title of my first autobiography, *Free Spirit*. She gave me the self-confidence that has helped me survive for eighty years.

4

BOILED DUMPLINGS

It ain't about how hard you can hit. It's about how hard you can get hit and keep moving forward.

—Rocky Balboa, as played by Sylvester Stallone

Luis Vonmetz was from Bolzano in South Tyrol. A few years older than me, he was a passionate mountaineer who was elected chair of the South Tyrolean Alpine Club (Alpenverein Südtirol, AVS) in 1991. He took this role very seriously. We got on well and remained friends until his death in 2022.

Before I finished school, I was already publishing my first newspaper articles. Journalist Josef Rampold proved a mentor who proofread my copy for his mountaineering pages in the *Dolomiten* newspaper.

Later, however, Rampold became disenchanted with me when I questioned the much-vaunted idealism of mountaineering and the colonialist behavior of flag waving on the world's highest peaks. I criticized the South Tyrolean Optants who, in 1939, were prepared, as part of the Hitler-Mussolini pact, to leave their homeland for the lure of Greater Germany. More than 200,000 of the 246,000 German- and Ladin-speakers opted to leave—some 86 percent of them. When I accused the Optants of betraying their homeland, all hell broke loose. I'd wanted to explore the recent history of our province of South Tyrol, to reappraise and clarify, not to level accusations, but the backlash and headwinds unleashed were merciless. It didn't matter that my views were factually correct—they were simply unacceptable. I learned to live with it, though not by keeping my mouth shut as my mother had recommended.

For my seventy-fifth birthday, Luis Vonmetz recalled our time together, including the later accusations, in the South Tyrolean Alpine Club (AVS) magazine, *Berge erleben*:

> At about the same time as my first rock climbing trips, Reinhold was climbing with his brother Günther. Their tours were getting harder and harder. And they started to gain more and more recognition. Around the

mid-1960s, Reinhold applied to the AVS head office to take the mountain guide course.

Emil Schorn, the somewhat older AVS secretary, looked Reinhold up and down and gave him the following advice (in his strong South Tyrolean dialect): "Go away, eat boiled dumplings for a couple of years, then come back, sonny." Of course, Reinhold wouldn't put up with this.

Instead, he went straight to the Italian Alpine Club headquarters (Club Alpino Italiano/CAI) where he was immediately accepted for the course. Long afterward, Reinhold founded a mountain rescue center, which is still linked to the CAI today. As you can see, the South Tyrolean Alpine Club has to accept its own share of the blame here.

By 1969, the Messner brothers' achievements were impossible to overlook. Reinhold solo climbed the two most difficult mountain routes in the Western and Eastern Alps: the Droites North Face and the Philipp Flamm route on the Civetta. That year he joined our alpine mountaineering group, known as the HG (*Hochtourengruppe*) in Bolzano. Reinhold immediately took on a leading role and became HG delegate to the AVS management committee. In 1970, he and his brother Günther were invited to join the Nanga Parbat expedition organized by Karl Maria Herrligkoffer. The goal was to climb the highest mountain face in the world, the 4,500-meter Rupal Face. The South Tyrolean Alpine Club launched a fundraising campaign for the brothers. On April 2, 1970, we gave Reinhold a send-off at the Hotel Mondschein. The landlord and AVS chairman Heinz Mayr said a few words: "Reinhold, you're not the first to set out from here to conquer the world's mountains. We said goodbye to Erich Abram sixteen years ago in this very room as he left for K2. Our friendship goes with you. Come back safely!"

Reinhold and Günther were the first to climb the Rupal flank to the summit, having set up each high camp themselves. It was the first full traverse of an eight-thousander, but Günther never returned. In 1972, the AVS erected the Günther Messner bivouac shelter in his memory under the north face of the Hochferner. Today, it's situated at the Mountain Museum Corones on Kronplatz.

In 1971, Reinhold made the first solo ascent of the north face of Puncak Jaya, which is comparable with the Solleder route on the Civetta Northwest face.

In 1972, when he married Uschi Demeter, I still remember how we celebrated in Villnöss with funny posters and South Tyrolean sparkling wine. In the same year, he climbed the south face of Manaslu where two team members died.

The direttissima (super direct) style of aid climbing was introduced to the Dolomites in 1958, using fixed ropes, etriers, expansion bolts, and hand drills with the first direct ascent of the north face of the Grosse Zinne/Cima Grande. Reinhold saw the use of bolts as a mistake. Instead, he remained loyal to the Paul Preuss philosophy, and succeeded in forcing the alpine climbing world to think again. As a result, for years none of the classic Dolomite routes were equipped with modern bolts. Reinhold went on to revolutionize Himalayan mountaineering. Drawing inspiration from his role models Hermann Buhl and Walter Bonatti, he succeeded in establishing the alpine style in the world's highest mountains. This meant no supplementary oxygen, virtually no fixed ropes, and no porters on the mountain. By minimizing weight and climbing fast and light, the amount of time spent in the death zone was significantly reduced.

In the summer of 1973, Reinhold invited me to join him for the first ascent of the Marmolada. Our HG climbing friends—Jörgl Mayr and Jochen Gruber—came along too. Reinhold led virtually every pitch, hammering in pitons but placing no bolts. Shortly before the exit pitches, Jörgl took over the lead and climbed the difficult crux, which Reinhold called grade VII, though "officially" the seventh grade didn't even exist at the time. On the summit, Reinhold mentioned that he knew a new route on the northwest face of Monte Pelmo. We arranged to meet the next weekend. The weather was poor, the climbing was hard, and about one hundred meters above the start the face was split by a huge ledge. Jochen and Jörgl climbed the lower pitches. Reinhold and I bypassed the lower section and started climbing from the ledge itself. Reinhold was climbing magnificently. I belayed him pitch after pitch. We left pitons and ropes in place for the second team. About halfway up, around 400 meters from the summit, the weather finally took a turn for the worse. Reinhold and I stood there in the rain and thick fog. We decided to retreat to a bivouac spot we had seen below. Jörgl and Jochen had arrived in the meantime at this bivouac where an overhanging roof protected us from rockfall,

and we spent the night singing and telling stories until the bright, icy hours before dawn, when Reinhold and I set out again. We had left the rope hanging in place the day before so that we could climb the first pitch quickly and safely. The face eased, and we made good progress.

We reached the summit around midday and hugged each other. I got to know Reinhold in the mountains. He was a considerate, happy, and helpful climbing partner. I couldn't have wished for anyone better to climb with. . . .

Later in 1981, Reinhold fell out with Josef Rampold, the then editor-in-chief of the popular *Dolomiten* daily newspaper. Up until that point, Rampold had supported and admired the Messner brothers. But he withdrew his backing when Reinhold questioned the "often feigned nature of mountain comradeship" and accused South Tyrolean Optants of having betrayed their homeland for Hitler's Germany in 1939. He claimed that his handkerchief was his only flag, and that it would go with him to the world's highest summits. There was an almighty row, which was continued in many South Tyrolean Optant families.

I was declared persona non grata by many, but Luis remained a friend.

In 1977, the HG celebrated its twenty-fifth anniversary, and Reinhold Messner left. He also left the AVS. He said later that the South Tyrolean Alpine Club was too *völkisch* (right-wing) and didn't do enough to represent the interests of mountaineers, that the alpine mountaineering group had plenty of talk of comradeship but was dominated by envy and resentment. Which he thought was a shame.

In the Himalaya, he enjoyed his most outstanding success yet, the first solo ascent of an eight-thousander. In 1978, Reinhold climbed Nanga Parbat in just three days by a new route up the Diamir Face. With Peter Habeler, he then made the first ascent of Everest without bottled oxygen. He was initially criticized by nearly all the medical experts, which only made the climb even more sensational. He went on to invite the best young South Tyrolean mountaineers to his later Himalaya expeditions. He wanted to show them a way to climb the eight-thousanders. In 1984, his back-to-back alpine-style summits of two eight-thousanders—Hidden Peak and Gasherbrum II—with Hans Kammerlander was further testimony to his methods.

After completing all the eight-thousanders, Reinhold applied his creativity to new goals and adventures. From 1989 to 1990, he and Arved Fuchs crossed the Antarctic on foot, trekking 2,500 kilometers via the South Pole. In

1993, he traversed Greenland on foot. In 2004, he crossed the Gobi Desert, a 2,000-kilometer trek through the wilderness, on foot carrying up to 40 liters of water on his back. He was sixty years old.

In 1991, I was elected chair of the AVS, and a journalist asked me about my plans. I said I regretted that South Tyrol had no alpine museum and that the AVS should do something about it. Reinhold quickly promised to help. At the Alpine Club we weren't able to pull the project off. However, Reinhold pursued the issue and applied to the provincial governor for permission to renovate Sigmundskron Castle near Bolzano for the purpose.

This endeavor caused a lot of controversy. As the AVS, we didn't want to argue: we were always in favor of an alpine museum—why not use the empty, tumbledown Sigmundskron Castle?

In my position as head of the AVS, I supported Reinhold's project. South Tyrol has a rich tradition of mountaineering, which an alpine museum should underscore. Just as in the mountains, however, Reinhold once again found himself facing a strong headwind. Fortunately, he was able to weather it, right through to the end. Today, everyone admits that Sigmundskron Castle is a huge success. Now that it has been restored, it is popular with both locals and tourists. Reinhold went on to create more mountain museums to represent alpine history—and mountain peoples—with cultural and art collections. The five museums finance themselves and require no subsidies.

These days Reinhold is dedicated to mountain film. He has so many stories to tell. His films are authentic, honest, and exciting. There has been a reconciliation with the Alpine Club.

When I was a rock climber, I once failed in my attempt to link up all the Geisler/Odle Peaks—from east to west, from the Kampiller Turm to the Kleine Fermeda—by climbing them on my own in a single day. I abandoned my plan at the Villnösser Turm, the summit with its two little horns, even though it was only late afternoon. I had an appointment I needed to keep down in the valley. Between the Kleiner Odla and the Villnösser Turm, I picked my way back down over easier, craggy terrain. Near the bottom, down in the cirque, I allowed myself to glissade, sliding down the fine, flowing sand that lies in the gullies between the coarse scree. Pushing my boots into the soft slope, heels first, I felt weightless. I knew that probably no one would ever descend this exact same line, formed by the water and winter snow in the cirque. Leaping and sliding in great bounds, I reached the valley in mere minutes. Had I come down a few meters to the right, I would have gotten stiff knees and used ten times as much energy.

It was abandonment to nature—being alert, letting myself go, and becoming one with the downward-flowing scree. I followed the ever-changing cirque not the well-trodden path. Nature, despite its mercurial quality, guided my footsteps and taught me to trust in it completely.

I'm often distrustful of people. They do what they do for their own benefit, out of selfishness, vanity, and hypocrisy. I have often gone out on a limb and faced the wind—and have been criticized and ostracized for it. And rightly so, perhaps. However, I still prefer to be courageous and face the wind head on than be patted on the back.

5

A HUT AT THE EDGE OF THE WOODS

Adventurers have a mental map of the world. We see a landscape full of possibilities in our heads. We move through it according to our own rules. However, anyone pushing the limits and introducing new ideas will face resistance from within the ranks.

—Reinhold Messner

When I came of age in Italy at twenty-one, my dreams were crushed for the first time. I met resistance from all points of the compass. Without asking me, my father had read through the logbook I kept of my climbs. He added a moralizing message to declare that I should start a proper career, and that mountaineering was just a hobby.

After going to Switzerland for a winter attempt on the Bonatti Route on the north face of the Matterhorn, I was late getting back to school, although I had permission from my headmaster for the time away. My German teacher was angry. Until that point, I had always gotten good marks in his class, but he started to harass me and I ended up failing my school-leaving certificate. I wasn't prepared to be treated like this by my teachers.

In those days, it was possible to retake an exam in autumn, which allowed me a second chance. I had just returned from Switzerland again, this time to climb the Walker Spur on the Grandes Jorasses in Mont-Blanc. My fingers were battered, but I was tanned and feeling very sure of myself.

My teacher was not impressed: "Have you been climbing again?"

"Why not?" I replied, and he failed me a second time.

On the day that one of my classmates brought the results to our house in Villnöss, I was working with my brother in the chicken shed, which meant that my father heard the news first. He stormed in and shouted: "You can do what you like, but you won't get another cent from me to finish school."

I stood up, put down the hammer, and walked out. I never set foot in our chicken shed again.

I wanted to live my own life, to be free to follow my own dreams. That was how I saw my future.

A few days later, I climbed a route on the Piz Ciavazes, alone, a free solo as it's called today. High up on the face, I experienced a freedom that had nothing to do with school grades. Where would I live? I didn't need a house. A small hut would be fine, somewhere to leave my belongings while exploring the wilderness—which was becoming scarce even in those days.

Standing on the summit plateau of the mighty Sella massif in the Grödner Dolomites, I watched the choughs playing on the thermals, circling over the void.

What was I going to do? I had failed my school exams and felt ashamed. Sitting on a rock, I looked out over the Dolomites. It felt like the choughs were trying to tell me something. Were they not doing what they loved best? Was this not their way of expressing their love of freedom? They dove, soared, and hovered in the air with their yellow beaks shining in the sun. It was not their acrobatics, but the way they hovered that was fascinating. They seemed to be able to float on the wind.

This was what I had dreamed of. To lead the life I loved, in spite of the bans and the angry voices. This was how I reacted to the attempts to restrict my freedom. I was going to face the wind and copy what I saw in the natural world around me.

How I hated "bourgeois morality" in those days. I also resented the power of the state over the individual.

I was no hippie; I had no intention of turning on, tuning in, and dropping out. But there was no way I was going to let anyone stop me from living the life I wanted. I was not interested in owning things; it was doing things that made me happy. Climbing the Walker Spur on Grandes Jorasses, one of the three great north faces of the Alps, was more important to me than passing my school exams.

At first everything was provisional. I didn't really have a plan. I wanted to build myself a hut. Not a house to last for generations, but a hut that would serve as a nest and a home base, an expression of my semi-nomadic way of life.

In those days, I was an obsessive rock climber and saw alpinism as a way of gaining access to the shrinking wilderness, to enable further mountain adventures.

For me, the history of alpinism reflects the continually evolving adaptation of our thoughts and actions to reality. However, the level of expertise was growing, but the wilderness was shrinking, with no end in sight. And this was threatening traditional alpinism. What interested me most were the ways that we adapt.

On a hard rock route, it's all about climbing up, meter by meter. "If I can keep this up, I'm going to reach the summit." Going over the whole route in your head in advance—including the difficult sections—helps provide an overview. However, as in life, you only recognize the real cruxes when you get to them. Assessing an entire route is like finding the right path. Overcoming difficulties, without losing sight of the big picture—this is the art of finding your way in life. I believe that we should follow Paul Preuss's motto: "It's our ability that determines what we are capable of." After all, we cannot simply climb wherever we choose to in the mountains. Our level of expertise needs to match the routes that we intend to climb.

We cannot just read nature like a book. The mountains will always be an uncertain environment. But it is precisely this uncertainty that fuels our sense of adventure.

I built my hut on the Gschnagenhardt Alm a few years later: at the edge of the woods, where I had enjoyed my first taste of freedom with my brothers and sister as a child.

6

THE RED ROCKET

Günther Messner was never earmarked for the summit. But he knew that Reinhold Messner, who supposedly merely wanted to reconnoiter the Rupal Face, would never settle for that but head for the top instead. So, he left Gerd Baur behind and said: "No, I'm following my brother, because he's going to the summit."

—doctor and expedition organizer Karl M. Herrligkoffer

On the Herrligkoffer Foundation's website, there's a report from the Siegi Löw Memorial Expedition to the Rupal Face of Nanga Parbat in 1970, entitled "A New Attempt":

> Confident of his chances of success, Herrligkoffer set out in May 1970 with a strong team of mountaineers from Germany, Austria, and South Tyrol to make a further attempt on the Rupal Face. The expedition team consisted of German mountaineers Michl Anderl (deputy expedition leader), Gerhard Baur, Günther Kroh, Hermann Kühn, Gerd Mändel, Hans Seler, Peter Scholz, Peter Vogler, photographer Jürgen Winkler, Austrian mountain guides Werner Haim and Felix Kuen, and well-known South Tyrolean alpinists Günther and Reinhold Messner. Wolf-Dietrich Bitterling from Berchtesgaden was responsible for transporting the equipment from Germany to Rawalpindi. He was assisted by Elmar Raab, who was also included in the expedition team. A pharmacist called Alice von Hobe provided the medical expertise and Max Engelhardt von Kienlin joined the expedition as a guest.
>
> On June 3, brothers Günther and Reinhold Messner climbed with Felix Kuen and Peter Scholz in poor conditions to reach the Merkl Icefield. They fixed ropes up the steep ice face—which was up to fifty degrees in places—and deposited equipment. On June 14, bad weather forced the whole team to retreat to base camp. Following a forecast for a spell of fine weather, the team continued up the Rupal Face. On June 25, the Messner brothers reached the start of the Merkl Gully, where Scholz and Kuen pitched a tent

the following day to establish Camp 5 at 7,350 meters. They then climbed back down to Camp 4.

During a radio message on June 26, I suggested a plan to the expedition leader.

Gerhard Baur's recollection is as follows: "I heard that Reinhold Messner had said a red rocket would be fired to indicate if bad weather was looming. In that case, he would make a solo attempt on the summit, in other words, climb as far as he could." If good weather was expected, Herrligkoffer would send up a blue rocket. Then the summit team would fix ropes up the Merkl Gully to guarantee maximum safety during the attempt on the summit.

On the evening of June 26, Gerhard Baur and the Messner brothers reached the tiny Camp 5. At 8 p.m., a red rocket was fired, despite the good weather conditions. This was a mistake. Blue wrapping on the rocket had concealed some small print saying that it was a red rocket, which meant that the team back at basecamp didn't notice. Reinhold Messner started to make preparations. He explicitly told his brother and Gerd Baur to wait until he returned to Camp 5. On June 27, Reinhold Messner got up at 2 a.m. and prepared to climb. By the light of his headtorch, he forced a trail up the 50-to-60-degree steep Merkl Gully and climbed sections up to 45 degrees on grade III rock.

At 350 meters from the summit, a ramp leads up right to join the South Shoulder.

Glancing back down the face, Messner saw a figure climbing the gully. It was his brother. While fixing the ropes to secure the gully, Günther had become so enraged with a tangled accessory cord that he cast it into the snow angrily and spontaneously decided to try to reach the summit himself. He climbed most of the Merkl Gully in under four hours, covering around 400 meters of elevation.

At 9 a.m. that morning, the two brothers started climbing together toward the summit, which they reached at 5 p.m. After an hour at the summit, they started to descend. According to Reinhold Messner, his brother was so exhausted that he lacked the confidence to downclimb the Merkl Gully without a rope. After considering their options, they decided to try to find a way back down on the west side, via the Diamir Face. At around 8,000 meters, they were forced to bivouac. Günther suffered severe altitude sickness during the night. On the morning of June 28, Reinhold reached the notch above the upper end of the Merkl Gully on the western ridge. From this Merkl Notch, he could look down to the gully, where he saw two people climbing slowly upward. It was Peter Scholz and Felix Kuen and they were roped up. Once they were within earshot at last, Felix Kuen asked Reinhold if the brothers had reached the summit, and if everything was OK. Reinhold confirmed that they had and that they were fine.

Reinhold said he knew that his brother was suffering from altitude sickness. He realized he needed to get him out of the death zone as fast as possible. And that the best way down was the Diamir Face. He went on ahead to find the way down and discovered a way to negotiate the two large serac zones. Downclimbing over bare ice, the brothers reached the Mummery Rib. Messner described their situation as follows:

"Sometimes, there appeared to be three of us. But I knew that this was just an illusion. Around midnight, we stopped to bivouac again at the top of the Mummery Rib. The moon appeared at 3 a.m. and Günther had recovered somewhat. We continued to head down, reaching the easier firn slopes to the left of the two lower ribs at daybreak.

The plan was to pick our way between two glaciers to reach the green slopes. We agreed to wait for each other at the first spring on the grassy areas below. We walked down a hard firn slope behind each other. I was moving faster but kept stopping and waiting. We had done the worst part."

Reinhold reported that he was about one and a half hours in front of his brother and had lost sight of him. He said that he stopped to wait for him for a long time and then headed back up to where he had last seen Günther. At this spot, he found the remains of an ice avalanche that had not been there before. He remembered calling and looking for his brother, but to no avail. He spent the whole night searching for him among the wreckage of the shattered ice debris. And continued searching the next day. On the evening of 30 June, he crawled under a block on the glacier and tried to sleep.

The next day, July 1, he limped off the mountain into the Diamir Valley. Local people found him, exhausted and incapacitated with serious frostbite on his feet. Sometimes they had to carry him down. Reinhold Messner was then taken to the Bunar bridge in the Indus Valley. Here a Pakistani officer drove him in his jeep to nearby Gilgit. No one knew where Günther and Reinhold had come down the mountain. Both the Rakhiot side and the

> Rupal side were possible options. A search party headed up into the Rupal Valley, to see if the brothers had come down the West Ridge.

Over fifty years have passed since this tragedy and this report is still available online. There are a lot of mistakes in it, but I never commented on it at the time, nor do I plan to do so today. Factually, this first article by Herrligkoffer about the first ascent of the Rupal Face is more or less correct. However, our expedition leader was soon spreading several lies—whether they were excuses or justifications, I leave open to debate. I couldn't simply ignore his comments, or Felix Kuen's accusation that I had other intentions at the Merkl Notch. This is what Herrligkoffer says in his first report:

> During our radio call on June 26, Reinhold Messner requested that we fire a rocket to indicate the weather to Camp 5 at 8 p.m., as it had no radio contact with the other camps. A blue rocket would mean good weather for the summit, a blue rocket and a red rocket dubious weather, and two red rockets bad weather.
>
> Reinhold explained to me that if the weather was good, then they would secure the gully together to make a push for the summit with Kuen/Scholz the next day. He also said that if the weather was unstable, they would attempt the summit. But that they would *not* attempt the summit if two red rockets were fired. We arranged to fire the rockets at 8 p.m.
>
> At basecamp, we had two rockets with blue wrapping and two rockets with red wrapping. We thought that we had two blue and two red rockets. In fact, all four of them were red ones.
>
> After announcing the good weather forecast at 6 p.m. to all the camps with a radio, Michl Anderl fired what he thought was a blue rocket at 8 p.m. We were shocked to see that it was red. We wanted to follow up immediately with a blue rocket, but we didn't have one. We hadn't arranged to talk to the other camps until the next morning, so there was no way of getting a message up to Camp 5.
>
> Despite the red rocket, we hoped the Camp 5 climbers would use their mountain expertise with weather conditions to make the right decision the next morning, in other words, to secure the gully *or* push for the summit. I can't understand why Reinhold Messner interpreted the red rocket as a prompt to attempt the summit alone. We had agreed exactly the opposite.

However, this made no difference because at 3 a.m., Reinhold decided to head to the summit alone.

The Messner brothers called for help between 6 a.m. and 9 a.m. on June 28. An hour later at 10 a.m., Reinhold Messner was spotted on his own on the ridge and Günther was nowhere in sight. It's a well-known

> fact that the human body starts to deteriorate in the death zone, even with full rest and sufficient food. The only way to sustain normal bodily functions is to use bottled oxygen.

Herrligkoffer's comments were full of contradictions. However, his claim not long afterward that Günther had died and remained in the Merkl Notch was the final straw. Herrligkoffer alleged that "He sacrificed his brother to his own ambition." This allegation was Herrligkoffer's weapon of choice for his version of the events. His goal was to permanently blacken my name. This was my response to our expedition leader Karl Maria Herrligkoffer in my letter of 26 August 1970:

> Dear Karl,
>
> Your account in your letter of August 13, 1970, is untrue. Furthermore, I ask you to withdraw your claim of involuntary manslaughter (page 3/paragraph 2). I expect you to do so within ten days. In addition, I hope that you refute the many libelous claims that you made about Günther and me to the press and in other reports.
>
> I had no intention of publishing articles about what happened on Nanga Parbat in newspapers or magazines. However, due to your incorrect and biased reporting, I am left with no choice but to respond. I owe this to my brother Günther. Equally, I will strive to ensure that the whole truth about Nanga Parbat is made public.
>
> You have misrepresented or distorted the facts from Nanga Parbat and therefore the contract won't stop me from defending myself. Fortunately, this isn't the Wild West. I feel deeply offended by your letter of August 13. Given your numerous misrepresentations, I would have expected an apology, not an ultimatum. It feels like you're using my numbness due to Günther's death and my convalescence in hospital to dismiss our actions as foolish. At present, I am still in bed and can't defend myself. After our meeting in Gilgit, this wasn't what I expected from you. I'm saddened that it all has to end like this. However, you will understand that I have my reputation to consider and that I will not simply sit back and accept this defamation of character. I will never be able to forgive you for the false things that you have written about Günther. You are exploiting his death.
>
> Yours, Reinhold

Herrligkoffer responded with a letter (No. 5, dated September 5, 1970), the purpose of which was to silence us mountaineers:

To everyone participating in the Sigi Löw Memorial Expedition Nanga Parbat 1970

You will all be aware that since the return of our successful expedition, some very regrettable things have happened. Instead of discussing differences of opinion within the team, some people have talked to the press, who have reported, in some cases extensively, on the expedition.

It has now transpired that the editor of *Alpinismus* magazine is in possession of correspondence between expedition members, including myself, which is due to be printed in the October 1970 issue. I assume that it concerns the "red rocket affair." The letters are from eight participants. Nobody objects to discussing our differences and opinions about what happened on the expedition privately. However, I consider it a breach of team spirit should these sorts of letters be sent to others outside the expedition organization, especially if intended for publication. I therefore assume that none of the authors has given permission for publication of their letters. Furthermore, I expect that anyone who has written a letter informs the editor of *Alpinismus* that they are opposed to publication. I therefore request that you all write immediately to the following address by registered post and send me a copy:

Registered letter
To the editor: *Alpinismus*, Herring Verlag
8 Munich 25
Ortlerstrasse 8
All you need to write is as follows:
If you have received letters or manuscripts from me, I explicitly request that these are not published. I do not give my consent for them to be printed.

I also request everyone to reread the Participant Contract signed with the German Institute for Foreign Research (the Herrligkoffer Foundation). Section 4, paragraph 2 states: "Given that the expedition goal can only be achieved if all participants work together, participants will refrain from communicating information about the expedition to the press. All participants are responsible for ensuring that their letters and other reports or photos etc. are not published by third parties. Furthermore, participants will not divulge information to third parties about the expedition, unless the Foundation expressly exempts them from this obligation.

Anyone reneging on the conditions of this Participant Agreement, should be aware that the institute's relevant court of arbitration may impose a contractual penalty that could be high. Please refer also to sections 7 and 8 of the Participant Contract, and the Arbitration Agreement.

I mention all of this only by way of precaution, as I don't expect that anyone would seriously consider mocking the success of our expedition in public.

Yours,

Dr. Karl Herrligkoffer (Sigi Löw Memorial Expedition)

"The Rocket Affair" was published in issue 10 of *Alpinismus* magazine. "Nanga Parbat 70" was my contribution:

We were a good team and became friends although we hardly knew each other beforehand. However, the relationship between the team leaders and members could have been better. The most extreme example of the problems is the red rocket affair. On Wednesday, June 26, I talked to Dr. Herrligkoffer by radio from Camp 4. Every evening from 5:30 to 6:00 p.m., he said he would listen to the special weather service for our expedition. He expressed no reservations about my offer to attempt the summit on my own, even in the event of poor weather. He had no idea of the technical difficulties, but said: "You're saying exactly what I'm thinking."

On the afternoon of June 26, we agreed that if the weather report from 5:30 to 6:00 p.m. forecasted bad weather, he would indicate as such to me at Camp 5. This camp was out of radio contact, so he would fire a red rocket. To quickly finish the whole endeavor, I would then make a summit attempt alone. If the weather report forecast good weather, he would fire a blue rocket. Before we agreed on blue as the color, Dr. Herrligkoffer put down the radio and went into the tent to check that we really had blue rockets and said: "We only have blue and red rockets." All well and good. I moved up to Camp 5 (7,200 meters) with my brother Günther and Gerhard Baur. At 6 p.m., my team members in the lower camps heard from Dr. Herrligkoffer that the forecast was good. Two hours later (8 p.m.) a red rocket lit up the sky. I understood that bad weather was in the offing and only a solo ascent could be feasible. If a blue rocket had been fired, I would never have set off on my own without a rope or bivouac equipment. Equally, we would have fixed ropes in the Merkl Gully and all four of us would have made the push for the summit together. Given the good forecast, the climbers in the lower camps were surprised by the red rocket. The next morning, they contacted Michl Anderl, the expedition mountaineering leader to question the firing of a red rocket. Michl Anderl said that Dr. Herrligkoffer would explain later at midday. Dr. Herrligkoffer said that he had picked up a red rocket by mistake. When he was asked why he didn't fire a blue rocket immediately afterward, he said that there were none left.

Of course, it was only after those terrible and tragic days, sparked by the red rocket, that I got to hear the story about the rockets in Gilgit. And I couldn't understand why Dr. Herrligkoffer omitted all mention of the most significant moment of the whole expedition in his article in *Bunte*, Germany's popular illustrated magazine. On the morning of June 27, at 2:30 a.m., I set out from Camp 5, to try to climb the final 1,000 meters to the summit. I deliberately chose to leave the rope behind, to save weight and move fast. My equipment included two emergency space blankets, two hats, four pairs of gloves, six layers of clothing, and some dried fruit. The terrain was comparable with the north face of the Matterhorn. Around 8 a.m., I reached a ramp that led to the South Shoulder. Suddenly, I saw my brother coming up the Merkl Gully below me. I waited for him. We then climbed the South Shoulder together. The level of technical difficulty eased. At around 5 p.m., we stood on the summit. We embraced, completely exhilarated. This was the most beautiful moment in my life, because Günther was there to share it with me. We spent about an hour on the summit taking photos and filming. [Editor's comment: The camera and film were lost with Günther.] Günther didn't feel able to attempt the tricky descent—around grade IV—unroped. Therefore we decided to go down the Diamir side of the ridge, to try and reach the Merkl Gully lower down via easier terrain.

By the time it started to get dark, we had reached the notch above the Merkl Gully. We bivouacked here (at approx. 8,000 meters). It was a very cold night, and Günther's condition deteriorated. On the morning of June 28, I saw that there was no way of traversing down to the Merkl Gully without ropes. At 6 a.m., I called down the Merkl Gully for a rope. At about 10 a.m., I saw Felix

Kuen and Peter Scholz on the ramp to the South Shoulder. They were about 80 to 100 meters away. But Kuen was unable to help us. We couldn't hear each other properly. Kuen called out again to ask if everything was OK and I assured him it was. What else could I have said? There was nothing he could do to help us. I had to get Günther down as fast as possible.

It was our only chance. We started to climb down the Diamir Face. By midnight, we'd reached the Mummery Rib (about 6,300 meters). Three hours later (June 29, 3 a.m.) we started climbing down again. Everything was going to plan. We reached easier terrain and the firn slopes, pausing to drink from the glacier streams. I went on ahead. We agreed to wait for each other by the first meadow down below. I called back to show him the route I planned to descend. Günther descended by a route that was closer to the mountain. He was caught by an avalanche.

My ordeal before I reached human beings and my fellow expedition members is a story of its own.

[Addendum from the editor] From initial reports, we could be forgiven for thinking that Reinhold and Günther Messner had planned to traverse the mountain right from the start. This was not the case (we spoke to Reinhold Messner, Felix Kuen, Werner Haim, and Wolf-Jürgen Winkler). The fact that Dr. Herrligkoffer didn't write to express his consolation to Günther Messner's parents or contact them in person might have nothing to do with the red rocket affair, but it does say something about Dr. Herrligkoffer's character.

This was Herrligkoffer's reply:

Alpinismus No. 10/70 contains the article "Nanga Parbat 70" with a further report on our Rupal expedition this year.

1. It claims to have the "statements of seven participants" that contradict mine. At the time of the call on June 26, Günther Kroh and Peter Vogler were in a camp without radio contact. Therefore, their statements have no relevance. Elmar Raab signed a document previously to confirm that my account of the red rocket affair was correct. He revised his explanation at a later juncture. Therefore, only four participants corroborate the Messner version. The team consists of eighteen members.
2. The editorial in *Alpinismus* 9/70 states that the article by Reinhold Messner is an "authentic report." This is also inaccurate. Reinhold

Messner has simply provided his own view of events, which differs to mine and that of the other participants.

3. Furthermore, the magazine's editorial claims that my letter of August 13, 1970, to Reinhold Messner was a "threat." Referring to a contract that was signed voluntarily is not a threat. In addition, calling for collective team spirit when it comes to evaluating our expedition, is also not a threat.
4. In his "statement regarding the rebuttal," Max von Kienlin claims that during subsequent discussions: "the expedition members had always shared the same opinion" that the red rocket was fired "as arranged" and that this triggered Reinhold's push for the summit. Right up to the end of the expedition when we reached Munich, it is alleged that I: "never claimed anything else" and "never expressed any surprise at Reinhold setting out."

   Only when the "red rocket" issue was raised by Reinhold Messner in his report, did it transpire that the expedition members saw things differently. So, they didn't "always share the same opinion" about Messner's alleged "agreement."

   It's incorrect that I have never claimed anything else and therefore agree with Messner's account. In fact, I've always stated that after the mishap with the red rocket, we immediately planned to fire a blue one so that the team at Camp 5 didn't waste the spell of good weather. On the morning of June 27 at 6:10 a.m., I observed signs of movement via the telescope in the Merkl Gully and saw Reinhold Messner, Baur, and possibly Günther Messner also climbing up. As a result, it seemed to me that the mishap with the rocket was no longer important, which is why I didn't mention the matter in my initial report. I also first heard of Reinhold and Günther Messner's push for the summit on the evening of June 27 from Baur. I was more shocked than surprised because a push for the summit of this nature hadn't been agreed to by the expedition leaders. What's more, I had heard from Baur that Reinhold had only intended to climb as far as he could in order to return to Camp 5 on the same day without needing to bivouac.
5. When the editorial team of *Alpinismus* magazine contends that the red rocket had "turned into an incident," it fails to mention that it was only the case after a lawyer was appointed concerning my rebuttal of August 18, 1970. It appears that the magazine's editorial team has no interest in allowing all parties to express their opinions.

Munich, October 9, 1970

Dr. Karl M Herrligkoffer

Each rebuttal was followed by a further rebuttal, until the facts were virtually obscured in a whiteout.

October 4, 1970

Regarding Dr. Herrligkoffer's report on the 1970 Nanga Parbat Expedition in the German Alpine Association (DAV) publication (No. 5, 1970), I [Messner] feel forced to clarify a few points:

1. Günther and I reached the summit at 5 p.m. on June 27. We started to descend at 6 p.m.
2. The approaching monsoon (cloud banks to the south and west) meant that we created plan B on June 26, in case the report predicted bad weather. The weather report was good. Nevertheless, Dr. Herrligkoffer fired a red rocket to signal bad weather, indicating that I was to attempt to reach the summit as quickly as possible. If I was able to overcome the problems in the Merkl Gully, then I wanted to get to the summit before the weather changed for the worse. Bad weather would have meant the end of the expedition, and the only means of success was a solo ascent. Dr. Herrligkoffer was very happy with my suggestion.
3. Dr. Herrligkoffer is incorrect when he cites Felix Kuen. Felix and I didn't call to each other on a spur on the South Summit, but at the upper end of the Merkl Gully. [Kuen and Scholz were on the ramp to the South Shoulder; the Messners were at the notch above the Merkl Gully 80 to 100 meters away. See *Nanga Parbat 70*, Messner's account.] Felix Kuen and Peter Scholz had a rope when they saw me. Felix Kuen reported this differently, and I can't understand why he doesn't defend himself when Dr. Herrligkoffer quotes him, and spreads lies using his (Kuen's) name.
4. The Merkl Gully was not secured all the way and Felix Kuen himself maintained that it was only the first two sections. This makes Kuen and Scholz's achievement all the more impressive, as they both climbed up and abseiled down the Merkl Gully.

   Even if the gully had been secured all the way to the end, where we exited it to the right, we would still have had to descend via the Diamir Face on June 28. Because after talking to Felix Kuen we had no other choice.

   My brother feeling weak from the impact of altitude and unable to descend via the Rupal Face, as well as the red rocket indicating the approach of bad weather, triggered the chain reaction that led to us descending via the Diamir Face.

5. After Dr. Herrligkoffer realized that we had descended via the Diamir Face, he neglected to send a search party to the Diamir Valley. If you consider that Mummery took twenty hours (in 1895!) to reach the Diamir Valley from the Rupal Valley (basecamp in 1970), the "rescue measures" undertaken by Dr. Herrligkoffer beggar belief. (He was familiar with all sides of the mountain!)
6. You can probably only understand why Günther and I weren't together when we reached the base of the mountain if you've been in a similar situation. Felix Kuen was also one and a half hours ahead of his climbing partner when he reached the summit. Sigi Löw lagged behind during the descent from the summit in 1962 and fell. The very nature of the glacier also caused us to be so far apart. I've been in similar situations again and again in the mountains, but thought nothing of it, because everything had always turned out fine. With hindsight, I now see that it was wrong to not go down together.
7. When Günther didn't appear, I went back. I don't know how late it was nor did I look at my watch. Later, I saw that it had stopped working on June 29.

> I didn't continue down into the valley "the next day" as Dr. Herrligkoffer writes, but the day after that, so two days after starting to search for Günther. All that time, I expected that someone would be coming to help me. The fact that my fellow expedition members had no reason to expect that we had descended from the other side of the mountain only added to my worries and desperation. I had no way of informing them. I was on my own and I could hardly walk.

We did each tell our own side of the story (in the town of Bad Boll in 1971), and I did so again in Munich after Herrligkoffer's death, but no consensus was reached. Even though I was fair in my accounts; see, for example, my response of December 29, 1970:

> A rebuttal: I would like to underline that I have never personally accused our expedition leader Dr. Herrligkoffer of being responsible in any way for the death of my brother. If this impression has been created by incorrect reports in the press, I repudiate this.
>
> However, one fact is irrefutable. The wrong rocket caused us to make an unnecessarily hasty dash for the summit. Our descent route was not the wrong way down but the *only* way down. My brother Günther was suffering from altitude sickness, so descending via the much harder Merkl Gully would have been impossible.
>
> I categorically reject the accusation that I allegedly said that I would stop my attacks on Dr. Herrligkoffer in return for money. This slander once again left me feeling deeply disappointed. Due to the one-sided reporting from Dr. Herrligkoffer, I feel that I have no option but to take a stand, even if Dr. Herrligkoffer is doing everything possible to prevent me from doing so.

It took me years to win back my freedom from this conflict. The more I defended myself, the more heated the debate became.

Herrligkoffer succeeded in stopping me from publishing my book about the expedition called *The Red Rocket on Nanga Parbat*. He also managed to have the fees for the first edition frozen and the insurance money for my frostbitten feet withheld. The contract, literally a gag order, that we all signed with Herrligkoffer's institute prevented us from doing virtually anything. For years, I had my fees for talks deducted, as per the contract.

I joined the Rupal Face expedition full of optimism and in great physical condition. It was going to be my first eight-thousander. As brothers, Günther and I looked out for each other more than the other expedition members did. The downside is that amateur mountaineers neither understood nor sympathized with how we climbed then; they just sowed discord. The history of alpinism is full of similar examples.

After the tragedy and years of legal disputes, I didn't have the financial means to continue following my dreams. I wondered how I was going to fund my own expeditions. I had no financial resources, no community standing, and no support.

Back then, I asked myself who might be prepared to back, encourage, or trust me. Confidence in my own abilities was one thing I didn't lack.

During all those days sitting out stormy weather in the high camps, Günther and I often discussed writing a book about our first expedition to the Himalaya, and giving talks to fund our next trip. We mulled over setting up a mountaineering school. We were full of ideas and big dreams.

Now I was on my own. I had nothing but castles in the air. I went back to working at a secondary school in Eppan near Bolzano, where I had acted as a supply (substitute) teacher for maths, nature studies, and sports. On the weekends, I would climb in the Dolomites and walk the forests. It wasn't the world that was unfair, but people who lacked empathy. My enthusiasm for extreme rock climbing faded. My amputations meant I couldn't manage the difficult climbs of the past—so I started looking for other ways of pushing my limits. I wasn't going to let my life be destroyed by self-important expedition leaders, ambitious climbers, or moralists. I had become exploitable, and yet I valued my independence over everything else. My freedom had been sold off. I was caught in a trap.

7

NOT A GOOD WRITER

There's no textbook on coping with major crises. You can't control nature, or your foes who fan the flames of a crisis for their own gain.

—Reinhold Messner

In 1968, Jürgen Kemmler, an editor at BLV Verlag, a German publisher, sent this internal message (Munich, November 29, 1968):

> Subject: Young sportswriter
>
> During a visit to Bolzano, a number of people mentioned a young sports student. He's twenty-one years old and famous for his free climbing routes. He regularly publishes well-written mountaineering and skiing articles in *Dolomiten*, the South Tyrolean daily, as well as in Austrian newspapers and (reportedly) in magazines.
>
> This young man's name is Reinhold Messner from Villnöss near Brixen.
>
> According to our sources in South Tyrol, this two-line address suffices. If you'd like to get in touch with Reinhold, he comes recommended by Dr. Steger, and the senator, Dr. Brugger. They're both respected in South Tyrol, and happy to vouch for Reinhold Messner.

This early praise from two South Tyrolean politicians was pivotal to my journey as a writer. This is exactly what I wanted to do in life—to climb and commit to paper these stories about the mountains. And who should approach me in 1970, but the most successful German mountain writer at the time.

> Walter Pause
> September 10, 1970
>
> Confidential
> Dr. Egger, Managing Director BLV publishing house, Munich 13
> Reinhold Messner, Villnöss (and father)
> Dr. Herrligkoffer, Munich 25

Albert Bitterling, Berchtesgaden
RE: Nanga Parbat 1970
Dear gentlemen,
On August 18, 1970, a Munich-based magazine asked me to pen a public rebuke to counteract the dangerous and escalating speculations in the trade and daily press about the last Nanga Parbat expedition. I agreed immediately. Further public debate by the expedition members could only lead to an embarrassing repeat of the affair of 1953 and therefore damage alpinism's international reputation. This could lead to future international expeditions losing what is their bedrock—the trust of the general public, the alpine associations, and the industry.

I was the press officer on the first Nanga Parbat expedition in 1953 under Dr. Herrligkoffer, where Hermann Buhl succeeded in his groundbreaking solo summit ascent. Today, free of all the shackles of unpleasant controversy, this episode is seen as one of the most important in alpinism's history. Therefore, I'm only too aware of what goes on before and after expeditions to the Himalaya. I also realize that many issues aren't discussed in public. Furthermore, as a sixty-three-year-old climber, author, and mountain literature aficionado, I understand much about the risks of the extreme physical and mental exposure that mountaineers have to deal with in the world's highest mountains, far from civilization. Over the years, these pressures have repeatedly led to expedition members returning home to Europe divided and arguing—whether they were successful or not—and not as alpine heroes.

In any case, I'd like to do my utmost to avoid a repetition of this high-alpine tragicomedy. I have neither the time nor much inclination to get involved. However, I think it's important to offer my services as a mediator. I intend to speak to all parties and draw up a definite plan so that we can resolve all the thorny issues that have arisen over the past few weeks in a way that's acceptable to all those involved. I spoke to Reinhold Messner's father in Villnöss on 1 September to give him the gist of my discussions as follows:

Yesterday, I had a second discussion with the managers of the BLV publishing house in Munich. The managing director, Dr. Egger, backs this plan, which I'd like to outline to the parties involved. I should add that I offer my services as mediator and editor for the following proposal *only* if it is treated as *strictly confidential* until a mutual agreement has been signed by all parties at the BLV's premises.

The press, who have so far viewed the recent disputes as a welcome opportunity to create plenty of hot air and make fun of mountaineers, would then be informed *after* my proposal has been agreed upon, in a joint press release written by me.

<u>My proposal is as follows:</u>

1. The gentlemen receiving this letter, if they were part of the expedition, will immediately cease all mutual recriminations, and agree not to publish further reports and to end all legal action.

2. Following agreement with the management board at the BLV publishing house in Munich, *two* Nanga Parbat books will be produced as quickly as possible for simultaneous publication, if feasible in spring <u>1971</u>.

   a) The foundation's publication will be a large coffee-table format book (25.5 x 21.5 cm, the same format as Pause books) with the best color and black and white photos from the 1970 expedition. It will include a twenty-page report by Dr. Herrligkoffer with an outline of the expedition. In addition, it would contain carefully written, detailed captions. Walter Pause will assume editorial responsibility, although he won't be credited on the cover.

   b) A small-format book, in other words, a modern book by Reinhold Messner, where he publishes his objectively written, factual expedition report including his tale of the events during the push to the summit and its consequences. It will be a straightforward and direct account. To help boost sales, it will contain 8, 12, or 16 single-page black and white photos to underpin Reinhold Messner's account. Because the camera was lost, this may prove difficult. Here too, Walter Pause will also assume editorial responsibility, and won't be named as author or coauthor.

3. My personal involvement in this matter is solely to act as a mediator, at the express wish of the publisher. My task is to quickly settle this dispute and to implement the plans for both books, in a style that finally updates the (previous) image of books about the Himalaya. I would offer my editorial services for the book texts (liaising with both authors closely in the process) and, above all, be responsible for selecting the right pictures, the layout, modern typography, etc. . . .

4. The idea of publishing two books (at the same time by the same publisher) would enable the foundation to grant the participant most affected by the expedition a deserved special position and exempt him from paragraph 5 of the participant contract. The details of this mutual financial agreement should be agreed upon amicably as per the contract signed by all parties.
5. The expedition's contentious issues that have been irresponsibly divulged to the press should *no longer* be discussed in this manner as a matter of common sense. The goal is to stop hungry journalists from fanning the flames and escalating the libelous claims on both sides, and to enable an important period of reflection.
6. If all participants agree with me and/or the BLV about this proposal in principle, I will release a statement to the press over the next few days that would be signed by *all* parties. I would also be prepared to wait and discuss this press release (whose purpose is only to provide clear and reasonable reassurance and won't address any of the contentious issues) in a short meeting at the publisher's or at my home. In other words, I could wait until all parties can meet here in Munich.

Gentlemen, I consider my proposal to be the only solution. I see no alternative (other than an embarrassing continuation of this dispute, which benefits *nobody*). I ask you not to dismiss my proposal without due consideration. If you should reject it, I won't raise this matter again at any juncture. I have more than enough to do than is good for me or my health. The fact that I could convince BLV to take on both books is not a tactic on my part, but more of a coincidence. We would all have the chance to produce two contemporary, professional, and readable books about the Himalaya, which would sell like hot cakes without doubt. Don't forget, apart from two or three exceptions, the previous (at least forty) books about the Himalaya were *not* a success. Either for the publisher, or for the author.

I wondered whether I should trust the proposal. After all, Walter Pause was Herrligkoffer's press officer during the controversial 1953 Nanga Parbat expedition, where Hermann Buhl reached the summit with an incomparable solo climb. Pause had already written to various publishers by the end of August 1970 and openly expressed his interest in the matter. His verdict was that "Dr. H. (Herrligkoffer) is not a good writer."

Walter Pause
August 30, 1970

To BLV publishing house, Munich, Dr. Egger
RE: planned book Dr. Herrligkoffer Nanga Parbat
. . . Let's cut to the chase. Yesterday, I spoke to Dr. Herrligkoffer. I was his press officer in 1953 when Hermann Buhl made the first ascent of Nanga Parbat solo. I wanted to, or rather I'd been requested to, write an opinion piece, a column for the German *Bergsteiger* (Bruckmann) magazine about the latest dramatic Nanga Parbat expedition. During my interview with Dr. Herrligkoffer, we discussed the planned book about this expedition, and I asked him to consider publishing it with BLV.

This would mean I could be responsible for editing it as an expert on the subject and the situation in 1953 and since. Dr. Herrligkoffer had two quotes, one from the *Süddeutscher Verlag*, the other from his previous publisher Lehmann. I had to rewrite the first Nanga Parbat book published by Lehmann/Munich. I told Dr. Herrligkoffer it was time he started producing contemporary books on the Himalaya. And that this applied to both the pictures and the text. All the previous books—except the French Annapurna book—were written, presented, and contained pictures in a style that seemed outdated. They reflected the tradition of previous mountain literature, which was written by brilliant climbers and mountaineers, who couldn't write to save their lives. As a result, they always ended up getting stuck in a somewhat fake style. There's a lack of cosmopolitan experts who can really write about the mountains. I told Dr. Herrligkoffer that I would edit the book, if he published it with BLV. I'm only interested in working on the project to show what a *good* book on the Himalaya could be like. And to prove that it can be commercially successful. Up until now, the only bestsellers have been the French Annapurna book (*Premier Huit Mille* by Maurice Herzog) and the Hermann Buhl book (*Achttausend drüber und drunter* by Nymphenburger Verlag, with 120,000 copies sold by 1968).

In any case, I plan to interview Dr. Herrligkoffer on the 9 or 10 September and take minutes to combine all the statements in a binding

> form. These will then form a basis for the documentary report that is going to feature in the book. . . .
>
> Jürgen Winkler was also on Nanga Parbat as the photographer selected by Dr. Herrligkoffer. He told me a lot about the expedition over two evenings.
>
> Jürgen Winkler is also invited to accompany Dr. Herrligkoffer on his expedition to Mount Everest in 1972, along with other members of the *Extremen Fels* (Extreme Rock) team [*Im Extremen Fels* is Walter Pause's famous book of 100 alpine routes]. Manfred Sturm and others have also been invited to take part.

In the meantime, I had committed my experiences on Nanga Parbat in 1970 to paper. I had written it as a film script, to avoid having to refer to myself in the first person. It was called *The Red Rocket on Nanga Parbat.*

Walter Pause continued to write to me. His efforts to resolve the dispute and pave the way for future expeditions were genuine. Although, unfortunately, he was more interested in telling Dr. Herrligkoffer's side of the Nanga Parbat story. First and foremost, he intended to rewrite my manuscript as he saw fit. He told me what he thought about my writing.

> The publisher sent me your manuscript for a Nanga Parbat book, or rather the copy of an unfinished manuscript, which was obviously a first draft and not ready for publication.
>
> Nevertheless, I have read most of it and feel that I can judge it properly. Mr. Kemmler from BLV has also read it. We both came to the same conclusion. It doesn't work as a book in its current form. To print it at the moment would damage both the reputation of the author and the publisher. However, another publisher—in the mountain literature segment—might still be prepared to print it immediately. The result would resemble all those hastily produced books of the past few years. This is not literature. Let's face it, writing is hard. Anyone who is too ashamed to learn to write properly, shouldn't be doing so in the first place. Writing is always torturous. It's a matter of quiet, patient persistence, and above all mental discipline. He who can write, is already a man. Please don't take my carefully considered words the wrong way.
>
> You have such a fine reputation, my dear Reinhold, that I want to protect you, a highly experienced, and in this exceptional case, very responsible and

intelligent player on the stage of mountain literature. I wouldn't want you to commit a youthful folly. A book is something permanent. Once published, it remains in the literary sphere forever.

It will shape people's image of you, how people see your physical achievements and how they view the spirit that enabled you to triumph. To put it bluntly, the current manuscript would *not* make a book, even if we omitted the attempt made over the first twenty pages. My dear Reinhold, please note that I've also been told the same thing myself on several occasions.

As a fellow climber and writer, I'm happy to share with you openly and in a friendly manner what works, what doesn't, and how you can turn this into a *good* book. One that will catapult your name forever to a position that's unfortunately rare in the world of mountain literature. Let me be completely honest. My criticism may be difficult to accept. I appeal to your obvious intelligence, not to the emotions you might have at the moment.

1. There are many ways to write a successful book. In your case, *only* a personal account works—in other words, in the first person. Your attempt to avoid the almost traditional first-person narrative of this adventure, which surpasses the realms of any drama imaginable, and to write it in the form of a film script is *not* an original idea. Quite the opposite. *It spoils everything* about your tale that could make it an outstanding read and a good book.
2. Allow me to say again (as I told you in person) that what you experienced needs *no* embellishments. It requires no special treatment or presentation. What you experienced can *only* be related in a concise and disciplined way. There should be *no* psychological or philosophical pondering. I know this won't be easy for you. However, these emotional reflections and interjections will *ruin* the book and destroy your reputation too. I repeat, keep it short and simple, make greater use of the huge range of words the German language offers. Ask yourself what happened, what did I see, what did I do, and what did we do? Or what did our surroundings look like? The way that you write about what you thought comes over in such a stiff, cramped, and therefore less believable manner. I appeal to you to leave these passages out altogether. Knowing what to *leave out* is the real art of writing.
3. Knowing what to omit also requires rising above certain issues and leaving out the angry attacks on Herrligkoffer. You are no ordinary writer, you

are no Hiebeler, whose grudges spoil each book he writes. You need to demonstrate the intellectual discipline required to write a book.

In ten, twenty, fifty, or one hundred years, your book will be one of the classic works of mountain literature, but *only* if you can write it as succinctly and as well as I ask you to. In ten, twenty, or fifty years, *no* reader will be interested in people's behavior or the mistakes they made—especially in such exposed positions. The only thing that will interest them is the good story that conveys the experience, because it was written concisely. I beg you to be man enough to forget Herrligkoffer and focus solely on narrating the Nanga Parbat tragedy in all its detail. Clearly, concisely . . . and with a more varied use of vocabulary.

4. Keep your sentences simple (many of your sentences are excellent, because they are short, not long and confusing). And then you need to work hard to describe what you see, with more precise and varied vocabulary. The Rupal Face is different from the Droites, Jorasses, or Civetta. As a reader, I want to be able to picture it exactly. "Glorious" . . . is not a word you should be using, it should not be used more than once in the book.
5. The BLV will only take on this book, and would publish it immediately, if it was written the way as I have described—and if an agreement can be reached with the foundation regarding the publication date. If you are not capable of writing it in first-person narrative, then it will have to be rewritten. Buhl was only able to write such a good book because it was edited by a writer. Who should edit it? I offered to help both you and Herrligkoffer, as a backup solution. I didn't receive an answer. Therefore, I will not edit anything by him. Sadly, this means that I will not be able to edit your book either, although I would do it immediately. I would like to add that the purely descriptive passages in your book made a strong impression on me. However, I need to save my resources for things other than mountain literature and am desperately short of time. I cannot do it. . . .

Copy to BLV, Mr. Kemmler

Around the same time, I received a copy of a letter by registered post from Dr. Ludwig Delp, a lawyer, which was addressed to the Nymphenburger publishing house, for the attention of Berthold Spangenberg, 8 Munich 19, Romanstrasse 16, on December 16, 1970. It threatened to block publication of my book.

RE: Your intention to publish Reinhold Messner *The Red Rocket on Nanga Parbat*
Dear Mr. Spangenberg,

I regret having to contact you in my capacity as long-standing legal counsel for the German Institute for Foreign Research, 8 Munich 25, Plinganserstrasse 120a, regarding the aforementioned affair.

Please find attached, a letter, which was obviously written and distributed by Mr. Reinhold Messner, one of the participants in this year's Nanga Parbat expedition by the German Institute for Foreign Research. In it, he claims that the above-mentioned book is due to be published by you in spring 1971 (probably March).

However, it appears that this letter was neither written, nor authorized by your publishing house. This also applies to the contents of this letter, which advertises the book, using slanderous claims about third parties.

To prevent this dispute, which was started by Mr. Messner, from spreading to your publishing house using the legal measures at the disposal of the German Institute for Foreign Research, I ask you to do everything in your power to immediately withdraw this letter from circulation and to prevent any repeat of the slanderous claims in connection with your publishing house.

Furthermore, I would like to make you aware of the following: as is standard procedure, on October 19, 1969, Mr. Messner signed a participant contract concerning his involvement in the Nanga Parbat 1970 expedition. Please find enclosed a certified copy of the contract. In particular, I refer to section 5, paragraph 4 of the contract, which details the regulations applying to book publications by climbers reaching the summit. In particular, I refer to the relevant embargo period and the relationship between the expedition report and the entire book.

You have already been made aware of the contractual provisions in the letter of September 5, 1970, from the German Institute for Foreign Research.

The authentic expedition report by the German Institute for Foreign Research has not yet been published. It is not possible to give a more exact publication date at this time. As a result, the contractually agreed embargo period has not yet started. It will certainly not have expired by spring 1971. Therefore, your publishing house cannot announce that it intends to publish Mr. Messner's book in spring 1971—if the contents of the letter are to be believed.

Mr. Messner transferred copyright regarding all forms of communication about the events of the expedition regardless of the media on which they are reproduced and in terms of time and space and gave the exclusive rights to the German Institute for Foreign Research. See section 5, paragraph 1 of the participant contract. As such, this transfer of rights also applies to the planned book publication. Mr. Messner is therefore not permitted to act on the manuscript or to legally transfer you the right to publish the work without the express permission of the German Institute for Foreign Research. Notwithstanding, if this was to be attempted, it would constitute an infringement of the exclusive rights of the German Institute for Foreign Research with the corresponding injunctions and compensation claims.

Pursuant to the same contract provision, the manuscript belongs to the German Institute for Foreign Research and moreover due to the particular clauses in section 5, paragraph 4, it has a right to obtain information regarding the expedition report and the overall scope of the book. This means that the Institute may request to see the manuscript to carry out this inspection. Referring to the book, Mr. Messner talks of "large numbers of photographs and illustrations." The provisions of section 5 of the participant contract between the German Institute for Foreign Research and Mr. Messner apply here too.

Given his claim, it would seem that Mr. Messner has withheld a number of images subject to exclusive rights by the German Institute for Foreign Research. This does not alter the fact that he has no legal right to use this material. In this respect, the German Institute for Foreign Research also has the right to prohibit their use, claim compensation, and publish them here too.

Should the announcements in the letter be true, your publishing house is also passively involved, irrespective of the fact that there is already a lawsuit against Mr. Messner at the Munich County Court.

Just a few days ago, the German Institute for Foreign Research became aware of a letter from Walter Pause to Mr. Messner, which indicates that, on behalf of BLV, Pause is considering the same manuscript from Mr. Messner. In the correspondence, Pause outlines the editorial conditions and other factors under which the BLV would publish the book. Among other things, Mr. Pause makes it a condition that there is an agreement with the Institute (i.e., the German Institute for Foreign Research) regarding the publication date.

This leads me to conclude that there is no contractual agreement between Mr. Messner and your publishing house, and the aforementioned letter was sent without your knowledge or consent. I cannot imagine that such a respected publisher as yourself would enter into such an agreement, especially in this form.

Nevertheless, the fact remains that your publishing house was said to be publishing the book in spring 1971 in violation of other rights.

In addition, this statement was connected to a number of defamatory and slanderous claims. I am sure that you will understand that the German Institute for Foreign Research will make immediate use of all types of legal redress at its disposal to defend itself.

Therefore I request your prompt reply to explain your position on the issue and the claims made by the German Institute for Foreign Research by December 23, 1970, at the latest.

I sincerely regret that I am obliged to bother you with this matter as the year draws to a close.

Yours sincerely,

Dr. Ludwig Delp, Lawyer

The book was published and a temporary injunction stopped any further sales. There I was, a disabled man, humiliated and without any prospects for the future.

However, both my books were well received. Reviews of *Zurück in die Berge* (Back to the Mountains) called it "the most interesting mountain book for years" and *The Red Rocket on Nanga Parbat* the "insider expedition report." Nevertheless, I wasn't happy with them. My first two books were later reproduced in a different form and reissued—and are still in print. They are quoted as "portraying the power and language of the young generation of mountaineers." I still feel grateful toward Walter Pause for the advice he gave me.

At the time though, I was disappointed for two main reasons.

First, the dispute prevented mountaineers from understanding how the Nanga Parbat 1970 tragedy occurred. They found it hard to see how anyone could descend from an 8,000-meter peak without help. And secondly, they believed everything that our expedition leader said, even though he could only have made it all up, as he wasn't there at the time.

Seven of my toes had to be amputated. I would never be as fit for rock climbing again. What's more, Günther's death was perceived as being my fault, and not Dr. Herrligkoffer's—though by summitting, Günther and I had made his expedition successful. The use of every possible form of legal action, lies, and contradictions against me meant that I came up against the stark realities of the real world. Instead of reacting, I should have just stuck to telling my story, as Walter Pause had advised me to do.

Today, any doubts have long since been cleared up. Dr. Delp went on to describe Herrligkoffer's version of the events on Nanga Parbat 1970 as speculation. My fellow expedition members, as well as many well-known alpinists who stood by the expedition leader at the time, have since effectively shown themselves to be *Schafsköpfen* (blockheads) for reacting this way.

I was made a member of the International Climbing and Mountaineering Federation Safety Commission (UIAA), a group spearheaded by Fritz Wiessner—and I was entrusted with new responsibilities.

This gave me a solid standing in international mountaineering. Still, I hadn't learned how to deal with strong headwinds. It turns out that my mother's advice to "know when to hold your tongue" was something I had yet to learn.

8
NO LIMIT

Whenever I found myself facing a new challenge, others seemed to know immediately that it wouldn't be possible.

—Reinhold Messner

After the Nanga Parbat expedition, though I couldn't forget the accusations leveled against me, I was able to forgive my expedition leader.

Dr. Herrligkoffer, I thought, must have assumed that we (Günther and I) died in the Merkl Notch. That was why he didn't send a search party to the Diamir Valley. Nobody believed that we could have survived the descent of an unknown route. When I suddenly turned up alone and unexpected in the Indus Valley, Herrligkoffer imagined that my brother had died in the Merkl Notch, something he believed right up until his own death. Even if this public conjecture was a way of protecting himself, however, it meant that I was accused of acting in a calculated manner: that I had been planning to traverse Nanga Parbat all along. His speculations triggered my response—and a dispute that lasted over fifty years.

In October 1970, I was invited to join the UIAA's Executive Committee, and Ugo Graf Vallepiana asked me to sit on a commission formed by Fritz Wiessner to redefine the difficulty scale and grade system for climbing routes. I had very strong opinions on the matter: "The scale should never have a ceiling, and climbers should decide whether they're skilled enough to manage the route," I said. The minutes go on to say: "Messner's convinced that we'll revert to a simplified scale in a few years. Vallepiana agrees. If the scale's too complicated, then it's of no practical use. It's impossible to measure every meter of a route."

The commission, which was selected by the UIAA Executive Committee, included many famous mountaineers, such as: Jean Juge, president, Geneva; Werner Munter, UIAA, Mühlethurnen (Switzerland); Colonel Peter Baumgartner, ministry of defence, Andermatt (Switzerland); Bernard Amy, FFM, Paris; Reinhold Messner, CAI, Villnöss/Funes (Italy); Peter Baumgartner, OeAV, Vienna; Günter Sturm, DAV, Munich; Vitali Abalakov, Russian

A rock climber in the 1960s

Mountaineering Federation, Moscow; Frank Solari, president of the material commission (ex officio); France Avĉin, vice president of the material commission (Slovenia, formerly part of the Federal Republic of Yugoslavia).

I particularly enjoyed talking to Fritz H. Wiessner back then. He used to be in contact with Dieter Hasse and Manfred Sturm and was an excellent climber himself, a living alpine legend. Born in Dresden in 1900, he learned to climb on the Elbe Sandstone Mountains in Saxony. Later he moved to the US, where he influenced the development of extreme mountaineering. In 1925, he made the first ascent of the southeast face of the Fleischbank (Wilder Kaiser) and the north face of the Furchetta.

On the fiftieth anniversary of these mighty routes, in 1975, Wiessner celebrated his seventy-fifth birthday. He let me interview him:

RM: How does it feel to have been an extreme climber for half a century?

FW: The mountains were always an important part of my life. It wasn't about the competition, it was about the mountain itself. I'm glad that I had fifty years of extreme climbing without any serious accidents in the mountains.

RM: How many serious falls did you have?

FW: Five, and always while leading. One of them was a massive fall in the Elbe Sandstone Mountains. I've never injured myself in a fall, apart from this summer, where I slipped on a rock at my local Elbsandsteingebirge crags and fell awkwardly. . . . I was watching some other climbers.

RM: Who were your role models?

FW: I admired Preuss and Fehrmann, and followed their philosophy as far as I could. I climbed the Fiechtl-Weinberger on the Predigtstuhl completely free. Until 1950, I hardly ever climbed as a second. In the Elbe Sandstone Mountains, there's a crack, where I put up the first ascent. It was graded VIIc, *Meisterklasse*.

RM: And then in 1925, you had your big breakthrough—the Furchetta North Face. And you were on Nanga Parbat in 1932, weren't you?

FW: I was supposed to lead the expedition. Welzenbach invited me. However, it was too difficult to organize everything from America, so Welzenbach's friend Merkl took on the role. I climbed with two other Americans to bring most of the supplies up.

RM: The 1932 Nanga Parbat expedition wasn't successful. But you were very bold in attempting first ascents—in the Tetons, on Devils Tower, in the Black Hills.

FW: . . . I developed some 40 new climbing areas.

RM: And then you went to K2?

FW: K2 left a big impression on me right up to this day. I was at peak fitness and we got so close to the summit. We were climbing with minimal equipment, no radio, no oxygen.

RM: Were US climbers who focused on free climbing following *Elbsandstein* ethics and rules? [In the Alps, pitons are used more widely.]

FW: I probably had a big influence.

Jean Juge and I went on to climb some big Dolomite routes, and I'm still friends with Bernard Amy to this day. I gained insights and learned a lot from all of them about the early years of alpine climbing and the world of mountaineering before I came on the scene.

On December 23, 1970, I wrote to Fritz Wiessner in Vermont with a final correction regarding the standards and difficulty scale:

> Dear Fritz, forgive me for having taken so long to write to you. Herrligkoffer's distortions of the facts are getting worse and worse and making life difficult for me.
>
> Here's my opinion on the difficulty scale: replace "upper limit of what is humanly possible" with "current limit of what is possible in free climbing." It's not necessary to explain the grade because it speaks for itself.

I continued to think about the difficulty scale. In 1973, I published my book entitled *The Seventh Grade*. In the book, I proposed extending the upper limit of the Welzenbach scale, which with its six grades had become the UIAA difficulty scale for rock climbing.

On this issue I didn't make any friends either. On the contrary, I was accused of arrogance, and even of being a con man, although I was only correcting a mistake made by Welzenbach. He had defined grade VI in rock climbing as the upper limit of what it was possible to climb, citing a tour as an example, namely the Civetta Northwest Face. Based on this logic, Emil Solleder's route on the big Dolomite face would remain the hardest free-climbing route forever.

Today, the standard of international climbing has catapulted into the realms of the virtually impossible. I didn't see this coming—the return to free climbing and the launch of indoor climbing as an Olympic discipline. The notion of infinite development of the sport is part of our instinct, not some no-limit credo of individual climbers. While we all have our limits, as a climbing community we continue to push those boundaries.

Skeptics have stirred up strong winds in this debate. Thankfully, these headwinds have helped me to recognize and admire—not criticize—the continually burgeoning skills of ever-younger climbers.

9

THE BOLT WAR

The resistance that I faced, in some cases for many years, suddenly seemed to disappear, because I no longer took it seriously.

—Reinhold Messner

In a letter to me in autumn 1969, Toni Hiebeler wrote: "If you carry on like this, you'll end up dead." A year earlier, Günther and I had led the team of Hiebeler/Maschke through the Eiger North Pillar, climbing slowly due to the bad weather.

Shortly afterward, Toni invited me to Munich to meet with his publisher, Dr. Walther Heering. They were intending to offer me a job writing for *Alpinismus*. At that point, *Alpinismus* was *the* most progressive climbing magazine and Toni Hiebeler, editor-in-chief.

While I was waiting for the interview, I got chatting with Toni's secretary, Frau Heilmannseder. "If you start as a journalist, there'll be no more time for climbing. You'll be stuck in the office," she warned me.

After a brief interview, Heering and Hiebeler offered me the job. I turned it down, because they couldn't agree to a clause I wanted enshrined in the contract, allowing me to spend half my time outdoors.

Around this same time, I met the famous climber Dieter Hasse. Nine years earlier, with three others, he had created the new route on the Cima Grande that went down in alpine history as "the direttissima." Their route signaled the dawn of a new dimension of climbing in the Dolomites and found many imitators. Although Hasse had drilled bolts to climb the overhanging sections in the middle of the wall, it was a bold climb.

Hasse and I got to chatting by the side of the road under Sass Pordoi and talked about Saxon climbers, the great free-climbing routes in the Dolomites, and how the bolting of routes from the ground up reduces the exposure. We talked about the idea of "leaving no trace," of adventure climbing, and the use of aid.

We parted ways not as opponents, quite the contrary. I have a lot of respect for Hasse. However, he became a vehement critic of my stance on "climbing

Messner with Hans Vinatzer

safely, without bolts." He dismissed my work for the UIAA Safety Commission, and later my book *The Seventh Grade*, as "mad philosophy." The early Dolomites free-climber Hans Vinatzer saw things differently; he was my salvation.

Erich Vanis wrote as follows in the Austrian Alpine Club publication, the *Österreichische Alpenzeitung* (*ÖAZ*):

> I was interested to follow our club member Dieter Hasse's critical views on the passages in Reinhold Messner's book *The Seventh Grade* that mention Dieter's alpine achievements (January/February edition of the *ÖAZ*).
>
> I believe it was important to give Hasse plenty of space in the *ÖAZ* to rectify all the errors and distortions of alpine history. If this article hadn't been printed, then young climbers in particular might have believed the

dogmatic opinions espoused by the G(C)OAT (Greatest Climber of All Time—Messner). And despite his major impact on the alpine climbing world in the 1960s and early 1970s, Hasse would have been characterized as the over-cautious, over-bolting buffoon.

In the 1960s, using pitons as climbing aids was par for the course. Climbers in Europe, myself included, had little contact with the new generation of top young climbers from the US, such as Royal Robbins, and their new "clean climbing" ethics. I had no idea of the developments in Yosemite, California, at the time. I followed Paul Preuss's ideas and routes and tried to use as few pegs (pitons) as possible on my first ascents. This attitude—adventure climbing—jarred with the later generation of climbers, who followed different ideals than Mummery's "by fair means" philosophy. I developed my ability to discover new routes that I could climb by skill and fair means, and turned that and my own climbing skills into an art.

Other climbers were better climbers, but I was fascinated by finding ways to link moves while climbing on lead and being bold enough to venture where others hadn't dared. I never once fell while leading. As a result, I attempted more and more difficult first ascents and repeated the hardest routes on the biggest faces. I enjoyed putting ideas into practice.

Toni Hiebeler wasn't the only one, though, to prophesy my premature downfall. The climbing community also claimed that my luck wouldn't last. Claude Barbier, the outstanding Belgian mountaineer whom Italian climbers called "il divino Claudio," commented:

> Messner says: "Although I've climbed over a thousand tours in the Alps and been on twelve expeditions, I've never fallen. Which is more important to me than all my other successes."
>
> 1966: On the Walker Spur? "It once took me six attempts at the end of a corner (dihedral) to make the final move onto the ledge above it; I kept slipping back."
>
> 1968: On a winter ascent of the Pelmo North Face, Messner fell 30 meters.
>
> And in 1969, in the Droites: "I peered over the lip down into the ten-meter-deep crevasse. . . . Suddenly I was carried over the edge and into the void."
>
> 1971: In *Mountain* magazine, Messner admitted to having fallen a couple of times when aid climbing, "Never while free climbing, but I've fallen once or twice on artificial when a piton came out."
>
> Readers can make of this what they will.

I climbed with Claudio Barbier in the Sella Towers in the Dolomites and knew about his free soloing prowess. He was well aware of the difference between "falling off the wall" and "falling when roped up and seconding." Nevertheless, during the public debate on placing protection, I came out as the loser. I'll admit that I was also lucky. Above all, because I was in the right place at the right time and met the best possible teacher: Sepp Mayerl from East Tyrol in Austria.

I was eighteen; he was twenty-five. The seven-year gap made him an experienced teacher and me a keen student. We climbed a lot of long routes together, such as Tofana, Sella, Civetta. At first, he led everything; he showed me his secrets, and his first ascents. He also sang the praises of his favorite climbing partner, Peter Habeler from Zillertal, Austria.

In our second year of climbing together, I was allowed to lead some of the time. In the third year, we started swapping leads and I met Peter. In 1969, following our successful Andes expedition, where I climbed the whole time with Peter, Sepp let me lead everything.

So, I had the good fortune to learn from the most experienced climber there was. And then with Peter, who was just three years older than me, I went on to push the boundaries of alpine climbing.

In 1970, Sepp Mayerl and Rolf Walter made the first ascent of Lhotse Shar. Sepp then climbed numerous other first ascents in the Himalaya. We lost touch over the years, unfortunately, until, fifteen years later, we worked together on a book project. It was due to be called *Im Schatten der Grossen* (In the Shadow of the Greats). As the title could have been misleading, Sepp changed it to *Der Turm in Mir: Zu Schwierigsten Gipfeln der Erde* (The Tower in Me: To the Most Difficult Summits of the Earth). Sepp was a church tower roofer who didn't use scaffolding.

Blasl, our nickname for Sepp, taught Peter and me the skills to go one step further, and we became pioneers of high-alpine mountaineering. It was good fortune and Sepp's expertise that made this possible. We definitely didn't want to overshadow him—quite the opposite. After our success on Everest, we never forgot him.

There was a lot of jealousy among mountaineers back then. Maybe not everyone got their share of good luck. Falling out of the wall is not the same as slipping from a hold.

I remained mired in the "bolt war" for many years. For two decades climbers argued whether the slab on the Heiligkreuzkofel Central Pillar could have been free climbed in stiff boots in 1968. I think a handhold broke off some years later.

Anyway, I'm still alive. If I had fallen out of the wall back then, both my climbing career and my life would have been over. There would have been a lot of questions, but few answers. I know I am lucky to have made it, and I'm grateful for that.

10

"STOP THIS DESPERADO"

I was always accused of moralizing. At some point,
I stopped comparing my ideals to others.

—Reinhold Messner

In autumn 1970, I left hospital as an invalid. Seven of my toes had been fully or partially amputated. And a few of my fingertips were gone too. It was obvious that I would never be able to climb as well again.

During his first lecture on the expedition in Munich, Herrligkoffer's verdict was devastating: "He abandoned his brother." I felt ashamed having to respond—his damning conviction nearly tore my family apart. It was only because I knew the truth of what had really happened that I was able to bear this awful accusation that I had somehow sacrificed my brother.

I had used up all my savings to venture out on the Nanga Parbat expedition, so I was left with no choice after this but to get a job. I started working again as a secondary school teacher in Eppan near Bolzano, but then left after four months to lead trekking groups to Mount Damavand in Iran, Tilicho Lake in the Annapurna range of the Himalaya, and the Carstensz Pyramid in New Guinea, where I climbed a few first ascents.

Hannes Gasser, a well-known mountain guide, wrote in *Tiroler Tageszeitung*:

> Reinhold Messner, who came to the attention of the public due to the tragic Nanga Parbat expedition last year, plans to lead a European expedition to the Carstensz region next year.
>
> He plans to step up the research started on the Indigenous peoples there, who have had little contact with civilization. Messner also returned to Nanga Parbat this autumn to search for his brother's body, who, as is well known, was killed in an avalanche after successfully reaching the summit. The avalanche situation made further searches impossible.

In 1972, as part of the Tyrolean Himalaya expedition led by Wolfgang Nairz, I climbed the South Face of Manaslu. Franz Jäger and I set out for the summit from the last camp on the southwest ridge of the huge summit plateau. The plan was to make it to the summit and back to camp within the same day. Franz soon gave up and headed back down over the flat, windblown snow. We didn't think there was any risk.

I reached the summit on my own, got caught in a snowstorm that turned into a hurricane, and lost my bearings on the way back down. Stuck in a whiteout, I spent hours going around in circles. Luckily, I found the tent; Andi Schlick and Horst Fankhauser were inside, but no sign of Franz. Franz and

I had flattened the tent and weighted it down before we had set off. Yet when Horst arrived, the tent had been set up. Had Franz come back only to set out again to call out for me? To help me find the way? Andi and Horst went to look for him and spent half the night searching the plateau.

They dug snow holes to shelter from the storm and the cold. Andi became disoriented and disappeared in the whiteout. He never returned. Franz wasn't found. When Horst came back to camp alone the next morning, it was clear that tragedy had struck. And I was to bear the responsibility for it.

Back in Europe, a campaign sprang up against me, which was also linked to the death of my brother on Nanga Parbat. That profound tragedy, now joined by the tragic events on Manaslu, was to brand me inhuman once and for all.

Hannes Gasser wrote in the *Kurier*:

> In my opinion, Reinhold Messner is responsible for this disaster. You should not leave your climbing partner on their own during a storm on the summit. The zone between 5,000 and 8,000 [meters] has such significant risks that a mountaineer who is exhausted or struggling mentally will seldom survive. Even if Franz Jäger had instructed Messner to go on alone, Messner should have gone back down with him.

Gasser contacted Max von Kienlin, a guest on the 1970 Nanga expedition 1970, and asked for his support. Von Kienlin sent documents to Toni Hiebeler. As Hannes Gasser wrote in a letter to von Kienlin, he wanted to "stop this desperado Messner."

Max von Kienlin replied: "Don't you already have enough to finish Messner off without my help? I'd be surprised if you didn't." In other words, Baron von Kienlin felt his support was unnecessary, as this time the collective accusations in mountaineering circles would already be enough to finally destroy my reputation.

11

GOING SOLO

My raison d'être increasingly became to focus on my own ideas and put them into practice. I was less interested in success, preferring to climb successfully in the present. Crises were also par for the course. I accepted them and criticism as part of my life.

—Reinhold Messner

After two summits and three deaths, I found myself asking whether this style of high-alpine climbing was justifiable. It wasn't. The risks were just too high. I could justify "fast and light" summit ascents in the death zone for myself, but not for others. Günther followed me up Nanga Parbat of his own free will, but then got altitude sickness. Our only hope of survival was the Diamir Valley, where Günther disappeared within an avalanche basin on the Diamir Face.

On Manaslu, two of my fellow climbers died in a snowstorm. Horst Fankhauser and I were able to make it back down into the valley.

If Günther and I had turned back at the South Shoulder on Nanga Parbat, we might have made it back to Camp 5, though we wouldn't have reached the summit.

Günther followed me, and maybe climbed too quickly to catch up. He wanted to reach the summit. On Manaslu, it was the opposite: Franz Jäger didn't feel up to attempting the final push to the summit and headed back. Andi Schlick braved the dark and the cold with Horst to go and look for Franz. Both Andi and Franz went missing. Both accidents, which are the greatest tragedies in my mountaineering life, are linked to my determination to attempt to reach the summit. So, I have to bear the responsibility for their deaths—to this day. I'm not apportioning any blame in this respect. Both partners—Günther and Franz—made their own decisions and took their own risks.

In the summer of 1973, I attempted to climb Nanga Parbat solo, but failed due to the scale of the task. The exposure on the vast Diamir Face was so huge that I just couldn't cope with it.

Six months later, I led a small expedition to the Andes, to the South Face of Aconcagua. The chair of the South Tyrolean Alpine Club (Alpenverein Südtirol, AVS), Luis Vonmetz, said this about it:

> In 1974, Reinhold planned a new route up through the South Face of Aconcagua in South America. He was accompanied by his wife Uschi, a doctor named Oswald Oelz, Konrad Renzler, Jochen Gruber, Jörgl Mayr, and Ernst Pertl as the filmmaker. The first attempts on this 3,000-meter-high face went well. Only Jochen overexerted himself while setting up high camp. He got altitude sickness and had to be brought back down to base camp by Oswald Oelz. Reinhold left high camp in dubious weather to head to the summit alone. This proved successful. Jörgl was supposed to wait and assist Reinhold on the descent, but instead he followed Reinhold, who refused to let him continue climbing. Back in South Tyrol, this resulted in an argument. Jörgl felt cheated of the summit. In his book, Reinhold said that Jörgl would never have coped with the challenging conditions without a rope. Looking back, Reinhold's decision is understandable, especially considering the fatal accidents on his earlier expeditions.

After these two tragedies, I wanted to rule out any risks for my fellow expedition members. Jörgl was an excellent climber on rock, but he was visually impaired. How would he negotiate the 1,000-meter summit face should it turn out that he couldn't climb fast enough to keep up with me? Speed was a condition for making it to the summit and back in a single day. I understood why Jörgl was annoyed. But what if he had followed me and then gotten lost? How would I ever be able to live with the reproaches from the mountaineering world?

I increasingly retreated from mountaineering circles. I failed on a 1974 Makalu South Face expedition, but with Peter Habeler successfully climbed the North Faces of the Eiger and the Matterhorn in fast ascents. We weren't interested in breaking any records but in moving fast. My strategy was to climb safely, quickly, and independently. And the same went for high-alpine mountaineering, which was definitely possible with Peter more than with anyone else. He climbed quickly and securely in all kinds of terrain and could move without protection when it got steep. I knew that Peter was the ideal partner for the next level of big wall climbing in the Himalaya.

12

INTRIGUE FOR INTRIGUE'S SAKE

If the powerful and mighty hate you, it makes them vulnerable. First, they stumble because of their arrogance, then due to their shortcomings.

—Reinhold Messner

In the summer of 1975, Peter Habeler and I climbed Gasherbrum I, also known as Hidden Peak, in the Karakoram in pure alpine style. It had been climbed first by the Americans Peter Schoening and Andrew Kauffman. Habeler and I made the second ascent of the 8,000-meter peak via its north face.

During the previous months, I had been part of a big Italian expedition on Lhotse. I describe both climbs in my book *The Challenge*.

To me, writing had become more than a way to help fund my expeditions. Toni Hiebeler, the most influential alpine journalist of the day, wrote a review of my book that bordered on intrigue. I knew Toni Hiebeler personally: I'd climbed the North Pillar on the Eiger with him and published articles in his *Alpinismus* magazine. So why did he refuse to review my first book, *Zurück in die Berge* (Back to the Mountains), in his magazine?

In 1969, Hiebeler praised my achievements as a mountaineer, but later, when I became an author and public speaker, and effectively a competitor, he reacted with suspicion. In 1969, Hiebeler wrote:

> Messner has been climbing mountains since 1950. He's a fierce advocate of classic mountaineering, of free climbing—and an unparalleled critic of using bolts. We feel he is right. If only there were more Messners!

And in 1976, he commented that

> he only devotes twenty pages to what happened on the mountain. In the rest of the book, Messner describes his experiences on the abortive Italian

> expedition to the South Face of Lhotse (8,511 m) in the Himalaya, before he climbed Hidden Peak. Over half the book is about the preparations and trek to reach the mountain, which were all part of *The Challenge*. It's an exciting read, both for climbers and other readers. And it was an amazing feat, although often somewhat overrated. Because everything that Messner describes as a challenge has been seen before. And it was often improvised and therefore made more difficult, and more dramatic. . . .
>
> Reinhold Messner and Peter Habeler are the first climbers to climb an eight-thousander as a team of two. They had the "lightest equipment available" and were "highly trained." Messner and Habeler are high-alpine professionals. And I'm not being glib with the term professional. They were fitter and had acclimatized to an extent that would be impossible for a conventional climber with a day job.
>
> These facts don't detract from their exceptional achievement on Hidden Peak; however, those seeking to imitate their success need to be very well prepared.
>
> As is so often the case, there were also problems between team members on Lhotse.

I thought it was paramount to write about the two very different expeditions, and the ups and downs between those involved. It helped me to see more clearly the differences between expedition-style climbing and alpine-style climbing. For me, writing about the experience was almost as important as the climbing itself. By criticizing my book, I perceived that Hiebeler also questioned my style of climbing. Just like Walter Pause, he saw my approach to high-alpine mountaineering as an attempt to become a professional in the scene, which it wasn't at the time. Hiebeler goes on to say:

> How having climbed two or even three eight-thousanders can go to your head! Messner's ambitious nature seems to make him overestimate the alpine public's interest. Even the most malicious of journalists wouldn't have minded two teams climbing the eight-thousander via two routes. The problem for Messner was that the Austrian team was also a mini-group who used no porters. [Hans Schnell led a small expedition to the summit via the normal route up the other side of the mountain to the summit.]

> . . . According to the book, a brand-new Reinhold Messner stood at the summit, freed from the shackles of fame and glory. "The atmosphere was one of all-embracing silence, not the silence of death, but a liberating silence—infinite, light, and carefree. All the sounds seemed part of this profound tranquillity. Any movement was neither work, nor action—merely being. And being was freedom. A sense of freedom remote from time itself."
>
> Further on in the book, the reader can breathe a sigh of relief—the adventure had a happy ending—the Hidden Peak is Reinhold Messner's first eight-thousander without the death of a team member or a brother. And that is, without doubt, the most positive thing about the whole expedition. After all, Messner has his own unique view of life. As he puts it: "How important is my life—in the scheme of things."

Ten years later, Toni Hiebeler came to see me at Juval Castle. I had just finished renovating it. In 1985, he wrote in *Berge* magazine: "Juval was pretty run down, but the thirteenth-century edifice is situated in an impressive location high up over the valley."

Again, he was unable to curb his somewhat spiteful side. But he couldn't hurt me anymore. Today, Juval Castle is open to the public for all to see and admire.

13

ONE-MAN SHOW

If we have our own "why" of life, we shall get along with almost any "how."

—Friedrich Nietzsche

Before I decided to attempt to climb the world's highest mountain without supplemental oxygen, I knew about Edward Norton and the British Mount Everest expedition's attempt to reach the summit without a mask in 1924. My projects were often based on attempts that had failed and taken place long before my time. I carefully studied my predecessors and read their books to learn from their mistakes. Norton was ultimately too slow and had to abandon his attempt at around 8,600 meters. To have any chance of success, I had to be faster.

After Peter and I had achieved the "impossible," climbing Mount Everest without masks, I talked about our ascent as compared to the near-successes of our predecessors. Somehow, this created the impression that I was the one in charge of the whole affair.

Other mountaineers asked Peter: "Why do you put up with this? Where's your self-respect? All your joint achievements are becoming the Messner one-man show!"

Peter made his view plain: "I would never have reached the summit without Reinhold. And he would never have made it without me." Exactly. From the start of our joint expedition to Hidden Peak, our concerted joint efforts heavily influenced the development of high-alpine climbing, and that remains the case right up to this day.

Peter Habeler:

> The ascent of Hidden Peak in the Karakoram—the Pakistani side of the Karakoram—in 1975 was a simple, two-man operation, with a tiny budget and minimal equipment. It was probably the smallest expedition ever to tackle a 8,000-meter peak. And, what's more, we made it to the summit without bottled oxygen. It might have appeared that Messner was the leader,

Filming of *The Eiger Sanction* on location in Kleine Scheidegg, Switzerland, in 1975, with cast members, including Clint Eastwood and Peter Habeler

> and me, the hanger on. I don't have a problem with this—it helps to sell the story. Public acclaim isn't important to me whereas Reinhold craves widespread recognition. There is this photo of me, on the summit of the 8,068-meter Hidden Peak. Reinhold took it, simply because I was at the top before him. The image was published all over the world and captioned: "Reinhold Messner conquers Hidden Peak."

I have never hidden the role that Peter played in our successes. On the contrary, I write about his summit push on Hidden Peak in my book *The Challenge*, and his role is the climax of the whole tale.

> The steepness of the face started to ease off. The higher we climbed, the more the slope tilted, forcing us closer to a seemingly nearby gully. Quietly at first, a roaring sound started to get louder and louder above us, like a giant pair of bellows. As Peter reached the ridgeline, the sun shone on his head and the wind blew through his disheveled hair. Below, where I was, everything was still and calm. I trudged on upward, hoping to film Peter's

ascent. Peter said: "This is the ridge to the summit." He was dead sure that we were going to make it. He pulled his axe out of the snow and climbed on. The wind was strong up here, but not unpleasant. It was loud enough to hide the noise of my labored breathing and heavy steps.

We reached the ridge between the Northwest Face and the Southwest Flank, and beyond the Eastern Summit of Hidden Peak the whole panorama of Central Asia opened up before us.

It was a spectacle that surpassed anything I had ever seen, a high-alpine landscape in grey and white fanning out from crest to crest as far as the eye could see. Individual ridges rose like petrified waves in a gigantic sea that had been turned to stone. To the left stood the highest peaks of the Karakoram—three eight-thousanders in one go—Gasherbrum II, Broad Peak, and K2—the frontier mountains between Xinjiang and Pakistan. Standing there like figments of the imagination, they towered into the blue-black sky, paralyzing our courage—a visual reminder that only heightened our own sense of altitude and isolation.

The isolation was overwhelming. When I think of how long it had taken us to get here, it seemed like eternity. Everything was quiet, a silent, transparent space above the summits, with only the stars in the firmament. Always I had been searching for this sense of solitude, and had worked for many years to have the independence to endure it. Now, for the first time I had found the inner peace to experience it.

Up here, close to the summit, the world seemed to stand still. The roaring wind and humming sound that seemed to come from within the mountain formed a blanket over the valleys, as vast as an ocean. This persistent, billowing sound. The colors in the jagged circle met at the summit in black and white. The atmosphere was one of all-embracing silence, not the silence of death, but a liberating silence—infinite, light, and carefree. All the sounds seemed part of this profound tranquility. Any movement was neither work, nor action—merely being. And being was freedom. A sense of freedom remote from time itself. I could hardly make Peter out in my camera's viewfinder. This dark figure seemed to merge with the black background of the sky. It was only when he moved that I could see his footsteps in the sloping firn of the Western Flank.

As he stood on the highest cornice, he seemed to melt away into nothing. I couldn't tell how far away he was.

> The thought of reaching the summit first after this tough ascent made him feel strong and exhilarated. I saw him shake off his tiredness and quicken his pace.
>
> He only registered that he was at the top when he looked down the western side of the mountain to the Abruzzi Glacier. To make quite sure he was right, he crossed to the other side to the first rocks, where he hammered in the single piton that we had brought with us to the summit. He climbed back up to the snow-covered summit, where we met and hugged each other. Peter could barely restrain his tears of joy.

I've always been criticized for stealing the show and downplaying my climbing partners' roles. Readers of my books will find the exact opposite. And not because it's easier to talk about your partner than it is to talk about yourself, but because my partners were often stronger than I was. Without Sepp Mayerl, Peter Habeler, Friedl Mutschlechner, Hans Kammerlander, and Oswald Oelz, I would have been unable to make my wildest of dreams come true.

None of them were hangers on. They were all beacons of hope, driving forces, and active players, just as I was.

14

PROFESSIONAL OR IDEALIST?

If you demand a lot from yourself but little from others, you will avoid resentment.

—Confucius

After my third eight-thousander and failed expedition on the South Face of Dhaulagiri in 1977, a new type of criticism of my climbing started to creep in. It concerned my endeavors to put my passion onto a professional footing.

Herrligkoffer had taken me to court repeatedly to prevent me from finding funding for new, independent expeditions. I lost those cases in court due to the expedition contract.

Walter Pause continued to dispute my ability to write about mountaineering. This made me question my plan—to finance my own small, cost-efficient expeditions at least in part by publishing books and giving expedition talks.

My desire was to be a freelance adventurer, but the older generation saw no idealism in what I was doing; instead, they argued that I was driven only by money.

Idealism was something that I had questioned too. This was the case after the attempt on Dhaulagiri, which I wrote about in the June 1977 edition of *Bergsteiger* magazine. Peter Habeler and I also failed in our attempt there not long afterward—we retreated in fear of our lives.

Dhaulagiri's steep south face is threatened by avalanches at all times, on all sides, from the base of the wall all the way to the summit. The face itself is 4,000 meters high—it was then the world's highest unclimbed face. The Rupal Face on Nanga Parbat is higher, but not as difficult.

After succeeding (with around 100 porters) in finding a way through the Thulo Kholaden, which at that time was still considered inaccessible, we reached the foot of the wall, where we set up base camp near two small lakes in a previously unexplored grassy basin.

Although it had been snowing on twenty-six of the earlier twenty-eight days, we were able to establish a high camp at the foot of the south pillar of the south face. After many days of reconnoitering and observation, Peter Habeler and I managed to reach an altitude of 6,100 meters. In the end, confronted by loose rock, persistent storms, and constant avalanches, we abandoned the attempt. We called off the expedition at the end of April.

Dhaulagiri fascinated me, more than any face I had ever climbed. Our four-man expedition with Otto Wiedemann and Michael Covington was my most carefully prepared trip to date, yet never had the scale and reality of a project so far exceeded my expectations. Never before had it become clear on an expedition that continuing to try for the summit would have been tantamount to suicide. And yet I had never felt as even-tempered as I did after getting back down to the valley.

Dr. Karl Maria Herrligkoffer was quick to criticize the expedition in a letter to the *Süddeutsche Zeitung*:

> Regarding motivation toward climbing and attitude to risk, I find Messner's execution clumsy and ignorant of the facts. This is the idle blathering of a professional mountaineer, who makes a living out of climbing mountains, and is now attempting to cloak the business-driven nature of his actions with idealized justifications.

I shouldn't have responded to Herrligkoffer. His "idle blathering of a professional mountaineer" was an accurate description of himself. But I did respond:

> He claims to represent the "high ideals of mountaineering teamwork," yet uses clichés about climbing and is subjective and biased. Although he surely recognizes that most expedition teams are partnerships of convenience. A man like Herrligkoffer, who expects his companions to sign contracts with him poorly understands that mountaineering has less to do with "defeat or victory" and more to do with surviving—with authentic experiences.

The issue was discussed in detail in *Bergsteiger*, edition 9/1976:

B: In an interview with the *Frankfurter Allgemeine Zeitung*, you said that you're an alpinist so that you can be a mountaineer. Can you explain what you mean?

RM: I describe myself as a "freelance alpinist" because I don't earn a living from mountaineering but from the activities associated with it. I don't get paid for my expeditions or climbing trips. I'm a speaker, author, and filmmaker. This gives me the freedom to spend a few months of the year doing what I love best.

B: So, you're a professional?

RM: That depends on how you define the word. "Professionals" are professional sportsmen. People who get paid to take part in sporting competitions, for example, Cassius Clay, Franz Beckenbauer, or Niki Lauda. However I have never been paid to climb a route. On the contrary, I have paid out of my own pocket, with considerable sacrifices to climb the Rupal Face, the Eiger North Face, and Hidden Peak. Of course, I always give talks after my expeditions and I'm now in a position to partially finance my trips in advance with the proceeds from speaking tours, books, and films. But to come back to the word professional. In English, "professional" also means being "skilled and educated" and "an expert." This also applies to artists. I'm happy to be called a professional based on this definition.

B: You're without doubt an expert. But what about using the name Reinhold Messner in advertising?

RM: I provide consulting services to half a dozen companies who use my name to promote their products. In doing so, I get paid for my expertise. Who better than us experienced mountaineers when it comes to developing equipment? I see this as useful work, and don't see the point in philosophizing about it. It's not as if I'm doing advertising for margarine or Coca-Cola.

B: And what about your alpine training center?

RM: I'm the director and founder of the *Alpinschule Südtirol*, which for the most part I manage myself. I also employ mountain guides who follow my teaching methods and principles. It's a small organization, but it's a lot of fun.

B: Would you describe this as a professional venture?

RM: Even less so than my other activities. A mountaineering school is like a ski school. Naturally, mountain guides and ski instructors make a living from their sporting expertise and work in the mountains. But these people aren't being paid for their triumphs, they're just doing their job, the same as a teacher, builder, or travel guide. The fact that they're doing what they love shouldn't be held against them.

B: So, you're involved in a whole chain of activities connected to mountaineering?

RM: The same as you. You write articles for alpine magazines, so you're also living from mountaineering, broadly speaking.

B: In this respect, there are lots of people who make a living from activities associated with alpinism. Some earn vast sums, but most more modest incomes. Some people write articles, some sell photos, others give talks and presentations or offer consultancy services. However, the paychecks from these activities are generally not sufficient to fund even one single holiday. All these people have another job as their main source of income. Although you *don't* work as an architect, which you originally trained for.

RM: For the time being, I'm more interested in traveling the world and going climbing than in building houses. I pay for this freedom by dispensing with a solid, middle-class income. Everything comes at a price. If you want a steady income, then you pay for this by having your freedom restricted. If you want to remain free and independent, then you have to make sacrifices in other areas. We're all free spirits and can live our lives accordingly. There are no privileges.

There's one last thing I'd like to mention. I was a mountaineer when I was a schoolboy, when I was a student, and when I was a schoolteacher. Today, I'm a mountaineer in the shape of a freelance alpinist. I still enjoy climbing as much as I ever did, although paradoxically, I have less time to climb these days than I did during my time studying and teaching. I'm fascinated by the mountains, and I consider myself lucky that I can devote my time to them.

All the amateurs who criticize my mountaineering, fail to understand that they're only humiliating themselves.

15

"CALLED A FOOL"

Climbing up a mountain, only to climb down it again.
It's akin to Sisyphus on Everest. What started as an angry rebellion against competition and consumerism, has ended up as alpine hubris. Reinhold Messner's dream of "returning to the mountains" has turned into a nightmare. Rousseau returning to nature. The story of his unique career reads like a modern version of the Greek legend. There appears to be no way to escape from the torture of his desire to top each achievement, motivated by his obsessive belief in growth.

—philosopher Ludger Lütkehaus in Germany's *TAZ* newspaper

For over fifty years, people have been asking me about my ascent of Mount Everest without oxygen. Sylvain Tesson, a French travel writer, interviewed me for *Philosophie Magazin* in 2016. He's an enthusiastic mountaineer who knows all about the great alpinists. He describes mountaineers as the adventurers of the twentieth century. He asks, why do people climb mountains? Why torture yourself in this manner?

ST: Is the alpinist a happy Sisyphus, who's aware of the absurdity of human existence? Early alpinists were viewed with mistrust and irony.

RM: Alpinism is only just over two hundred years old. It's part of our culture. Mont Blanc (4,810 meters) was climbed by Jacques Balmat and Michel-Gabriel Paccard on August 8, 1786. Their success was then copied by a few eccentrics and a bunch of aristocrats.

In 1865, during the first ascent of the Matterhorn (4,478 meters), four alpinists fell to their deaths on the descent. The press response was highly sarcastic. The editor of the *Times* asked, "What right has [the mountaineer] to throw away the gift of life and ten thousand golden opportunities in an emulation which he only shares with skylarks, apes, and squirrels?"

There are as many reasons for climbing mountains as there are people who climb them. And these reasons are all neither good nor

> bad. My motivation was to rescue mountaineering from a paramilitary ideology and to promote what I saw as a "simplified alpinism" that reflected the zeitgeist of the 1970s. My initial premise was a simple one. I wanted to climb in the Himalaya the same way I climbed in the Alps. This meant independent mountaineering: climbing either as a team of two or solo and carrying all your equipment with you en route to the summit. Climbing in a minimalist style. Many famous mountaineers argued that this style was only suitable for climbing four-thousanders. I proved them wrong.
>
> In 1978, when I announced that I planned to climb Everest without oxygen, many doctors said I would die. They told me that the lack of oxygen at that altitude would destroy my brain. And that if I didn't die at the summit that I would come back with brain damage.
>
> Before I made it to the summit with Peter Habeler, we were forced to brave a heavy storm (at around 8,000 meters). I knew that if I was wrong, I would die. Nature is neither evil nor unfair. It has no objectives, it isn't interested in my fate. Therefore I knew that I had to develop the resources to survive on my own.

Surgeon and mountaineer Professor R. Margreiter from University Hospital Innsbruck thought it was possible to climb Mount Everest without oxygen (from *Medizin und Sport*):

> Of course, climbing eight-thousanders without oxygen means reaching the limits of what is physically possible. However, I think that you can climb Mount Everest, which, at 8,848 meters, is the world's highest mountain, without oxygen equipment in good conditions and after proper acclimatization.

Peter Habeler, my partner on Everest, was an outstanding mountaineer, and the best partner I had ever had. He moved well in all types of terrain, was a stylish rock climber, and his endurance was unmatched. His outstanding head for heights enabled him to cover ground fast at high altitudes. This characteristic is essential if you want to climb eight-thousanders quickly in just a few days, which is what we ultimately did.

When we returned from Everest, I dared to call into question all the jingoism, heroic alpinism, and placing of flags on summits. I couldn't stand all that

overly patriotic ideology. My home country was both somewhere I came from and somewhere, through climbing, that I escaped from. Once I announced that my handkerchief was my flag, I was celebrated no longer as the hero of Everest but vilified as a traitor who disrespected his own country. The South Tyrolean press, a virtual monopoly, received hundreds of letters of complaint.

In addition to the South Tyroleans, the mountain writer Walter Pause also criticized my success on Everest. His response of October 2, 1978, to my Everest book is illuminating—not in terms of mountain literature but the depths of human nature.

> Letter from W. Pause to BLV publishing house, Munich:
>
> Please send me a copy of the new book by Messner (Everest), which you have concealed from me in such an embarrassing and petty manner. When Dr. Egger finally admitted that "he wanted to tell me in person" that there would be a book (the first in a series), that would finally challenge Pause's BLV success, calling it a "sensation" etc.—I was still none the wiser.

It states in our contract that you are compelled to inform me about any plans for other mountain books. *If* you had done so, then I could have suggested certain changes that would have spared you the bitter tone of the commentary in my beloved *Süddeutsche Zeitung* (*SZ*).

This is a new BLV scenario: apparently, your publishing house has nobody who understands how to assess literary and stylistic qualities. Furthermore, nobody will understand what the purpose of the (mild, yet still embarrassing) criticism in the *SZ* is. Mr. Messner is mercilessly unmasked in his self-congratulatory and above all godlike proclamations. . . . I could have given him subjective and precise advice (after all, Messner is not damaging me and my mountain books, but only the publishing house). This should have been the responsibility of your editors who appear to have been sleeping on the job.

But you failed to do so, which means you have brought it on yourselves. I am not affected, although I find the whole affair embarrassing. You build up a small publishing house to become a major player and even make it famous, and then *no one*, neither the managing director nor the editor, not even the publisher does the *obvious*—to approach Walter Pause the expert (after all *that* is what I am when it comes to writing and *producing* books).

I refrain from commenting further on your mortifying performance. The *SZ* found a few positive things to say, however there are other critics who are going to expose you and your folly. . . .

Let me reiterate that as long as I'm an author of carefully written books, not just any old hastily produced literature, who has turned a poor publishing house round and still can, I'm entitled to be critical. I'm sure that you will say that I'm just jealous and that I know what it means to *write* in the broadest sense of the word. Or that I, as a BLV author, have *no choice but* to criticize a book that has been kept secret from me (in the meantime the *SZ* has done the job for me and there are dozens of similarly critical reviews to come). Nevertheless, it is outrageous that your editor has dared to approve the printing of such a sensationalist book as this one. I doubt that they have even read it.

When will the BLV appoint someone who is *capable* of identifying and dealing with publishing problems? By the way, have you actually understood the underlying sarcasm in the *Spiegel* review? All I can say is good luck to you in the future.

Forty years later, it was obvious which of us had the most enduring stories. Here's an excerpt from an interview with the *Schwäbische Zeitung* from May 2018:

SchZ: Mr. Messner, do you view May 8, 1978, as your greatest alpine triumph?

RM: No. It was only the outside world that saw it that way. It was a story that attracted a lot of publicity especially due to the large number of critics it had beforehand. As so often in my life, I experienced strong headwinds. Doctors, physiologists, even mountaineers said that I shouldn't even attempt a climb like that and to climb and survive above 8,500 meters without bottled oxygen was impossible. They even did the math to prove it. It looks like they got their math wrong.

SchZ: Didn't that all worry you beforehand? There were warnings that your brain would suffer irreparable damage if it had to function at an altitude like that for such a long time without enough oxygen.

RM: I've already been on several eight-thousanders, each time without masks or oxygen. Peter Habeler worried that we might be taking too big a risk. To me, it was a clear-cut decision; if there was no way forward, we'd turn back. Nobody wants to die up there.

SchZ: By climbing Everest, were you trying to prove something to yourself or your critics?

RM: Well, mountaineering has taken a particular direction. The dawn of the new alpine style (fast and light) arrived in 1968. In 1967, the US climber Royal Robbins had written an article "Nuts to You" about "clean climbing." Without being aware of what he'd written, I penned "Murder of the Impossible." The crux of my argument was that people are drilling more and more and climbing less and less. Technical aids, such as pegs and bolts, are making alpinism obsolete.

SchZ: But there is a difference between climbing in the Himalaya and climbing in the Dolomites without technical aids. Especially above 7,500 meters in the "death zone."

RM: Our reduced-to-the-max, fast and light alpinism was initially based on climbing in the Alps. But in 1975, Peter Habeler and I climbed Hidden Peak, an eight-thousander, without any of the usual technical aids. So, no masks, no high camp, no fixed ropes. That really was back-to-the-roots alpinism. It was only afterward that we started to discuss whether this style was feasible on Everest. My approach was not to talk about it but to actually try it out.

SchZ: What was the hardest thing about the ascent?

RM: The summit push on May 8. We knew it was our last chance. There was a raging storm through the night, and we hardly got any sleep in the tent. The wind was pummelling the walls and the seams so hard, we thought the tent would be torn apart. We had to wait for daybreak; without fixed ropes it would be impossible to find our way in the dark. We left as soon as the first rays of sun appeared.

SchZ: But what about the storm?

RM: There were breaks in the wind. It was minus 30 to minus 40 degrees Celsius. To stop ourselves from being blown off the ridge, we had to keep kneeling down as we were moving.

SchZ: And then you reached the summit. Did you feel overjoyed, or would you describe your mood as one of satisfaction or relief?

RM: I felt shattered. Peter was very emotional. I don't remember my feelings as clearly, I can recall breathing a sigh of relief. But I was acutely aware that in mountaineering you're only successful if you make it back down. The descent wasn't a problem, it wasn't hard, and the storm eased off. We were more grateful than euphoric when we'd made it back down successfully.

SchZ: You talk about breathing a sigh of relief. How does it feel to breathe at nearly 9,000 meters?

RM: You end up panting like a dog. You hyperventilate. You only manage a few steps up before you have to stop and rest. You need to bend over, ideally over your ice axe, to open up your chest. Gasping and panting hard, you take fifty breaths and then do another two steps. It's never-ending and takes every last vestige of willpower. It's not just your legs that are done, the blood supply to your brain is no longer adequate. This affects your ability to think and make decisions. In short, you're a bit like a zombie up there.

SchZ: And you never wore an oxygen mask on an eight-thousander afterward?

RM: No. After climbing Everest, I realized that it was possible to do the big mountains without it.

SchZ: Forty years later, Everest has become a mass-tourism destination. Is it still the same mountain that you knew?

RM: Everest is still Everest, even if it is increasingly made light of. People have turned the mountain into a consumer product. Today, you can book Everest as a package at the travel agency—base camp to summit and back down again if all goes well.

SchZ: So, exactly the opposite of your back-to-the-roots, fast and light alpinism?

RM: Yes, I call it *Pistenalpinismus* (mass alpinism). The organizers spend months every year constructing a safe route from base camp to the summit. It's the Sherpas who do the work. There are oxygen dumps, doctors, and cooks in the camps, fixed ropes to ensure that everyone finds their way, bridges over crevasses, and ladders on the steep sections. All this work costs millions and needs repeating every year because the ice on Everest is always shifting. Clients can only be brought up over the slopes once everything's ready. However, if a young climber is looking for a new route and finds one by climbing independently, then Mount Everest is still the same mountain.

SchZ: How did you then and how do you now feel about Everest?

RM: I like all mountains that have a story to tell. Storytelling is as important to me as mountaineering itself. And Everest is a mountain with so many stories, from the failed attempts of the 1920s to the first ascent by Edmund Hillary and Tensing Norgay in 1953, and the traverse by Norman Dyhrenfurth in 1963. Every time I see Everest, I think of all these stories. And it's only because of them that the mountain still retains a special place in my heart.

On April 25, 2015, Khunde Hospital, founded by Sir Edmund Hillary, was destroyed by an earthquake. The Everest 1978 expedition leader Wolfgang Nairz and I helped finance its reconstruction with the help of two charitable organizations. The Messner Mountain Foundation and Nepalhilfe Tirol joined forces to meet this new challenge. We wanted to help the Sherpas and were grateful for everything that we had experienced on Mount Everest.

I wondered if the Sherpas had speculated whether Peter and I had mini-oxygen bottles as small as cartridge cases with us in 1978. Walter Pause contacted me to contribute ideas and routes for his book *Im Extremen Fels* (Extreme Rock). The Bavarian mountaineer Hans Engl, who climbed Mount Everest in autumn 1978 without an oxygen mask, was heralded as my adversary and depicted as the silent hero, while I was called a con man.

Isn't that all forgiven and forgotten now? Everything has been straightened out. Today, the Sherpas are successful mountain guides. Many of them climb Everest year after year without oxygen. Publishing house BLV, which published Pause's books as well as my own, has since been acquired by another company. Hans Engl was onstage at the Oktoberfest in Munich. My Everest book is not my best, but it is the most successful of my books, and, despite Walter Pause's criticism, it's still in print today. In the long run, the upset isn't worth it because it always returns to haunt those who started it.

16

K2 AND BROAD PEAK

It's better to love what is right than to know what is right.
And it's better to be enthusiastic for what is right than to love what is right.

—Laozi, founder of Taoism

A year on from the Everest ascent, I led a small team to climb K2, the second-highest mountain on earth. Our original goal, the Magic Line on the South–Southwest Pillar, had become unrealistic after we got held up for over two weeks in Islamabad, Pakistan, at a time when the former president Zulfikar Ali Bhutto was to be tried and executed.

Robert Schauer, a top young alpinist from Graz, Austria, was with us on the team; he'd showed exceptional qualities on Everest the year before. After I was reported as saying that it would be impossible to organize a rescue attempt to the summit of K2, he commented on this in the press in a rather moralizing way: "If a climber gets injured, we can't just shoot them to put them out of their misery and leave them up there to die!" Moreover, he went on to add, referring to the 1978 Mount Everest expedition: "Reinhold was snowblind in Camp 4 after returning from the summit. He hollered and wailed the whole night. Peter Habeler describes it in his book. What would have happened if we had just left him up there?" The two Sherpas, who had waited with Eric Jones for us to return from the Everest summit push, would have done everything they possibly could to accompany me back down from Camp 4 to Camp 2. Just as Peter had accompanied me, as if it were the most natural thing in the world.

On K2, it was our speed that enabled Michl Dacher and me to reach the summit before another bout of bad weather hit.

According to Schauer: "No one had ever made it to the summit as fast as Reinhold Messner and Michl Dacher. However, claiming that it was 'alpine style' was a bit of an exaggeration. We all helped to set up the three camps on the mountain with essential supplies. It was only really 'alpine' from 7,400 meters!" The way that we had organized things on the mountain had paved

the way for the other rope teams to attempt the summit. However, only Dacher and I reached the top. Schauer didn't make it.

Robert Schauer's response: "I don't feel that I need to comment on that. I have no desire to attack others due to the anger and frustration I felt at not making it. I just want to explain why I feel that Messner is no longer an acceptable expedition leader."

I can live with this. The experience from numerous expeditions has taught me to accept that I have both good and bad characteristics. It's only narcissists who like to create an unrealistic picture of themselves.

Robert and I made up later in life. He went on to set up the mountain film festival in Graz, Austria, filmed amazing shots of Mount Everest as a cameraman, and made the first ascent of the West Face of Gasherbrum IV with Voytek Kurtyka—an exceptional achievement. Schauer also succinctly described how I operated when I led small teams: "Reinhold likes to think of himself as democratic, he claims that everyone on the team should speak their minds. But thanks to his powers of persuasion, he always wins others around to his point of view at critical moments. At least, he convinces the majority anyway. Then there's a vote and it always goes Messner's way!" Motivating others, getting them to share your vision, preparing projects so that a team can pull them off—these are the ways to reach exceptional goals. Narcissistic personalities—who often criticize others—can't motivate other people; instead, they make people's lives hell, wielding judgements, putting them down, whittling away at the truth, and ultimately bringing out the moralistic cudgel.

They hide their own weaknesses by demonizing others.

At the same time as our K2 expedition, a group of Austrian mountaineers were on neighboring Broad Peak. As Dacher and I had got back from the summit earlier than planned, we had time on our hands. Why not try another eight-thousander? I had wanted to give all the team members a chance to climb K2. We contacted Mr. Awan in Islamabad, the man responsible for expedition permits, to ask for permission to attempt Broad Peak. This angered the Broad Peak expedition leader, Dr. Franz Berghold, whom I was on Dhaulagiri with. The letter he wrote to Germany's *Der Spiegel* magazine clearly shows how he felt:

> Our Austrian expedition only received a mountaineering permit for the period of June to September 1979 after years of applying. We worked hard to prepare a route up the west face with high camps and fixed ropes to enable a summit attempt. We only heard of Messner's intentions a few days later, by chance. We were very disappointed by this. We should have been informed and asked if we were OK with it. When we heard by accident that Messner planned to simply override us with his ambitious plans, we were naturally extremely annoyed. If we had known of his plan, we would have refused to agree to Messner's attempt to climb Broad Peak this summer by the only possible route.

On September 15, 1979, Berghold sent a similar letter to Toni Hiebeler, the most influential mountaineering journalist at the time:

> A few days after Messner/Dacher had summitted K2, Michl Dacher visited our base camp at Broad Peak. We were just getting ready for our second attempt on the summit. After a few hours chatting, the purpose of his visit suddenly became clear. Messner had sent Dacher to inform us that they also intended to climb Broad Peak (and make use of our 1,800 meters of fixed ropes and three fully equipped high camps). Of course, he would still claim that he was climbing "alpine style." . . . Apparently, he had tried to contact us by radio and via the *Spiegel* messenger in Rawalpindi out of politeness. Fortunately, Mr. Awan from the ministry of tourism wouldn't be intimidated, which considering the somewhat corruptible nature of authorities in that region, is nothing short of a miracle. If the weather hadn't been so miserable—it cost us the summit—he would probably have just marched in, and simply expected that we would step back to allow Messner, the mountain god, to head on up. I expect that Michl Dacher couldn't live with the idea—probably due to his friendship with the Woergoetter brothers, which is why he sneaked over to us to at least let us know.

Berghold's team didn't reach the summit, despite fixing 1,800 meters of ropes up the mountain. Mr. Awan rejected our application because in those days the rule in the Karakoram was to only allow one eight-thousander per expedition.

Three years later I climbed Broad Peak in alpine style with no fixed ropes. I climbed with two local Pakistani mountaineers, and we took three days to go from base camp to the summit. It was the final ascent in my attempt to climb three eight-thousanders in a row. Nobody tried to hold us back, and we met no other climbers on the mountain. Upon our return, it was a joy to behold how excited the locals were about what we had done. It would appear jealousy remains the preserve of us western climbers.

17

HILLARY'S SON

Your life will soon be over, and everyone will have forgotten you.
Check the brutal impulses of the passions. Take care to ensure that you do not react even to brutes with passion, as brutes often react toward others.
He who sins, sins against himself. He who acts unjustly, acts unjustly toward himself, and damages himself, by making himself worse.
Men are often unjust by omissions as well as by actions.
Idle tongues will blame virtue herself with harshest words.
Of the free will there is no thief or robber.

—Marcus Aurelius

In the autumn of 1979, I traveled with a small group of friends to the holy mountain Ama Dablam, one of the most beautiful mountains in the upper Khumbu region of the Himalaya in northeast Nepal. Wolfgang Nairz led the expedition and organized the expedition permits.

Arriving at base camp, we met four New Zealand climbers who planned to ascend the 2,000-meter unclimbed Mingbo Face on the western side of the mountain to the summit. Peter Hillary was their leader. This was a very bold undertaking.

The small team—all of them top climbers—were well prepared and well acclimatized. They set out from base camp the next day. Maybe they were worried that we would get ahead of them.

However, we were heading for the south face of the mountain and we first needed time to acclimatize. We planned to climb first to acclimatize before deciding which route to attempt.

The Mingbo Face looked an interesting challenge, but our Tyrolean team felt that it was too exposed to falling ice. High up on the face below the summit there are three seracs (ice cliffs)—in Sherpa mythology, they're known as "Mother's Necklace"—that could break off at any moment, turning the concave face below them into ice avalanche hell.

Solo-Khumbu District in northeastern Nepal

We watched the New Zealanders and followed their progress over the next few days. They made good time to just below the left ice bulge on a steep ice arête. Suddenly, a large ice avalanche came off the central serac directly under the summit. Huge blocks of ice exploded over the climbers and then swept down the face, taking everything in its path with it.

Although all their protection had been ripped out, Hillary and his team were miraculously left, still clinging to a rocky tower. Through the telescope, we could see that one of them was hanging on the rope under the overhang. He wasn't moving. The other three were moving, but very slowly. Before they could start abseiling, they had to cut the rope to their dead teammate. It was the only way they could free up the rope to escape.

They started to descend. Would they be able to make it back down the steep 1,200 meter face with so little gear left? They were probably injured too.

We had to help. It was almost a reflexive action. First, we tried to climb up and reach them from the side, but it was impossible to reach them this way.

Oswald Oelz, our expedition doctor, decided that we should try to reach them from below, by climbing up to them via the central gully. We knew it was dangerous. But it was the only way to help the three survivors and get them back down to the foot of the wall. The attempt was a success, and Wolfgang had them flown to the hospital in Kathmandu.

Nine months later I read in Germany's *Süddeutsche Zeitung*:

> Edmund Hillary seemingly has huge respect, but no liking, for Reinhold Messner, the first man to reach the summit of Mount Everest without oxygen, a mountain that has since been climbed by 110 people. Last year, Messner rescued Hillary's son Peter when he was hit by an avalanche on Ama Dablam. It was a risky operation, which Messner promptly exploited as self-promotion and later turned into a book.

"Messner is in certain respects a prima donna. Yet, I admire his amazing climbing skills," Edmund Hillary is said to have commented.

For my part, I admire Edmund Hillary for the things he achieved in the second stage of his life: building an airport in Lukla, setting up schools for Sherpa children, and founding a hospital in Khunde. He had a strong sense of social responsibility to improve health and social welfare facilities for the Tibetan ethnic group of Nepal, who made his success possible. This is an aspect of his personality I admire even more than his 1953 climb of the last step of the unclimbed Mount Everest.

On May 29, 2023, on the seventieth anniversary of the first ascent of Mount Everest by Hillary and Tensing, my wife Diane and I opened the new Everest museum in Namche Bazaar. The Sherpa Culture Museum and Mount Everest Documentation Center is dedicated to the Sherpa people and celebrates their part in the ascent of the world's highest mountain. The mountaineering photos, documentation, and Sherpa art and history that Lhakpa Sonam Sherpa has been showing people visiting Nepal for decades has finally found a worthy home. In 1980 Edmund Hillary said, "I want to see the Sherpa people proud and capable of successfully adapting to the changes in Nepali society." His vision and vocation has become my vocation, too.

Thanks to Edmund Hillary, today the Sherpas are successful tourism experts and entrepreneurs who are highly respected in Nepal. They are unrivalled tourism operators for the highest mountains of the world. Whether exploiting eight-thousanders will remain sustainable is another matter. The mystery that the Sherpa clans have respected in the Himalaya and Transhimalaya for more than five hundred years is now fading as vain tourists from all over the world flock there.

18
THE OPTION

You have to be able to sacrifice your homeland for Greater Germany.

—Norbert Mumelter, a leading member of the Völkischer Kampfring Südtirols (VKS)

In 1978, during celebrations for the first summit of Everest without supplemental oxygen, I made a comment that triggered a big row back home in South Tyrol. My words of thanks following a speech by a politician—who had referred to the flag of South Tyrol on the summit of Everest—were seen as a provocation: "I am my own *Heimat,* and my handkerchief is my flag."

The following night my car was vandalized: someone painted the words *Heimatverräter* (traitor to the *Heimat*) on it. Over the following weeks, the *Dolomiten* newspaper printed letters from readers accusing me of "putting down my own homeland" and other malicious comments. I can't say that my father didn't warn me. An Italian journalist asked me how I would respond. My reply was even harsher. I said that in 1939, we South Tyroleans betrayed our homeland as part of the "Option."

Newspapers in Bavaria, Germany, started reporting on the row, and I was soon painted as a homeless vagabond incapable of loving the place I grew up in. The well-known South Tyrolean writer and film producer Luis Trenker got involved in the debate. The *Abendzeitung* newspaper (Munich) reported:

> What just happened is bound to have further implications. In Tyrol, it has caused huge waves of emotion, like the flooding of the River Etsch and River Eisack as the snowmelt thaws. The old man and the younger man have only one thing in common. They are the best-known South Tyroleans in the world. And both of them climbed mountains in search of wealth and fame.

Luis Trenker, the famous author of *Mountains on Fire* and *The Prodigal Son,* had also turned against me. Nobody wanted to defend me. My father, who himself had been active in the *Völkischer Kampfring Südtirols,* showed no mercy. His response was "I told you so."

With Luis Trenker and his daughter

The *Abendzeitung* later reported:

> In August 1981, on the fiftieth anniversary of the first ascent of the North Face of the Ortler in Sulden, there was a reconciliation of sorts between Luis Trenker and Reinhold Messner. They were both in a group photo and shook hands with the first ascensionist, the Munich climber Hans Ertl, who lives in South America today. But then things flared up again. Messner's

latest interview on Italian television had both mountaineers back at each other's throats.

Bolzano's *Dolomiten* newspaper reported facts that might have escaped most South Tyroleans, who tend to get their information via Austrian and German television. The newspaper is no fan of the best-selling Villnöss author, ever since Messner decided not to publish his books using the paper's own Athesia publishing house. According to the *Dolomiten*, during the interview, Messner explained that South Tyroleans constantly refer to values such as *Heimat* (homeland) and *Vaterland* (fatherland), but do so in a very superficial manner.

On the other hand, Messner says he loves his home with all his heart. He might have traveled to some of the most beautiful corners of the world, but he's still the boy from Villnöss. And he says he would never leave his home for a "political system" or a "Führer" in Germany, which (as he bluntly points out) the majority of South Tyroleans did in 1939.

Eighty-six percent of German-speaking South Tyroleans opted in favor of Hitler's Germany, and were ready to leave their homes to move to the Third Reich. Ethnic-racialist *völkisch* values triumphed over the often-quoted *Heimatliebe* (love of the homeland).

Howls of anger are echoing all over beautiful Tyrol! Messner's latest scandal has reopened a painful chapter in history that South Tyroleans have still to come to terms with. In other words, the famous Option agreement between Italy and Germany during the Hitler/Mussolini era negotiated by the two dictators. South Tyrol was to become Italian and brutally Italianized. German South Tyroleans were allowed to decide between emigrating to the Third Reich or staying in their homeland.

The Option created a deep rift in the native German- and Ladin-speaking community in South Tyrol and it divided families. In many cases, the wounds have yet to be healed. In the meantime, history has shown that it was mainly thanks to those who stayed, the *Dableiber*, that it was impossible for Italy to deny the existence of the "South Tyrolean Question" after the war. However, it's also well known that it wasn't the Optants who decided to go to Germany who divided South Tyrol in such a brutal manner, but the two fanatical fascist leaders.

> And then Messner's comments came and hit South Tyroleans like heavy rockfall: "I don't believe there have ever been a people who have betrayed their own homeland as much as we South Tyroleans."

I had underestimated the trauma experienced by the people of South Tyrol due to resettlement, war, and fascism. The *Abendzeitung* continued:

> The newspaper has received an avalanche of readers' letters, and now there is an important addition. From a prominent name, whose response has long been awaited, Luis Trenker.

Luis Trenker, of all people. During the Option he played a dubious role. He was publicly criticized by Goebbels, yet was able to intervene with Hitler himself—and not on behalf of his desperate fellow countrymen south of the Brenner Pass (South Tyrol) but to boost his own position in Berlin.

The *Abendzeitung* again:

> Yes, when it comes to politics in Tyrol, the two mountain goats hold rather different positions, as a West German Broadcasting (WDR) television interview with talk show host Werner Höfer showed a couple of years ago. Trenker upholds the ideal of a unified Tyrol (combining the northern part which has belonged to Austria for over six hundred years and the southern part, which has belonged to Italy since 1918). Messner, on the other hand, when asked the naive question by a TV host: "Are you Tyrolean?" replied: "No, I'm South Tyrolean."

There was no way I could win this discussion. But it did politicize me. It opened my eyes to another side of South Tyrol, and made me realize that its history should be questioned and reexamined. Here is a summary of Trenker's letter to the *Abendzeitung*. I could almost feel him pointing his finger at me with one hand and holding up his ice axe in the other.

"My dear Mr. Messner," writes Luis Trenker in his rather patronizing tone. "I find your claims outrageous. . . . If you had climbed as carelessly as you talked in your interview, then you would never have reached a single Himalayan summit." Messner has "no idea of how much the South Tyroleans suffered" during fascism, says Trenker angrily, and shows no understanding of the very difficult decision his fellow South Tyroleans faced back then, holding presumptuous opinions about a period that he didn't have to live through. And he concludes: "Today you live with us in South Tyrol, which is now in a more fortunate position. You should be grateful. Take note, my friend, this sort of arrogance never does any good in the long run, and a lack of respect is worse than superstition."

I've never had much time for superstition, nor for false representations of historical events. Instead, I decided to bring out a book about the Option that was published in 1989.

The *Abendzeitung*'s final say on the matter:

> This brought about an initially abrupt end to the discussion. Now all is quiet on the mountain front, as Messner is off on his travels again. However, we're curious to see what he has to say on his return. Because even for Tyrolean mountain enthusiasts, Messner's personal scorn, insults, and questionable political opinions have become more interesting than anything else that he brings back in terms of stories from the mountains of this world.

Shortly afterward, another South Tyrolean publication, *ff* magazine, wrote:

> Reinhold Messner has kept his promise. He doesn't just want to be seen as the "climbing monkey," but also wants to contribute to intellectual issues.
>
> As such, he is helping to establish a more liberal climate in South Tyrol. During his search for a "different South Tyrol" he met Alexander Langer, who was also looking for new perspectives. At a conference at Maretsch Castle in Bolzano, the first indications of this different South Tyrol became evident. . . . Reinhold Messner showed his more tolerant side:
>
> "We need to talk to all the people of South Tyrol, including people without much interest in politics. We must avoid sectarian factions." It's all about breaking down stereotypes, cleaning up the mess from the inside, at a cultural level, and using citizen's initiatives to press ahead with new ideas. We need to move away from political notions of "right" and "left." What is required is imagination and creativity.
>
> "We all need to change ourselves first," says Messner.

The campaign to ostracize me resulted in the harshest attacks I have ever experienced. My response was first to throw myself into politics, then to delve deeper into the history of our South Tyrol. And in 1991, I embarked on the *Rund um Südtirol* project, a long-distance hike and climb of over three hundred mountains in South Tyrol.

19
THE SEVENTH GRADE

If people tried harder to improve themselves, instead of saving the world—
if they tried to find inner peace, instead of trying to free all humankind—
how much more might they have achieved to really free all humankind?

—Anonymous

My success as a high-alpine climber continued after Everest, in part, because I had stopped rock climbing—my first great love. The loss of several of my toes and fingertips following the Nanga Parbat tragedy meant that I would never climb as well again nor regain my appetite for big wall climbing in the Alps.

My 1968 essay, "Murder of the Impossible," published worldwide, antagonized older climbers. In 1973, I published *The Seventh Grade*, which included a critique of bolted climbing. In 1979, in response to a new, extended edition, people questioned whether I was still capable of understanding how extreme rock climbing had become. And what was "professional mountaineering" anyway? During an interview in 1981, the editor of *Alpinismus* magazine asked for my opinion.

A: Do you feel the pressure to perform?

RM: No, I'm not under pressure to perform. . . . Neither financially, nor in terms of ambition. If I wanted to deliver new superlatives, then I'd have to do more writing than mountaineering. As long as I have the strength and the time, though, then I will carry on mountaineering and writing about it.

A: You once described a terrible vision of the future where the world's top ten climbers would climb the North Face of the Eiger solo against the clock in front of television cameras. Do you think that the tendency toward the commercialization of climbing is something that can be controlled?

RM: Whether this vision becomes reality depends entirely on how intelligent climbers are. A long time ago, Chris Bonington, Dougal Haston, and I were approached to do something similar for British television. We all rejected the idea, because we didn't feel we could accept the responsibility. I'm the first to oppose these kinds of timed competitions. The speed you climb is tied to safety. The conditions on the face are what make the difference. This kind of alpine climbing isn't suitable for competitions. I see a danger for sport climbers getting carried away and becoming something akin to gladiators. This could be possible at climbing walls and bolted crags. Sport climbing has great potential to push the limits, the same as in other competitive sports—and it has this element of gamification.

A: By reprinting *The Seventh Grade*, you've shown that you're still very interested in extreme climbing. Are you going to start rock climbing again? And what are your goals?

RM: I still climb on rock. Just not at the same level as I did in my best year—1969.

A: . . . then we don't need to mention your detractors who claim that you only know about the seventh grade from other people. Maybe you could tell us which of your first ascents might have this level of difficulty?

RM: Difficult question. When I was making those first ascents—for example the Central Pillar on the Heiligkreuzkofel (Sasso della Croce)—a

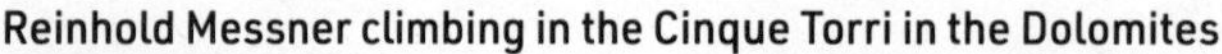
Reinhold Messner climbing in the Cinque Torri in the Dolomites

seventh grade didn't exist. As a result, I wasn't even able to think about giving them grade VII. Today, young climbers say that some of my first ascents deserved the seventh grade.

There are still some of my first ascents that have only been repeated by people using aid and placing bolts. The Heiligkreuzkofel Central Pillar has still to be repeated "fairly."

A: How do you define ideal free-climbing? Could you describe it for us briefly?

RM: To me, it means climbing all the way, from first pitch to summit, using only handholds and footholds. I have to admit that this is an ideal that I've lived up to on only a small number of routes. For example, on the North Face of the Second Sella Tower, where I used no pitons for aid. Back then, we didn't have the sport-driven attitude that climbers have today. We had strong ideals. The fewer technical means used to make progress, the more highly esteemed was the climb.

A: So how did you transition from free-climbing to expedition mountaineering?

RM: Originally, I was interested in vertical and overhanging rock. I grew up in the mountains, hiking and playing in the forests. I was an adventurer, not a sport climber. But after I'd spent months in the wilderness, and realized what that felt like, it fascinated me as much as rock climbing used to.

Today, I would much rather hike through Bhutan, cross the Gobi Desert, or walk to the South Pole than be given an expedition permit to climb an eight-thousander. My focus has changed—I'm more interested in the general notion of adventure. I think that this is ultimately the way it always goes for mountaineers who've been active for a long time. They start to see more than the sporting dimension and become more interested in nature and wild landscapes. This isn't some clichéd vision—I really mean what I say.

A: What impact has the ability to travel faster by plane between wild mountain areas and civilization had on you?

RM: In this century, we can go just about wherever we want. But we don't have the right to impose on others our culture, our knowledge, or our religion (if we have one) as being somehow better than theirs.

A: When you travel to Tibet or to other developing countries, don't you sometimes experience something of a culture shock at the underdeveloped economies and poverty in these regions?

RM: No, I've never felt this culture shock. In Tibet, people are poor. But they're richer than people in Nepal on the other side of the border. Remember that Tibet has a very small population, while Nepal is overpopulated. I come from a South Tyrolean farming family. I've yet to see the modest values I grew up with surpassed anywhere that I've been.

A: As a public figure, you're always in the spotlight. Public figures are role models. Is this a burden?

RM: The apparent need to be a role model isn't something that affects me much. I don't want to ruin my life by every minute thinking about how to be a role model for others. In the German-speaking world, I'm the most widely criticized mountaineer. This tempers my influence as a role model. If some young person climbs grade VII or attempts an eight-thousander and falls during the process, it's not my fault. I find it interesting that I'm often criticized here by the same people who boast about the falls they've taken. When I think about the many falls I've had, I feel ashamed, not boastful. The most important thing in mountaineering is staying alive. I've never let a compulsion to be a role model get to me.

20

YETI, BONATTI, AND JUVAL CASTLE

To pretend to know when one does not know is a fault.
To know but not look down on those who do not is virtue.

—Li An, the *Huainanzi*

As Tibet opened up to scientists and mountaineers, it became feasible and possible to climb all fourteen eight-thousanders, and in 1983 I announced that I intended to try. I'd also just bought Juval Castle. My father was the first to publicly speak out, saying it was "arrogance" and that "mountaineers don't live in castles." As a result, he never once came to visit.

My mother saw things differently, and she lived at Juval for some time during the renovations. I think she secretly hoped that reconstructing and funding it would keep me from going on dangerous expeditions.

Most mountaineers saw my investment as just showing off. There were lots of letters to the mountaineering magazines and no shortage of *Schadenfreude*.

Toni Hiebeler wrote: "Reinhold Messner, professional alpinist and eight-thousander collector, is now the king of the castle. He's purchased Castle Juval (927 meters elevation) that towers over the start of the Schnalstal/Val Senales. The thirteenth-century building is a protected monument and currently uninhabitable."

Its previous owner, a *Dableiber* (someone who chose to stay in South Tyrol during the Option Agreement), was a fine, cultivated old gentleman. He sold it to me on condition that I promised to retain ownership of the castle and restore it. Moreover, he sold it to me because he said I was correct in what I'd said publicly about the Option debate.

I climbed Lhotse in 1986—for once with a tailwind—yet I returned not as a victor but as a man subject to major criticism again.

Walter Bonatti wrote: "The world is full of Messners. However, you cannot be the Virgin Mary and abandon all your principles at the same time. You have to choose what you want and then be consistent. I'm not criticizing him for his financial affairs—that's his own business. But I do criticize him for his inconsistency and opportunism—what a disgrace! It's a shame, because Messner has done some wonderful things, not on the eight-thousanders—for me they're just a kind of gigantic collection of summits—but here in the Alps. I even dedicated a book to him once, though given what he has become, I'm sorry I did. Who is the real Messner? The man I met back then was on my wavelength, but he has changed so much. Or perhaps the man was like this all along, but didn't show it? I don't know."

It was none other than Walter Bonatti, the most prominent mountaineer in the world from 1950 to 1965, who delivered against me such a withering judgement, which other alpinists joined in on, commented upon, and spread.

My father was right: "A mountaineer doesn't live in a castle." Even if Juval was more of a fort than it was a castle, and neither a very comfortable nor convenient place to live. Nevertheless, for me to live there did appear pretentious. Juval became somewhere I could retreat to, but I was also responsible for its upkeep and stopping it from going to rack and ruin. Today, Juval is both a public museum and a private home. I later had the northern wing covered with a glass roof to prevent further damage from the weather. All those years of renovation are now a source of joy and satisfaction. What was a former ruin is now one of the most exciting places to live in the whole of the Alps.

Walter Bonatti and I went on to become good friends and almost like brothers. We celebrated his eightieth birthday in Juval. We spent long afternoons together and talked about the "mountain idealists." These were the people who discredited him following his 1954 ascent of K2. Or we talked about the "good, old teammates," many of whom still accused me of having sacrificed my brother like Cain did to Abel.

These similar, shared experiences made us kindred spirits. Together, we found that we could bear the wounds and the suffering that dogged us. As friends, we buried the hatchet, recognizing who had engineered the argument between us. And we made peace with each other.

Bonatti found it hard to believe that it was possible to organize independent expeditions around the world. Climbing expeditions used to last six months or more and were only possible with support from alpine associations, governments, or wealthy sponsors. My generation, though, we were able to give talks, write books, and organize sponsors ourselves to finance our projects, travel the world, and make our dreams come true.

These days you can book an eight-thousander, including helicopter support. The spectacular adventures that Bonatti paved the way for us in the mountains—K2, Gasherbrum IV, Cerro Torre—have mutated into tourist attractions. Neither of us wanted this. But we have learned to accept it.

We traditional mountaineers have always respected and submitted to nature. Mountain tourists, on the other hand, believe that they can control nature. Using fixed support and technical equipment, they prepare the mountain for their own use, which makes it all a bit fake. Tourists and adventurers talk, but without ever understanding one another. They go their separate ways.

This became clear when my yeti story unintentionally entered the public arena.

In the summer of 1986, before I'd climbed the eight-thousanders Makalu and Lhotse, I hiked across Tibet from Kham in the east to the capital city of Lhasa, following the same trail that the Sherpa people had done five hundred years earlier when they migrated over the Nangpa La Pass to the Solo-Khumbu District south of the Himalaya, looking for a new home. Sherpa clans still move to the Solo-Khumbu area today.

My long trek, often following the yak caravans, frequently passed through wild, highland terrain where there were no trails. This gave me plenty of time to explore the story of what the tourists in Kathmandu called the yeti. In a small mountain village, I learned the true name of the yeti: *chemo* or *dremo*.

At a press conference upon my return from the Makalu-Lhotse expedition, I talked about the ascent of both eight-thousanders—and incidentally mentioned the yeti.

Because, while in Kathmandu, I had asked dozens of Tibetans who'd come south over the Himalaya to Nepal the same question: "What do you call the creature who the tourists here call yeti?" Without exception, they all said, "chemo." And on my trek, I had seen a giant chemo. The "monster" was a huge brown bear that stood up on its two hind legs. I had found an answer to the "yeti" phenomenon. The yeti legend had a zoological explanation, not a human one.

As soon as I mentioned it to the press, everyone wanted to know more, wherever I went. No one seemed interested in my main topic—the eight-thousanders. No one was listening properly.

And yet we cannot dispute facts. We humans are natural beings, just like chemo. By contrast, the "yeti" is fiction, an invention of society. However, it was impossible to get across that the yeti story was based on reality.

There was a popular joke at the time: Two yetis meet up. One yeti says to the other: "Guess who I bumped into yesterday?"

"No idea."

"Messner."

"Really, so he does exist then."

Explaining the legend both obscures and answers the riddle. The yeti remains a mystery.

It was perhaps stupid of me to discuss the yeti objectively in front of the press. It detracted from my actual intentions, and the derision I endured then still echoes today. Nevertheless, my answer to the yeti question is the only possible solution.

A column in the *Süddeutsche Zeitung*—just one of a hundred or so similar opinion pieces—is an example of how my yeti story became rich fodder.

> And then there's Reinhold Messner. The South Tyrolean has just returned from Nepal and is now giving interviews where he claims that the yeti has never existed. The yeti were just bears, who come over the passes from the northern side of the Himalaya from time to time, for example when in search of a mate. Some 99.9 percent of scientists agree with Messner.
>
> Now there are not one but two watertight arguments that dispute the nonsense. On the one hand, 99.9 percent of yetis doubt Reinhold Messner's existence—and we mean 99.9 percent of all yetis, on both the northern and the southern sides of the Himalaya. The last of the naïve yetis among them, the ones who still believe in him, argue that "He who wears the anorak" (as Messner is known by the yetis) has been spotted on top of all eight-thousanders. To which the more enlightened yetis always reply: "Why would anyone go and do that?" This normally puts an end to the debate. What the yetis couldn't possibly guess is that someone does that to spend years giving talks accompanied by slide shows in public halls all over Europe. On the poster advertising these events, Reinhold Messner, with his deep craggy wrinkles, thick bushy beard, and granite-grey complexion is increasingly starting to look part yeti, part Himalayan rock face.

> The yetis might be better off remaining in hiding in the deepest, darkest corners of the Himalaya, and continuing to warn their children with strange tales of "He who wears the anorak."

Ultimately, it was my own fault. If only I'd not felt the need to give my opinion on the wrong subject, in the wrong place, and at the wrong time—once again. After all, my mother had always warned me to "keep my mouth shut."

21

END OF A LEGEND

Power without magnanimity and sorrow without pain.
These are things I cannot accept.
—Confucius

Fifty years on from the South Tyrol Option Agreement, in 1989, I published a book about it with historians, writers, and friends. The book didn't receive much attention in South Tyrol, but was critically discussed abroad.

By now, Luis Trenker's attitude toward the Third Reich and his behavior during the Option were public knowledge. This didn't stop others from accusing me of treating South Tyrol's grandee badly—despite the fact that I had written positively about the mountaineer, filmmaker, and storyteller in 1987 and had made no mention then of the letter that Trenker had written on February 27, 1940, to Adolf Hitler to apologize for Trenker's dithering during the Option. (After much hesitation, Trenker had opted to leave for Germany, although his parents remained in South Tyrol.) He had written the letter to avoid falling out of favor with Goebbels and Hitler.

"I ask for your opinion and will do as you advise. . . . You, my Führer, know my work from *The Rebel* to *The Fire Devil* and you can rely on me to know where I belong and where I stand when the time comes."

By 1989, Luis Trenker was an old man. We had met often over the years. He came to Juval, and we talked about his time as a mountaineer. I was grateful to hear his stories, which are part of alpinism's narrative.

Here's an extract from my April 1987 article in Germany's *Bunte* magazine:

> In August 1914, two of the best rock climbers were hanging high up on the north face of the Furchetta in the Grödner Dolomites (Val Gardena). We're talking about Hans Dülfer and Luis Trenker. The rock was poor and the protection sparse. They had climbed 600 meters. Luis Trenker, the young mountain guide, was standing on a narrow rock and belaying. Holding the hemp rope, he looked up at his partner high above him, who

Juval Castle in South Tyrol

seemed stuck to the vertical rock face. The valley was some 600 meters below them.

Dülfer hadn't moved for over half an hour. Suddenly it started to snow. The mist moved in, obscuring all visibility, and they beat a hasty retreat and descended. Their attempt on the hardest route of the day had failed. Trenker and Dülfer were the same age, both born in 1892. Trenker was born in the Gardena Valley of South Tyrol, whereas Dülfer was born in North Rhine-Westphalia, Germany, far from the mountains. Enthusiasm for the mountains had brought them together. The Furchetta was their first climb together. It was also their last. Hans Dülfer was killed in World War I in northern France a few months later. He had volunteered to fight at the start of the war and joined the Bavarian Snowshoe Battalion.

Luis Trenker fought in the Dolomites. His experience as a mountain guide and goatherd on the Seiser Alm and the Langkofel/Sassolungo came in useful while he was a soldier and lieutenant fighting against Italy in the mountains. After the war, Trenker studied architecture and worked briefly with Austrian architect Clemens Holzmeister. In 1921, he helped the nature-loving German film director, Arnold Fanck, with his mountain films shot in the Alps.

Born during the Imperial and Royal monarchy when the Habsburg monarch reigned simultaneously as both Kaiser (Emperor of Austria) and König (King of Hungary), Trenker found it initially difficult to come to terms with life under Mussolini, especially given that his South Tyrolean *Heimat* had been annexed to Italy.

Trenker was a film producer, director, author, and actor all in one. His striking looks made him well known and vast audiences flocked to see the Trenker films. He became a folk hero.

His *Bergfilme* (mountain films) are well known. For instance, *Struggle for the Matterhorn*, *The Prodigal Son*, and *Mountains on Fire*, where Trenker relays his experiences fighting on the front in the high peaks of the Dolomites.

Using clever techniques and a few cinematic tricks, he brought realistic-looking climbing situations to the screen and engendered a love of the mountains in millions of people.

Trenker's enthusiasm inspired a young team of actors, camera crew, and mountain guides. An articulate raconteur, he entertained moviegoers and directed thousands of extras in his famous crowd scenes.

In Walter Schmidkunz, Luis Trenker found a sensitive and educated coauthor to write his best-selling books. Schmidkunz, with his profound knowledge of mountaineers and the history of mountaineering, was a rich source of ideas and material. He understood what mountaineers wanted to read. Together they published a series of illustrated *Wunderwelt* books with breathtaking photos of the mountains. No one has depicted the wonderful world of the mountains so well as Luis Trenker.

Luis Trenker was at the climax of his career shortly before the Second World War. At almost fifty, he was fit and bursting with ideas. His craggy features fascinated people and audiences, and many saw him as the perfect hero. The fact that Goebbels and Hitler planned to drop him, was due to Hitler and Mussolini's plan for the South Tyrolean population, the Option Agreement.

Trenker, who was popular in both Berlin and Rome, couldn't decide whether to "opt for the Reich." Himmler criticized Trenker for what he perceived as his ambiguous and therefore suspect political opinions.

After the Second World War, Trenker returned to the mountains. He didn't climb, but produced films, as he had done between the two wars.

Later on, he appeared in documentaries talking about his time in the mountains and during the war, of his brothers in arms. Once again, an audience of millions followed and loved his tales of adventures and the mountains.

Four and a half years after Luis Trenker died, on September 19, 1994, I received an open letter from Dieter Lehner of the Luis Trenker Archive:

> Dear Mr. Messner,
>
> In reply to your comments in *Alto Adige* on September 15, 1994, in the *Società & Kultura* section, I would like to respond as follows.
>
> If you were still young and therefore spontaneous and imprudent, then leniency and persuasion might be appropriate when it comes to Trenker. However, the distress caused by an older Messner cannot simply be condoned.
>
> I contend that you are jealous of the grand old man because your choice of words can hardly be attributed to ignorance or carelessness.
>
> And if they are due to carelessness, then this is unworthy of and unforgivable in a mountaineer.
>
> Your attitude to Trenker, I assume, is due to some psychological trauma, which would explain why you are unable to control your jealousy toward someone who is better, more prominent, and a bigger person than you. Despite what you claim, Trenker did have political ideals. He never collaborated with the Nazis, as you allege he did. Trenker had no skeletons in the closet.
>
> This debate challenges the honor of the venerable old man. So, I throw down the gauntlet on his behalf, so to speak, and challenge you to publicly debate the Trenker issue with me. If you believe you have enough courage and strength of character, then accept my challenge and justify your position. You would then be an honorable gentleman whose deeds are as good as his word.

And this is the letter that Dieter Lehner sent to the *Alto Adige* newspaper:

> Luis Trenker is Reinhold Messner's trauma.
>
> What possessed Reinhold Messner to vandalize a monumental figure and myth with his ineffective arguments and intellectual graffiti?
>
> Does Trenker cast an intellectually overpowering shadow? Is he the imaginary nemesis of a fifty-year-old mountaineer, who, now that he has no more eight-thousanders to climb, is stagnating in the absence of further challenges?

The way in which Messner chooses to attack the venerable old man reveals his base nature, and his envy toward intellectual heights that he himself will never scale.

Messner, who has acquired fame and riches solely by taking spectacular risks, has never become the intellectual giant that Trenker was.

Therefore, in the absence of sensational artistry on high mountains worldwide, he performs an indelicate high-wire act when it comes to Trenker, collaborating with semi-literate people who staple together photocopies from personnel files and call them academic papers.

Messner still has until his ninety-eighth birthday to emulate the most famous of all *Bergfilm* and nature film producers. Whether he achieves this goal remains to be seen. Time is on his side at least.

Everything else is an illusion. And so, Messner's wrangling as the naive sensationalist climber with this venerable Tyrolean personality will continue to be—and always remain Messner's trauma.

Messner should finally stand up and justify himself. I challenge him to a public debate on Luis Trenker. Let's see if he accepts?

—Dieter Lehner, Head of Luis Trenker Archive, Utting am Ammersee, Germany

Once again, I was the bad guy, although the research into Trenker's background and archives had been carried out by others who were experts in the field. I was unable to stay silent about new developments and discoveries, and felt obliged to respond to requests for comments.

And once again, I faced criticisms for publishing information first raised by historians and researchers, merely because my name made a better target for scandal than theirs. However, the stupidest thing of all was that my popularity continued to grow, ready for the next round of abuse.

22

THE SUFFERING GAME

Did I seek where the wind bites keenest, learn to live where no one lives, in the desert where only the polar bear lives, unlearn to pray and curse, unlearn man and god, become a ghost flitting across the glaciers?

—Friedrich Nietzsche, *Beyond Good and Evil*

In 1987, my friend Oswald Oelz wrote about my climbing all the eight-thousanders:

> No one has experienced the exponential impact of a lack of oxygen, solitude, and exhaustion as fully as Reinhold Messner, who has been testing these extremes since 1970.
>
> I first met him not long after he had climbed his first eight-thousander, Nanga Parbat, where he had lost his beloved brother Günther in an avalanche. He was in a hospital bed with frostbitten toes and bandaged fingers. Embittered and desperate, he had poured his anger and exasperation into one of his first books, which became the subject of a long court case.
>
> And now he can trace the journey from his first mountain, to his traumatic first eight-thousander, to his last in Lhotse, a climb which proved to be his salvation. The burden it must have been, to carry this desire to climb all fourteen of them, is perhaps most clearly expressed in the happiness, relief, and release on Messner's face on October 17, 1986, as he returned to the valley "freer than ever."
>
> At present, his next tragedy is not an issue. As Nietzsche puts it: "There are two types of tragedy in our lives. Not reaching our goals—and even worse, reaching our goals."
>
> The history of climbing the eight-thousanders is a long history of failure, suffering, and tragedy, interspersed with ego trips and absurd heroism. In 1895, leading English mountaineer Albert Mummery made the first known attempt to climb Nanga Parbat. He was never seen again. On June 3, 1950, fifty-five years later, Maurice Herzog and Louis Lachenal, with the help of

amphetamines, became the first to summit an eight-thousander—Annapurna. In 1964, the summit of the last eight-thousander, Shishapangma, was reached for the first time via its easiest route. Until 1975, not one mountaineer had managed to climb more than two eight-thousanders, and hundreds had died in the attempt. . . . Messner is one of the few survivors of this most dangerous form of mountaineering.

Two-thirds of the world's top high-alpine mountaineers have died on summit attempts over the last ten to fifteen years. And in the history of climbing Everest, there is a long list of mountaineers who have died during the attempt. With few exceptions, Messner didn't climb normal routes in the conventional manner, unlike many who tried to copy him. Instead, he chose to climb new, hard routes, or to repeat old routes in a new style. He is responsible for the key developments in modern Himalayan climbing, which stand apart for the sacrifices required and have rendered anachronistic big expeditions and siege tactics. Messner introduced alpine style mountaineering in 1975 on Gasherbrum I—dispensing with porters, fixed camps, fixed ropes, and expedition teams. He made the historical ascent of Everest without oxygen in May 1978 and then went on to climb alone, with no partners, on Nanga Parbat and again in 1980 on Everest.

In 1984, he decided not to head back down into the valley after climbing an eight-thousander, but climbed a second summit instead—the first ever 8,000-meter-peak double traverse. Only people who understand what it means to be utterly exhausted and the importance of tranquillity, water, and feeling secure in this dangerous world can really appreciate Messner's total dedication to reaching his goal. He longs to return home, to unwind, to feel safe, to be with his partner; he's hungry for love, recognition, and human warmth. But instead, he climbs on.

This is why he was disappointed when the first ever eight-thousander double traverse was misunderstood "both by experts and the general public" in 1984. He complains that his achievements no longer attract the interest they once did. He feels the cold, hard nature of success that envelops him and notices others in his orbit using him to market their own accomplishments. He is deeply hurt by Walter Bonatti's attack on his business acumen, the same Bonatti who once praised him as the young and last great hope for classical mountaineering. He furiously held the mirror up to what he saw as Bonatti's self-promotion. Messner always described his enemies—perceived or genuine—as ignorant charlatans. So, for him it felt good to be recognized by the best mountaineers in the world, by his equals, such as Christophe Profit and Jerzy Kukuczka—the second man (after Messner) to climb all fourteen eight-thousanders and who is the best high-altitude climber in the world today.

This kind of recognition has helped him persevere, rather like persevering through the storm that swept in during his final eight-thousander. That storm was dangerous but also useful as it literally blew him up the mountain. He says that if he hadn't gained this recognition, he would have given up somewhere along the way, emotionally drained. Messner primarily survived his eighteen eight-thousanders (he climbed four of the fourteen twice) because more than anything else he wanted to live to tell the tale. Unlike other mountaineers, he knew when to turn back, whether due to the risks of avalanches, unstable weather, or insufficient physical or mental fitness. Over the years, as he acquired more and more experience, he became neither fearless nor reckless—in fact, quite the contrary.

Moreover, Messner might have developed his skills amazingly fast, but he has never run before he could walk, so to speak. He was always terrified of falling and being killed. This mindset started during his time as an alpine rock climber. He never took a big fall while leading, a feat which is very rare. I also feared for my life during our horrific climb on Ama Dablam's Southwest Face, where we were constantly threatened by enormous ice avalanches. We hadn't chosen to climb there, but instead had gone to help rescue a party of injured New Zealand climbers. Few of the belays were safe, and moving fast was the best way to survive. Reinhold hurried us up the wall. Whenever I started to climb more slowly or struggled for breath, he called over to me to keep moving—and it worked. He also still had his proven and unbelievably quick climbing reflexes.

Hans Kammerlander knows Messner well (today's more-than-forty-years-old Messner "who now suffers all kinds of aches and pains"). He recalls how, on the summit ridge of Gasherbrum I, he saw Messner about to step into the void then instinctively jump several meters to land safely on a steep, icy slab of rock. "In this kind of situation, even a highly trained sport climber would have fallen the length of the face."

Like others who have the imagination, ability, and vision to break taboos and brave new horizons, Messner can be difficult to accept. For instance, professors of physiology and medicine had claimed that it was impossible to survive at over 8,500 meters without supplemental oxygen, even for a short time. Messner and Habeler were both told they would return from the summit of Everest with severe brain damage.

Reinhard Karl and I met them at 7,400 meters, twenty hours after they had reached the top and were headed back down. They were clearly exhausted and Messner was suffering from snow blindness, but apart from that they showed no signs of serious health problems. Later, when it became clear that they weren't suffering brain damage, the quest for explanations started. Eminent scientists, such as John West, the president of the American Physiological Society, surmised and wrote that Messner and Habeler must possess exceptional physical capabilities, which allowed them to process oxygen even when under extreme stress in ways similar to world-class marathon runners. This was not the case. With other researchers, I carefully examined Messner and five other mountaineers who had climbed above 8,500 meters without oxygen masks.

Their maximum oxygen uptake values were disappointing. The average figure for the six high-alpine climbers was 57 ml/kg/min. This meant that world-class mountaineers were comparable with amateur marathon runners. Elite marathon runners have a maximum oxygen uptake of 75–85 ml/kg/min. Messner, the most successful climber in the group, had 48 ml/kg/min—the lowest figure. Further tests on his heart, lung, and muscle functions also showed nothing special; only Messner's breathing was unusual. In a decompression chamber, when confronted with low levels of oxygen (hypoxia), he automatically showed a higher and earlier ventilatory response than others and was therefore able to compensate for the "thin air."

This temporary hyperventilation mechanism is automatically controlled by the brain and is apparently the most important physiological characteristic in extreme altitude climbers for dealing with low oxygen levels.

Alongside these physiological characteristics and strategic tactics, which minimize the time spent at extreme altitude and therefore prevent rapid physiological and neurophysiological decline, Messner's outstanding motivation and exceptional drive are the most important characteristics. They explain why he has been able to climb the highest peaks in the world without supplementary oxygen.

As a result, he's not overcoming physiological barriers but mental ones to push the limits of what is feasible.

Messner's motivation comes from the joy of climbing and the aesthetic nature of mountaineering. The photos from the summit of Cho Oyu and Makalu clearly reveal happiness and fulfilment.

During moments like these, for Messner it's no longer a matter of asking why, because the intensity of the experience overrides the quest to get there. At the summit, he's "immersed in the void" where perfect calm is juxtaposed with total despair. The photo he took on top of Nanga Parbat, using a self-timer and fish-eye lens, shows these moments when he is at his most alone, cut off from the world below. Messner's summit experiences have "profoundly changed" him and he needs them again and again. He has become addicted to them. His search was not over after he had summitted all the eight-thousanders. Just seven weeks later, he went on to climb the highest summit in the Antarctic, completing his quest to climb the highest peak on every continent. Successes and summits are not something that he expects to fall into his lap. Messner relishes challenges where there's a risk of failure or even death.

This is why he maintains that he has no intention of climbing mountains "while they're sleeping" as his daughter suggested to him on his way to Kangchenjunga. If he did, this would mean that he would reach the top just as they wake up, and that would be too easy. The greater the effort, the stronger the current he has to swim against and, by turn, the tougher he gets.

Messner never uses the chemical stimulants that Herzog, Buhl, and others turned to, drugs that Herrligkoffer mandated be in every mountaineer's backpack first-aid kit. He doesn't need amphetamines, because he has an extraordinary drive to be the first and best, which allows him to push himself right to his very limits. In this way, he hopes to get closer to the ideal version of himself, which he discovered in Tania Blixen's writing: "The most irresistible person on earth is the dreamer, whose dreams have become true." By the time he set out to climb his last two eight-thousanders, he had developed the confidence to have "had enough and to conceal being strong with humility." Upon reaching the goal of his dreams, he quoted Max Frisch: "If someone has the courage to be openly selfish, then someone else will come with his damn morals." He has now shaken off, outwardly at least, the suffocating moralism of growing up in a narrow-minded Catholic

> valley. He lives in his Renaissance castle high over the valleys and identifies with the solipsism of philosopher Max Stirner and his extreme individualism and principal denial of all religious, ethical, political, and social ties: "My business is neither religious, nor human, it is simply mine."
>
> Messner has inspired hopes and dreams that few can fulfil. He went in search of happiness to the summits of the eight-thousanders. When he reached the last one, he only wanted to be back on flat ground, where it's warm, where he can rest, where his friends are. Down here he finds the happiness that he spent sixteen years looking for up there. Then as soon as he is back down, the elusive happiness evaporates to only reappear again at the points where all the lines of a mountain converge.

In the same year, 1987, Ludger Lütkehaus published a rather different opinion piece in Germany's major national newspaper, *Die Zeit*:

> Messner has many enemies, probably more than he has friends. He walks over dead bodies, is profoundly commercially corrupt, unscrupulously selfish and narcissistic, bad at maintaining relationships; intelligent yes, but ultimately no more than a talented alpine yuppie.
>
> But that's not what this article is about. We can leave Reinhold Messner, the man himself, as successful and as controversial as he is, to the gossip columns of sensationalist newspapers, marketing strategies, and alpine history. What's more interesting is the type of personality that Messner, in an extreme form, represents. And the story of his trajectory, which developed at breathtaking speed. He is a modern hero. He combines the power of resistance and ability to adapt so closely that he ultimately returns to the point where he started. And the tragedy of the mythical hero, whose traits he shows, turns out in the end to be a tragicomic example of our times and the society that we live in.

23

SEVEN SUMMITS

The parable of the mountain: You cannot stay on the summit forever; you have to come down again. . . . So why bother in the first place? Just this: what is above knows what is below but what is below does not know what is above. In climbing, always take note of difficulties along the way; for as you go up, you can observe them. Coming down, you will no longer see them, but you will know they are there if you have observed them well. One climbs, one sees. One descends, one sees no longer but one has seen. There is an art of conducting oneself in the lower regions by the memory of what one saw higher up. When one can no longer see, one can at least still know.

—René Daumal, *Mount Analogue*

Traditional mountaineering is inspired by ideas and the notion of being the first. Younger generations have always sought to repeat the "impossible feats" of previous generations.

In 1983, two millionaire businessmen from the United States set themselves a crazy goal. They wanted to be the first to climb in a single year all "Seven Summits"—the highest mountain on each of the seven continents. Dick Bass operated ski resorts in Utah and owned ranches in Texas and coal mines in Alaska. Frank Wells was the former president of Warner Brothers, one of the biggest film production companies in the world. Together they had a huge budget, the best mountain guides, and a whole team of advisors.

To land in the Antarctic, they had a plane specially rebuilt. They bought their way onto a Mount Everest expedition and traveled to Australia to climb Mount Kosciuszko, a "grassy hump" that's 2,200 meters high. It was then clear to me they wouldn't reach their goal of climbing the Seven Summits, which had been my objective for years too.

I had also climbed Kosciuszko but didn't consider it to be the highest mountain on the earth's fifth continent, as Australia itself is part of a larger continent—Oceania, also referred to as Australasia. This includes the island country of New Guinea, where, in the middle of the jungle, there's a steep, rocky

mountain called the Carstensz Pyramid or Puncak Jaya. It has an elevation of nearly 5,000 meters and in those days was very hard to reach. I climbed the Carstensz Pyramid in 1971. It rained nearly the whole time, and I had virtually worn the skin on my fingers to the bone by the time I had finished. After reaching the summit of Everest in 1978, I decided to climb the highest summits on all seven continents. Would I be the first man to do it?

Dick Bass and Frank Wells knew that I was planning an expedition to Mount Vinson, the highest peak in Antarctica. I couldn't afford my own plane and my attempts to tag onto flights with the Argentinian or Chilean military failed repeatedly. Moreover, the special skis needed for the conditions were classed in the US as strategically important, secret equipment. They proved impossible to get hold of. Yet getting there on foot was unthinkable. Naomi Uemura, the famous Japanese adventurer who had reached the North Pole alone by dog sledge, also failed in his overland attempt to reach Mount Vinson. This meant that he was out of the running in a competition started a year earlier, when the veteran Swiss mountaineer Dölf Reist announced that he had climbed the five highest mountains on all five continents. But something seemed fishy about his claim.

His continent list was Asia, Africa, North America, South America, and Europe, leaving out Australia and Antartica entirely. If you count North America and South America separately and include the Antarctic, which is today seen by geographers as a continent in its own right, you have seven continents.

A controversial point in the Seven Summits definition is which counts as the highest summit in Europe: Mount Elbrus in the Caucasus Mountains or the venerable Mont Blanc (4,810 meters) in the Alps. Wells and Bass had engaged a team of geographers to determine the "correct seven summits," and duly climbed Mount Elbrus in the former USSR. Its glaciers are supposed to be on the European side of the watershed, so that the mountain belongs to Europe, although it is the recognized continental boundary between Asia and Europe.

I was in a snowstorm on the 5,633-meter summit of Mount Elbrus in the Caucasus Mountains in 1983, just a few weeks after Wells and Bass had climbed it. Elbrus was not technically difficult to climb. So only Mount Vinson in the Antarctic was missing from my seven summits. It was still game on, especially since my million-dollar "competitors" had failed on Mount Everest. It felt good to know that you still couldn't buy your way up the world's highest mountain.

Then, wonder of wonders, in the winter of 1983–84, Wells and Bass invited me to go with them to Mount Vinson. How generous of them! Finally, I had my chance. I made my preparations, and put up the 25,000 US dollars that was my contribution to the expedition. At the very last minute, shortly before departure, I was informed by fax that I had been uninvited. Frank Wells and Dick Bass had realized that I was their only competitor to reach all Seven Summits.

Bass and Wells went on to climb Mount Vinson without me. When later they failed on their second attempt at Mount Everest, though, I still had a chance.

In South America in 1976, I had climbed Aconcagua, one of the Seven Summits, via its hardest side, the 3,000-meter South Face. In North America in 1976, I had climbed a new route on Denali—the Face of the Midnight Sun. Oswald Oelz and I stood at the summit at midnight in temperatures of minus 40 degrees Celsius. In Africa, in training for my 1978 Mount Everest expedition, I had climbed Kilimanjaro via its Breach Wall, a vertical face more dangerous than the north face of the Eiger.

I climbed these difficult routes for myself, not because of some race to reach the Seven Summits. I had already climbed Mount Everest twice, both times without an oxygen mask. But the only thing that mattered to the two Americans was who would be first to climb all Seven Summits. Frank Wells gave up in 1985. Mount Everest was too high for him. Dick Bass forged on. He finally climbed the world's highest mountain with Sherpa support and using bottled oxygen. Respect for such an amazing achievement at the age of fifty-four! He opted not to climb the Carstensz Pyramid in New Guinea.

In the first days of December 1986, Oswald Oelz, cameraman Wolfgang Thomaseth, and I flew in a private plane with the highly experienced polar pilot Giles Kershaw to the Vinson Massif in the Antarctic. The weather was good, and the sun never set. Some forty-eight hours after landing, I was on the summit of Mount Vinson. A layer of mist covered the seemingly never-ending ice sheet. According to the latest measurements, our summit was 4,897 meters high.

It was very cold. The sea of mist with the odd mountaintop poking through here and there looked surreal. It was like being in another world, a world of ice, not fit for human beings.

Pat Morrow, a Canadian climber, reached the last of his seven summits in 1986, a few months before me. He was the first Seven Summits Summiteer. Back from Antarctica, I went back to climb Aconcagua a second time with Oswald Oelz: a gift to a good friend because he had still to climb it.

24

NO END TO THE MADNESS

If you don't hold yourself back,
then nothing and nobody can stop you.

—Christian Bischoff, life coach and author

After climbing Mount Vinson in the Antarctic, out of pure curiosity I started investigating ways of moving efficiently in snow while pulling a heavy sled weighing up to 100 kilos. Was it possible to march for one hundred days over the vast ice sheet from the Atlantic Ocean to the Pacific Ocean on foot? Yes, I thought, and I started to read everything I could get my hands on about the Antarctic and previous expeditions there.

Arved Fuchs became my expedition partner for this one-hundred-day experiment. He describes his feelings on us finally reaching the South Pole at the end of 1989 as disappointing, although he was optimistic about the second half of the march:

> After slogging for weeks through snow and ice, we reached this place where, instead of a tent, there was the shiny, silver dome of the South Pole Station, and my dreams came crashing down. This pole was not the pole I had been hoping to find. After forty-eight days of living like the historic polar explorers, suffering from the freezing cold and hunger, I found myself in a futuristic building that robbed the Pole of its harsh dignity. For the first and only time in my life, I understood how Scott felt when he said: "So much hard work and not even the reward of being first."

For sixty years, I have been accused of being ambitious, not appreciating my partners' efforts, or wanting the fame only for myself. Each time it was historians and journalists who started the argument, thereby exploiting the story following a successful expedition as long as possible.

Following our 1978 Everest expedition, Peter Habeler and I reported in unison to the many skeptics that we were still in good spirits. We emphasized that it was neither ambition nor a death wish that enabled us to climb so high, but the desire to achieve this feat with as little effort possible.

By the time the Antarctica crossing was financed and ready to go, three years on from my last eight-thousander and after finishing the Seven Summits, Arved Fuchs and I were ready. We had read a lot of books, studied many maps, and prepared the logistics together. We were both very much aware what rivalry and ambition had led to at the South Pole, but didn't let it affect us. He and I shared the same goal, and we were able to cope with the agonies of the cold, the wind, and the whiteouts that we would endure for our three-month journey. Our attitude wasn't one of self-sacrifice but the willingness to accept injury, just as Scott, Amundsen, and Shackleton—our companions in spirit—had done. This is my report on their journey for Germany's *Frankfurter Allgemeine Zeitung* newspaper:

> When Robert F. Scott set out for Antarctica on a second attempt to reach the South Pole, he planned to beat the record set by Irishman Ernest Shackleton, who had got to within 160 kilometers of the Pole. On June 15, 1910, his ship, the *Terra Nova*, set sail from Cardiff, Wales. When Scott reached Melbourne, Australia, there was a telegram waiting for him: "Allow me to inform you that the *Fram* is proceeding south to the Antarctic." It was from Roald Amundsen. Scott understood what this meant, but remained relaxed and didn't change his plans. His opponent was Shackleton, or "Shack" as his men called him, not Amundsen. The Norwegian explorer could try to reach the South Pole with sled dogs, but Scott wanted to do it the British way, the same as Shack had done during his attempt a few years earlier.
>
> Amundsen kept his plans secret until the last moment. His team initially believed that he wanted to sail around South America into the Bering Strait and on to the Arctic. It was only when they were at sea that he revealed his real objective. None of his men backed out. They all agreed to follow him to the South Pole. On January 14, 1911, Amundsen's ship reached Walvis Bay. The Norwegians set up winter base camp on the Ross Ice Shelf, at Framheim.

Amundsen's planning and sangfroid make him an exception in the history of polar exploration. He was an excellent skier, and familiar with the equipment and survival tactics of the Inuits.

Robert Falcon Scott was a British Royal Navy officer with the support of the navy and their experience from a previous expedition to the Antarctic region. Otherwise, he had only a hazy idea of the challenges he would face. Scott arrived in the Antarctic ten days before Amundsen and set up base camp at Cape Evans. Both groups used the rest of the Antarctic summer to establish supply depots along their planned route. Scott, who had ponies, dogs, and motorized sleds, was convinced that he had the upper hand, as he was using the familiar Shackleton route. However, he was no warm-hearted leader and remained aloof from his men through the winter. The British base camp was organized in accordance with Royal Navy hierarchy, with separate rooms for the officers and the men.

Amundsen, although nervous about the journey, organized the Norwegian camp along more relaxed lines. Everyone had specific tasks. They checked their equipment, carried out repairs, and, if necessary, adapted and improved their ski bindings. When the weather made it possible to start out on October 20, Amundsen began his march to the Pole. He chose four companions: Oscar Wisting, Olav Bjaaland, Sverre Hassel, and Helmer Hanssen. They left with four sleds, provisions, and fuel for three months. Their sleds were pulled by fifty-two Greenland sled dogs.

Scott set out on November 2 with fifteen men. He took everything with him that he had: a motorized sled, ten ponies, and twenty-three Siberian huskies who pulled three sleds over the ice shelf. Both expeditions used skis—the Norwegians were experienced skiers; the British, definitely not.

Amundsen made quick progress. He laid a depot at each degree of latitude, and marked it with high snow cairns and flags. Upon reaching the foot of the Transantarctic Mountains, 550 kilometers from the Pole, the Norwegians had forty-two dogs left. Pulling with all their might, they managed the steep rise up to the South Antarctic Plateau. When they got there, Amundsen had twenty-four dogs shot, as they were no longer needed. They would require extra food and so would serve instead as a source of food for the remaining dogs. On December 14, 1911, Amundsen and his companions reached the Pole. There was no sign of Scott. Amundsen was victorious, but he said he felt no satisfaction. On the journey back, the further he got from the Pole, the less the South Pole appeared to mean to him. He increasingly felt that he'd come to the wrong Pole. Wasn't the North Pole meant to be his real goal? The Norwegians made it back easily to base camp in Walvis Bay on January 25, 1912, with eleven dogs and two sleds. It took them ninety-nine days to cover the 2,600 kilometers as the crow flies. Their average of nearly thirty kilometers a day was extraordinary. In fact, Amundsen's South Pole Expedition is still the fastest dogsled tour of our times.

By the time Scott reached the foot of the Beardmore Glacier, he had lost five of his ten ponies. He had the remaining ponies shot and stored the meat in a depot for the return journey. After the dangerous ascent to the 3,000-meter-high plateau, Scott sent his support team back. He then headed on with two sleds and six men to the Pole. Storms and difficult snow hindered their progress. It would probably have been a sensible idea to turn back now. But what does sensible mean in this context? Scott had to go on. He had to do better than Shackleton. He wanted more than the Pole; he wanted to outperform his rival. The British team was doomed to failure.

Amundsen wanted to be the first to get to the Pole. Scott wanted to be a hero. His decisions were influenced more by the rivalry between two men seeking recognition in the United Kingdom than the actual nature of the physical challenge. He was also prepared to show that British heroes are ready to die for their cause.

As Scott wrote in his diary: "I do not regret this journey, which has shown that Englishmen can endure hardships, help one another, and meet death with as great a fortitude as ever in the past." This type of self-sacrifice, no matter how pathological it sounds, is essential to survival at the South Pole. Yet, at the same time it's also deadly. By then, Scott's team was falling apart. On January 4, 1912, Scott divided up his team for the last time. He headed on to the Pole against all reason with just one sled and four men—reaching the South Pole on January 17, 1912. Yes, he'd beaten Shackleton, but Amundsen had got there before him. The Norwegian flag was fluttering in the wind on top of a triangular tent. Scott flew the Union Jack next to it.

The British team was demoralized, and the return journey turned into a nightmare. Edgar Evans and Lawrence Oates perished just 13 kilometers from a depot that could have saved them. Robert Scott died a hero's death. Eight months later, when his body was found, Scott's diary was discovered.

Its contents rendered him immortal. Scott's ability to describe the readiness on the part of his team to make sacrifices and the depth of his own suffering tick all the boxes for a tragic hero, even today. I had no wish to adopt this attitude.

His depiction of the suffering and dying obscured other issues, such as unusable motor sleds, poor planning, and the heroic posturing of the British expedition. This was not something I wanted to copy.

Scott's heroism inspired Shackleton to return to Antarctica in 1914. His Endurance Expedition provided a better blueprint for my Antarctic crossing with Arved Fuchs. We drew on the experience of all the great polar explorers—Amundsen, Scott, and Shackleton—but understood that the underlying motives for a journey to the end of the world are as different and varied as the characters undertaking them. For example, I wanted to complete Shackleton's quest (to make the first land crossing of the Antarctic continent), while Arved aimed to reach both Poles within a year. Our march across the vast polar plateau had equally become an undertaking involving adherence to specific time frames and motives. There seemed to be no end to the madness.

25

YETI HANGOVER

Progress is impossible without change, and those who cannot change their minds cannot change anything.

—George Bernard Shaw

In 1998, I published a book called *Yeti—Legende und Wirklichkeit* (My Quest for the Yeti), which started a "new yeti dawn." Here's what Axel Klemmer had to say about it in Germany's *Alpin* magazine:

> Just imagine the scene. Reinhold Messner has got a photo of the yeti, but instead everyone's talking about Jan Ullrich. Germany's top cyclist is just twenty-three years old. He's got shaved legs, freckles on his nose, a big gold earring. He's the hero of the Italian roads, our Jan—and the first German to win the Tour de France.
>
> Life is unfair. All Jan has to do is ride his bike as fast as he can wearing his yellow jersey and he appears on the front page of the papers, day after day. What about Reinhold Messner? You'll find him somewhere in the "other news" section toward the back. The *Süddeutsche Zeitung* even printed a few lines on the abominable snowman and the explorer next to an amusing story about football pundit Lothar Matthäus.
>
> Matthäus and Messner. Two men who used to be someone. Now here they are, making fools out of themselves. It's sad to see. On *Bayern Drei*, a Bavarian radio station, the famous South Tyrolean mountaineer was heard holding forth on how the yetis live. It was just too much. The interviewer cheerfully asked Messner if he might have suffered from a lack of oxygen. Messner responded grumpily that his brain got more oxygen than many radio reporters. This might well be true. But what about the rest? He just doesn't notice anymore. And yet, it could all be so easy. He says he took a photo. And it's a "razor sharp" photo. We can see it—in two years! Here's someone who wants to enthrall the public, but has forgotten that he's only fit for "other news," along with Lothar Matthäus and the lottery

This cartoon appeared in the *Kronen* newspaper in 1986. The sign on the bars reads: "Yeti—can only be seen by Reinhold Messner. Please do not feed the animals."

numbers. If he'd put the photo on the table in front of him, the press would have stampeded to Juval Castle. *New York Times*, *Le Monde*, *Bergsteiger* magazine. They all would have come, and led with a photo of the yeti on the front page. Messner would have been able to donate a home to the yetis, to carry on pushing limits for the rest of his life. He would never have to worry about money ever again. But what did people see instead? Jan Ullrich.

Back to the yeti though. Let's not forget that the yeti is one of the last great dreams of the civilized world, and our longing for the lost secrets of childhood. His story has become a myth to rival Nessie. He's something we enjoy being afraid of. How all the editors would have fought to see the real yeti in all his hairy splendor. Instead, they write about sensational events on Mars, where a robot clumsily bumped into some red rocks. No one came to see the South Tyrolean mountaineer. Yet he expected them all to come. With that photo in his pocket, in two years' time. . . .

Footnotes for posterity: Nanga Parbat solo, Everest solo, seventh grade rating, all fourteen eight-thousanders. Reinhold Messner is a

> mountaineering legend. As a media spectacle though, he's increasingly becoming a tragic figure. He still has a loyal following. He climbs down off his mountain to grace them with his presence. He makes his announcements to them. He sells his books to them. This is no laughing matter. Yet others prefer to watch Jan Ullrich with his shaved legs and clean-shaven face. They've already forgotten two seconds later what this bearded man wants to show them in twenty or two hundred years' time. Shame really.

I wrote to Stefan Aust, editor-in-chief at the *Spiegel*, in an attempt to introduce some objectivity. But it was in vain. I could cope with the malicious reporting of the yeti story. The monster was a bear, and I was a clown. I had only myself to blame. However, the legend, which had been passed down over the centuries, had a perfectly rational zoological explanation, and this was deliberately not mentioned. And that alone had been my discovery.

> However the story got into your paper, it's plagiarized, inaccurate, and full of preconceptions. The author neither read my book nor interviewed me. I'm not interested in being friendly or unfriendly, I'm interested in the facts of the matter. You'll understand that I feel the need to respond to the avalanche of malice, and headlines such as "Messner hat uns einen Bären aufgebunden" (Messner's been pulling our leg) that the *Spiegel* ran in Germany.
>
> The three articles on Messner and the yeti that *Spiegel* magazine published over the last thirteen years don't do justice to the topic. The first article is based on a television interview with Henry Glas. The other two online articles contradict each other. As editor-in-chief, you're responsible for the last one and I would be delighted to discuss it with you live on television. Alternatively, a discussion of the book, or a *Spiegel* interview on the topic and the way that the book was belittled, would provide an opportunity to address the prejudices that have been stirred up.
>
> As a long-standing *Spiegel* reader, your reporting of the yeti issue makes me doubt the intentions of the *Spiegel* editorial team. I'm all in favor of critical, investigative journalism, but a cynical and prejudiced *Spiegel* is not something I plan to continue to read. I intend to meet what is effectively character assassination with anger, not submission.

In his op-ed piece in *Alpin* magazine, Clemens Kratzer commented on the narrative surrounding the yeti issue:

> So, the yeti is neither a Neanderthal, nor an abominable snowman. The gutter press spreads its malice, and the rest of the world is frustrated. People will probably turn away from him. From this yeti. Then he might be left in peace. Hopefully. Will people also turn away from Messner? Unlikely.
>
> Climbers hope that Reinhold Messner will get back to what he's best at. Alpinism. Making mountaineering history accessible. This includes people who find the subject somewhat abstract. Who could be better than R. M. at collating, documenting, writing, and safeguarding it for eternity? Before this wealth of knowledge and the many feats, both great and small, become lost and forgotten.
>
> Let someone else, some other explorer of limits, set out on the trail of the yeti to garner the headlines.
>
> Alpinism needs the natural world, its untouched beauty, the honesty of the mountains. It's a world where dreams, wonder—and yetis—are still possible.
>
> For something to have a future, it must also have a past: Messner as a brilliant chronicler and honest, yet critical guardian of alpinism and mountaineering history. That would be a fine thing.
>
> And what about the yeti? The legend and the reality?
>
> Maybe it is like Heinrich Spoerl's novel *Feuerzangenbowle* (The Punch Bowl) where he says that "the only true stories are in our dreams."

In an interview with Germany's *Focus* magazine entitled "The Wilderness Changes Our Perspective," I tried to expand on this:

> **F:** Did you believe in the yeti before your first encounter?
>
> **RM:** No, I always thought that the yeti was just a figment of the imagination.
>
> **F:** And now the yeti is apparently just a simple bear?
>
> **RM:** The yeti is nothing more than a myth: so part animal, part legend. I would estimate that over a billion people have heard of the yeti. I see the yeti as the wild counterpart of man at the interface between civilization and wilderness.
>
> **F:** So what did you meet in the wilderness then?

RM: People in the Himalaya talk of the chemo, dremo, or yethe. There are different names for it. Yeti is the general name. From a zoological viewpoint, the yeti is a brown bear with human characteristics. The brown bear (*Ursus arctos*) should not be confused with the Asian black bear (*Ursus thibetanus*), which can also be found in the Himalaya.

F: But is it not just a bear then?

RM: In daylight, yes. However, if you meet one in the middle of the night in an inaccessible high mountain range, then this changes your view of things. The world suddenly looks rather different. The yeti is much bigger and ten times stronger than you—and you're unarmed. There's nothing you can do. If the chemo had attacked, he would have torn me to pieces.

F: Where does the yeti live?

RM: Over the whole of the Himalaya and in the Karakorum, but there have also been reports of sightings in Siberia and Mongolia. I don't want to reveal the exact details, to deter hunters.

F: Could the yeti be a type of human being or monkey?

RM: No. All the stories that locals have told me about the chemo or dremo match the descriptions of the yeti and my own observations. The tracks and the whistling are from the same animal.

F: How does the yeti whistle?

RM: It sounds like the warning call of a chamois. The locals always told me that if the yeti whistles, it means danger.

Finally, on September 24, 1998, I read a more conciliatory article in the *Süddeutsche Zeitung* under the headline "Reinhold Messner and the Yeti":

> Is it all just a scam? Depends how you see it. Reinhold Messner is known as a pioneer precisely because he made his passion for adventure his job. He is as experienced at dealing with the media as he is with a rope and climbing gear. And he plans his marketing campaigns as thoroughly as he does his expeditions. But it's this self-marketing that has been causing Messner a headache for some time now. His material is not the newest and now he's running out. And finding new material is no easy task. Among other things,

> because he's now fifty-four years old, an age where he's less likely to be involved in pioneering conquests.
>
> Maybe the yeti is the only one who could actually save Reinhold Messner. Early descriptions of a wild and hairy animal or monster that can walk upright date back to the late Middle Ages. European mercenaries reported encountering the mysterious beast in Mongolia. In more recent times, English soldiers and mountaineers found traces and tracks of the yeti on the slopes of the Himalaya.
>
> They repeatedly discovered huge, strange footprints, which they duly photographed. They were deemed to originate from the mysterious giant.
>
> Some even claim to have seen the yeti themselves. Their descriptions have many similarities, much to the satisfaction of the large number of "the yeti is real" conspiracy theorists. Yet the details were not precise enough to enable serious zoologists to classify the creature. Could it be an orang-utan? A bear? Or the long-sought-after missing link between man and ape? Both experts and laymen are irritated by the constant yeti reports. Surely, Reinhold Messner is the only one who could save them. What if he really did discover the yeti?

The fact that I was the one to clear up the mystery proved once again my undoing—I was accused of being opportunistic and motivated only by financial gain.

Four days later, in his column in the *Frankfurter Allgemeine Zeitung* on September 28, 1998, Freddy Langer drew a line under the discussion with some wise words:

> To say that Messner discovered the yeti would seem to be an incorrect description of his thirteen years of constant research. More accurately, we could say that he identified it. This would also explain, not excluding certain financial interests, why Reinhold Messner has been responding to questions about the yeti by referring to his large, 250-page book. It's about to be published and going to provide a sober, zoological explanation for the old legends told by the farmers and nomads of the Himalaya. However, the key to understanding the yeti is more than what you see on the three color photos. According to Messner, it's about "the relationship

between mountain people and their bears." Because it has always meant two different things to them.

There's the bear they might meet during daylight hours and then the mythical abominable snowman they encounter in the forest at night or in the meadows. It's a fantasy that even has erotic connotations, where the yeti becomes an animalistic mirror image. Is this not the end of another wonder in our unpoetic world? No, Messner consoles us, and confirms once again that enlightenment rarely gives people the answers they want to hear. Whether bear or yeti, the myth lives on and the irrational hunt for the abominable snowman continues.

26

ÖTZI THE ICEMAN

To sit alone in the lamplight with a book spread out before you, and hold intimate converse with men of unseen generations— such is a pleasure beyond compare.

—Buddhist monk Yoshida Kenkō

In autumn 1991, I trekked around South Tyrol's borders with Hans Kammerlander. During our forty-one-day round trip, we grappled with the issue of identity, looking within and beyond ourselves to reflect on South Tyrol's past, present, and future, and who we were as a people.

In the Ötztal Alps, we reached the Similaun hut. The young hut warden, Markus Pirpamer, told us that a corpse had been found in the ice at the Hauslabjoch, near the border to Austria. Hans and I had passed by that way, but hadn't seen anything.

The warden had sketched a picture of the axe he had seen near the corpse—with a wooden shaft and iron blade—and it made me very curious. It looked like the wood-chopping axe I was given in Damis, New Guinea, in 1971 in exchange for our ice axes.

Hans and I went back to where the corpse had been found; it must have been hidden by mist as we walked past. Lying in a pool of melted ice like an open grave was an emaciated mummy. It was only partly exposed, still frozen into the ice. Back at the hut, we reported what we had seen to the carabinieri. They told us that nobody was missing.

I felt that it was possible that the dead man might have been from the Ice Age. The Austrian police took the axe away for examination.

Was he five hundred years old, two thousand years old—or even older? The question had no quick answer. Certainly it was an important archaeological find. The body lay along the path that Hans and I had trekked along, on the South Tyrolean side of the border between Italy and Austria.

In South Tyrol, the media made fun of my report. Abroad, the find was quickly compared to the whole yeti affair. The *Kurier* newspaper in Vienna wrote on September 24, 1991: "Reinhold Messner—who 'discovered' the Himalayan yeti—just happened to pass by while on a mountaineering trip and was shown the find." Two days later, Munich's *Abendzeitung* printed similar prejudicial comments: "Is someone playing a macabre trick, by dumping a mummy in the ice? The fact that it was Reinhold Messner, of all people, the man who says he saw a yeti, will do little to silence the doubters."

The *Kurier* continued to run the story, and the account of the corpse in the glacier became more and more bizarre:

> The rumors about this archaeological find are getting somewhat fanciful. It has been suggested that someone deliberately placed the corpse for extreme mountaineer Reinhold Messner to find, as he has already made a fool of himself with his yeti story, Austria's *Krone* newspaper reported. During his trek around the mountains of Tyrol, he stayed at the Similaun hut and created plenty of publicity by cleverly managing the story.
>
> But who's going to steal an old corpse? And where would they get it? Not to mention the bronze age tools found with it. All just to play a joke on Messner? "Is someone playing a macabre trick, by dumping a mummy in the ice?" the *Münchner Abendzeitung* asked in yesterday's edition. They're referring to the yeti-man Messner. . . .
>
> Moreover, there's a pointless argument raging about who the iceman actually belongs to. Both the mayor of Sölden in Ötztal, in whose area the mummy was discovered, and the Austrian forestry commission, which also owns the area, are claiming ownership.

It was only when Professor Konrad Spindler from the Institute of Prehistoric and Early History at Innsbruck University contacted me regarding the iceman from Hauslabjoch that my opinions started to carry more weight. By now, the discovery site was confirmed as South Tyrol. Dr. Spindler requested my assistance to clear up the matter.

> As we've learned from various press reports, you visited the glacier site of the corpse, shortly after it was found, during your trek around South Tyrol with your climbing partner Hans Kammerlander.

You were the first to recognize the significant age of the find and to suspect that it might be an important archaeological discovery. In particular, it was due to your comments in the media that we were able to quickly recover the corpse and bring in forensic specialists to organize a scientific analysis of the body and the artifacts found with it.

For this purpose, our institute has set up a central documentation center, led by our research officer Elisabeth Zissernig on behalf of the South Tyrolean government. The center has been tasked with clearing up all the events connected to the find, from its discovery to its delivery to the forensic experts in Innsbruck, insofar as they are scientifically useful.

We would therefore be very grateful if you would tell Elisabeth Zissernig what you saw at the site of the find.

Ms. Zissernig will therefore contact you by telephone in the next few days to arrange a time and place for a meeting. Please let us know the best way to get in touch with you. Naturally, we will cover any expenses.

My meeting with Elisabeth Zissernig took place in December 1991 in Munich. Here's the report generated from that morning meeting:

On Saturday, September 21, 1991, as part of his hike around South Tyrol's borders with his climbing partner Hans Kammerlander, Reinhold Messner arrived at the Similaun mountain hut with local guide, Kurt Fritz.

As soon as they arrived, the hut warden Markus Pirpamer informed Messner that the body of a mountaineer with a strange axe had been found. He drew a sketch of the axe. The head was made of iron and his description made Messner think of an axe from the Ice Age. Messner said there was great excitement, and they discussed all the possibilities. At around 5 to 6 pm they decided to head to the site of the find.

Local historian Hans Haid and his wife Gerlinde Haid, who were also at the Similaun hut to meet Messner, accompanied the three mountaineers. They couldn't hike as fast and arrived at the site later.

It took Messner about half an hour for the ascent to the site. The three mountaineers arrived at the location described by M. Pirpamer at 5:30 to 6:30 pm.

As expected, they found a black plastic sheet. Messner and Kammerlander lifted the sheet to one side and saw a figure lying face down. It was a perfectly preserved mummy.

It had already been dug out of the ice up to its hips. The exposed parts of the body were completely naked.

There was no hair. And at the back of the head, there were signs of an injury. The skin was damaged, and Messner presumed there had been a blow to the head. Under the chin, there was some sort of string or braid. . . . He had burns on his back.

The arms were more visible than on Anton Koler's photo, which had been taken the day before. His right arm was almost fully visible, our group could see that the dead man had nothing in his hand. The hips were partially freed from the ice. But the legs were still covered by water and a thin layer of ice. There was no sign of fur or leather clothing, and there were no fabric remains. Hay was around the feet, which reminded Messner very much of the footwear worn in Lapland. He could only see one "shoe," because the legs were slightly crossed over one another.

Near the corpse was a small piece of wood with holes in it. Messner thought it might be a reinforcing section of a basket.

About two meters from the body, pieces of birch bark were found that were very similar to the piece shown by M. Pirpamer at the Similaun hut.

Slightly further away in the same direction, about three meters from the body's head, further objects were discovered slightly higher up on the rocks. Sticking out of the ice there was a wooden rod (maybe it had leaned against the rock) that showed signs of wear.

They tried to dig the rod out of the ice. It wasn't possible as the water kept flowing. This piece of wood reminded Messner of the hunting bows he had seen in New Guinea. It's interesting to speculate how it would have been possible to carve this piece of wood with an axe. A Swiss army knife would have been more suitable, noted Messner.

In a crevice, they also found fur remains and a lot of strings. Messner couldn't see any remains of the backpack.

The Haids had now also arrived. The group discussed the possible causes of death and took photos.

> After about an hour, at 6:30/7:30 pm, all five of the group, Messner, Kammerlander, Fritz, H. and G. Haid, left to hike back to the hut, having carefully covered the corpse again with the black plastic sheet.

In 1992, I was being accused of "castrating" Ötzi (the name the iceman was given as time went on) and damaging artifacts found next to him. Professor Spindler was quick to refute this suggestion. Germany's best-selling tabloid, the *Bild* newspaper, slogged on: "Did Messner put the iceman in the glacier?" The paper suggested that it was "a 'strange coincidence' that Messner happened to be so close to where Ötzi was found. . . . Maybe Ötzi is an Egyptian mummy. Did Messner put it there himself?" More cheap sensationalism.

In 1993, Michael Heim (a historian) and Werner Nosko published a book called *Die Ötztal-Fälschung* (The Ötztal Forgery), in which they claimed that Ötzi was a fake. They also asked:

"And why did the alpine airhead Reinhold Messner turn up as one of the first eyewitnesses?"

Should I have responded?

The whole thing culminated in a further publication entitled *Ich war Ötzi* (I was Ötzi), a book with the subtitle *Die Botschaft aus dem Eis* (A Message from the Ice). In the book, Burkhard Hickisch and Renate Spieckermann told the story of a reincarnation. Nobody seemed to want to ask why factual distortions and this kind of humbug seemed more popular than my amateur findings.

The yeti and Ötzi affairs made it clear that people were prepared to use my name to sell all kinds of nonsense.

27

SOLAR ROOF, BUREAUCRACY, AND SELF-RESPONSIBILITY

The Heimat *custodians, associations with an obsessive tendency to want to cultivate everything, are the smallest totalitarian unit that a state, a country, a people is capable of producing.*

—folklorist Elsbeth Wallnöfer

In the 1970s, obtaining permits to climb an eight-thousander involved jumping through all sorts of major bureaucratic hoops, whether it was in India, Nepal, or Pakistan. It invariably meant trips to Rome, visits to embassies, and years of correspondence.

Toward the end of the twentieth century, the depth of European bureaucracy overtook that of developing countries. I found this out the hard way from 1993 to 1994, when I wanted to renovate a small outbuilding at Juval Castle. I received a letter telling me to stop all work immediately. This was followed by an order to restore the building to its original condition.

I responded by writing to the mayor of Kastelbell and also sent a registered letter to the Provincial Council for Landscape Conservation in Bolzano.

From Reinhold Messner–Juval, November 18, 1993
To the Kastelbell Building Commission
For the attention of the mayor,
RE: Restoration of the *Häusl* (little house) at Juval
After acquiring part of the castle rock, the access road, and therefore also the *Häusl* (referred to in old documents as *Baumanns Häusl* and intermittently inhabited), in spring 1993, I acted quickly to prevent further decay by restoring the roof.

I therefore ask the building commission of Kastelbell to approve the restoration of this *Häusl* in the given form with the materials used (stone, wood, shingle roof).

As I believed that I didn't require planning permission for maintenance and repair work, I have already started the work. Please forgive me for this.

Kind regards,

R. Messner

Reinhold Messner–Juval, November 19, 1993
Provincial Councillor
Dr. Erwin Achmüller
Office for Landscape Conservation
RE: Renovation of the "Baumann"/"Tagwerker"/ "Wegmacherhäusl" building on Juval hill, also known as the *Häusl* (little house). Please note as follows:

1. I was denied access to the lower courtyard of Juval Castle (for transporting wood and materials) for ten years, and I was forced to buy it. Therefore, the second half of the "castle hill" and the former "Baumann"/ "Tagwerker" / "Wegmacherhäusl" house became my property. (Purchase agreement dated April 13, 1993; approval of the court commission dated March 1, 1993)
2. According to a deed, several witness statements, the document attached, and the architectural plans, this *Häusl* was built and used as a residential building. (The fact that it was repurposed over the last few years doesn't contravene any of these facts. The building was never a barn.)
3. The old, totally dilapidated feed house belonging to a farmer at the bottom of the castle is to be demolished when a new one is built in a more favorable location.

I restored our *Häusl* exactly as it was or should have been built, in good faith that I didn't need official permission for pure restoration work. I also used the original materials (stone, wood, shingle roof).

The only nod to modernity is the solar panels on the southeast wing of the gabled roof. As an environmentally-conscious South Tyrolean, living on sunny Juval hill, I can't condone any other method of heating water.

I ask for all these facts to be taken into consideration during the discussion about subsequent planning permission approval.

After restoring the semi-ruin that was Juval Castle and preventing the Oberortlhof from falling into total disrepair, I wanted to halt the decline of the *Häusl* which had once been part of the castle property and inhabited.

My goal was to preserve all my buildings within view of the castle to their former structure and appearance.

I see Juval not as a romantic quirk, but the work here as preserving and revitalizing a cultural landscape that is and should remain unique in its harmony.

I now see that I made a mistake from an official point of view by trying to restore Juval. Nevertheless, I have little understanding why the State Office for Environmental Protection launched what is effectively a public witch hunt on "Messner—the architectural and environmental sinner" without seeking to contact me first. And all this, regarding a project where I intended quite the opposite.

There is still a lot to do at Juval. The cleanup work and paving and landscaping will take another five years. If I succeed in the face of all the resistance to pull off my overall concept for Juval Castle, I don't expect any recognition. What I do expect here and now is the respect of all those who value culture and landscape. I also expect the respect of the provincial government. Therefore, I request that you withdraw the order to stop the building work and I await your instructions to rectify the situation.

I spent six months on this issue, organizing the building permit, the restoration work, the zoning, etc. Dealing with lawyers. It cost me a lot of time, all just to comply with bureaucracy.

It has since transpired that the little house was already used as a residential building in the eighteenth century. It has remained unchanged in shape and size ever since. Only the shingle roofing and the insulation were replaced by my work.

The restoration was finally approved. However, for landscaping reasons, a recommendation followed that the solar panels on the roof should be removed.

My response was as follows:

RE: solar system on the "Tagwerkerhäusl"

The "Tagwerkerhäusl" on Juval has been verifiably used as a residential building for estate managers or laborers on the surrounding farms for centuries. And I have prevented it from being demolished. I now see that, following your ruling of April 11, 1994, case no. 28.2 CA/cv/1915), I am

Juval Castle in South Tyrol

now forced to dismantle the small solar system on the southeast wing of the pitched roof.

In this context, I don't want to go into the serious transgressions which, when it comes to landscape protection in South Tyrol, are committed

> almost daily. In Juval, and this applies both to the castle and farms, I have imposed more stringent conditions on my property than those imposed by the provincial government. And not only because I wish to set an example in terms of environmental protection and landscape conservation, but primarily out of respect for nature and the unique, small-scale cultural landscape of the area.
>
> Although the solar installation in question should certainly remain from an environmental point of view and doesn't look unattractive (it takes time to get used to seeing new materials), I will defer to your ruling and therefore to an old saying that "There's no cure for stupidity."
>
> I am well aware that this matter has been hyped up in an envious society and has become far more important than it deserves to be. It is also obvious that the solar installation has fallen victim to the dogmatic attitude of your officials.
>
> But now I've grown tired of complaining. I will clear my roof. But I won't give up entirely. For me, environmental protection has top priority. One last thing, as I have now been branded throughout Italy as "an architectural and environmental sinner," I feel obliged in any future publication that mentions Juval to bring up the "Wegmacherhäusl" case and the prohibited solar roof. Because my castle and its outbuildings will be open to the public in the near future.

The next ban came from the Office for Hunting and Fishing. The office wanted to stop my small herd of yaks, which I had kept for years in Sulden am Ortler, from grazing on the summer pastures and keep them enclosed behind double fences at the farm. Why? Because until I received final clarification from the Ministry of the Environment in Rome, I didn't have a zoo permit for "wild animals."

My first reaction was to try and explain the situation:

> Unfortunately, the gentlemen in Rome don't seem to know that there is a difference between wild yaks (*Bos mutus*) and domesticated yaks (*Bos mutus grunniens*), as you will see from the enclosed documents. In Sulden, we only keep domesticated yaks and request that this is taken into consideration.

I enclosed documents from the German Yak and Camel Foundation and asked for my yaks to be allowed to remain on the pastures at Sulden am Ortler that resembled their habitat in Tibet:

> Yaks are high-altitude cattle and of vital importance to the mountain regions of Central Asia. Yaks have adapted to the steep slopes of mountain pastures and extreme mountain temperatures. They are excellent beasts of burden. They produce milk and other essential produce for Asian mountain farmers and nomads who live on the high plateaus of Central Asia. As information about this species is very limited, this article aims to contribute to the understanding of a species without which the survival of people in the high mountain regions of Asia would be impossible.
>
> There are 12 million yaks living in China and 50,000 yaks in Mongolia. Together, this figure accounts for over 90 percent of the world's yak population.
>
> The yak is mainly kept as a domestic animal on the high plateaus of Qinghai and in Tibet, which is surrounded by the Himalaya. This includes the provinces of Gansu, Qinghai, Sichuan, and Yunnan and the autonomous regions of Tibet and Xinjiang Uygur. Yaks are kept to graze on around 88 million hectares of high mountain pastures, which are used commercially and would otherwise be unsuitable, or only to a limited extent, for farming. This means that the Chinese yak has access to one third of China's total grazing land—an immeasurable source of food. Old traditions say that today's domestic yaks are descended from wild yaks, which were domesticated around 2,500 BC. The earliest domestication of yaks was in Tibet and on the northern slopes of the Himalaya. Wild yaks can still be found on the high plateaus of Tibet and Qinghai today. They are one of the few species of cattle living in the wild in China.
>
> Yaks are multipurpose cattle. As a beast of burden, and source of milk, meat, and wool, its commercial benefit is fourfold.
>
> Yaks adapt well to high altitudes, low air pressure, and low oxygen content—the conditions encountered on the high plateaus. Their natural habitat is mountain pastures 3,000 meters above sea level. Summer pastures in Tibet can even reach altitudes of up to 5,500 meters. Yaks have a very broad, deep thorax and long, curved ribs. Their trachea is remarkably thick and

> large, and the space between the cartilages is considerable, so that they can adapt to a faster respiratory rate.

I was away on expedition at that point. Summer came and went, but our animals had to remain down in the valley. Upon my return to South Tyrol, I was amazed to see just how much energy the bureaucrats had expended on them. Just think how much time I might have been able to spend developing visions that might have helped to make the world a better place if I had not had to deal with all these bans and restrictions. It was often really exasperating.

A further, final attempt to solve the situation also failed:

> Last December, we were unfortunately given the wrong advice. So, we made the mistake of registering the yaks in Sulden as *Bos mutus* with the Office for Hunting and Fishing in accordance with the Ministerial Decree of April 19, 1996, although our animals are only *Bos mutus grunniens* (domesticated yaks), meaning they aren't subject to the above-mentioned decree. By way of correction, we hereby withdraw our registration of December 17, 1996, and consider all correspondence on this matter as irrelevant.
>
> We therefore hope that the application by Seilbahnen Sulden GmbH for permission to graze our animals around the cable car mountain station will be viewed sympathetically.
>
> During the construction work on my farm in Sulden, we will build a sturdy fence to enclose the yaks, and carry out the specified veterinary examinations for the animals.

Finally, on September 22, I received permission from the Ministry of the Environment. Our yaks weren't considered dangerous animals. The document was signed by the Italian minister of the environment, Edo Ronchi.

How much creativity, energy, and joie de vivre do we lose in Europe with this growing bureaucracy? It's like a contagious, incurable disease that is incessantly spreading.

Politicians talk about cutting red tape, and establishing faster approval procedures and clearer legislation. But what we get is exactly the opposite.

Where is the self-responsibility, the common sense, the room to maneuver?

As a mountaineer and explorer, I have been exposed to the laws of nature, the wilderness, and its risks and dangers. I guess I'm a kind of anarchist. My slogan would be "no power to anyone." In everyday, middle-class life I kept seeing my freedom being restricted.

When I return from an expedition, I notice this in particular. It makes me feel very bitter. Fighting bans and restrictions that are ultimately lifted has sapped a lot of my energy. I often knew how to do things better than the legislators themselves.

28

EXPO HANNOVER AND MEMBER OF THE EUROPEAN PARLIAMENT

Choose a job you love, and you will never have to work a day in your life.

—Confucius

In 1999, I was selected as an independent (South Tyrolean) candidate for a Green Party list for the European Parliament elections in northeast Italy. Embarking on my new career, I had little political experience and was content with my role as a backbencher. In 2000, though, when the World Expo was held in Hannover, I was quickly confronted with the power games of politics at home.

The Tyrol–South Tyrol–Trentino Euroregion, without permission, had begun using my name to advertise the Expo Hannover. As they say, you can't have it both ways, and such extensive involvement and benefit required my cooperation and consent. I asked the organizers to refrain from using my name in any way for PR purposes at the Expo and wrote to explain why: "I am involved in the Expo 2000 using my name exclusively to advertise the Leitner Lift Middle Station. I therefore ask you to leave my name out of all publications."

The South Tyrol Euroregion wanted to use my name for advertising the Expo, yet not mention my involvement back home in South Tyrol. I decided to intervene with a suggestion. I knew that the Expo 2000 in Hannover hadn't gotten off to a great start.

> Given that the upper platform of Leitner's Skyliner middle station has become one of the most popular attractions for visitors to the Expo 2000 (some 45 percent of all Expo visitors come to see it), a display there would be the best possible way to advertise the *Euregio* pavilion and our home region. Our suggestion is to exhibit the famous painting of the Wildspitz Panorama

> (5 meters x 2.5 meters) by Diemer/ Malfatti—subject to prior agreement with Michael Seeber from Leitner. We, the people of Trentino, Tirol, and South Tyrol should focus more on the mountains and on the quality of our products—especially at the Expo. Visitors at world expos pass through quickly and are flooded with impressions. The only things that stick in their minds are clear messages and strong emotions. It would be a shame if the Expo did nothing to benefit our tourist industry.

Today, the Malfatti painting is on display in a museum in Bruneck dedicated to mountain people. My involvement in the Expo 2000 was never mentioned. Television and print media in South Tyrol didn't report it.

I issued the following press release on June 7, 2000:

> Although the Euroregion booth at Expo 2000, which was partly financed by the region, has proved a fiasco, the official media in South Tyrol stubbornly continues to refuse to report on Reinhold Messner's Mount & Mystery exhibition. And yet this showcase at Leitner's Skyliner cable car middle station has become one of the Expo's main visitor attractions. It's a high-quality experience about mountains and therefore acts as excellent advertising for South Tyrol and the entire Euroregion.

29

BRUSSELS BACKBENCHER

Politics is the art of compromise and persuasion. This was never my purpose in life. When I came to the EU Parliament, Europe and fighting to cut bureaucracy were important to me. But I wasn't able to achieve anything in the end.

—Reinhold Messner

In 1995, buoyed by our successful Greenland trip, my brother Hubert and I dared to attempt an expedition into the northern polar sea. Our plan was to cross the Arctic, from Siberia to Canada, via the North Pole.

On day one, during an Arctic night of minus 52 degrees Celsius and amid thin sea ice, we were followed by a polar bear. During the second night, we took shelter in our tent on an ice pack. Suddenly, with loud cracks, the pack began to explode, tossing huge blocks of ice into the air and opening crevices. We had to fight for our lives to reach solid ground. Hubert slipped into the water. The falling ice destroyed one of our sleds and nearly crushed us too. We were lucky to survive.

Back home in South Tyrol, at Juval it had been raining. Someone had forgotten to leave the key in its normal place, so I decided to climb in over the castle wall, but I slipped and fell down into the courtyard. It was wet and dark, and before the fall I couldn't see how high up I was nor do anything to help absorb the impact. As I landed, my right foot struck a granite step. I had badly fractured my right heel; part of the bone was sticking out. Did this mean the end of my adventures?

Later, after a tricky operation, I faced plenty of ridicule and even more malice, though I had only myself to blame for the accident. Once again, I had to get used to being an invalid. I was not going to give up though. Being successful in life means having the courage to dare. My journeys became about studying the sacred mountains. I had a new task—safeguarding the story of traditional alpinism.

Before I started making enquiries to the province of South Tyrol about whether and how the ruin of Sigmundskron Castle might work as a mountain museum, I wanted to know how a meeting place like that could work. Juval Castle was also once a ruin, so I'd already had experience testing out different forms of storytelling in a museum format.

There wasn't much sign of enthusiasm at a regional level for the project, although the mayor of Bolzano and the South Tyrolean governor showed interest. I didn't give up.

In 2004, I stood for reelection in the European elections because I saw that my museum project was threatened. My feelings of opposition and attachment to South Tyrol were conflicting.

I gave an interview to Florian Kronpichler in South Tyrol's *ff* newspaper, entitled "I've Had Enough":

ff: Reinhold, you've given the governor of South Tyrol a theme for the summer press conference: South Tyrol—a messed-up, stuffy, undemocratic mess.

RM: Yes, this is how I see it, even if the provincial governor disagrees. He might not share my diagnosis, but he probably agrees with me on the cure: South Tyrol needs to become more open.

ff: So you don't need to leave South Tyrol and emigrate as you announced you would last week?

RM: No, I'm still going to emigrate. In fact, I already have. I'm not there at all. I'm quietly quitting. I've spent ten years getting involved for this province. I've given my all for the good of this region. But it's no use. People mock me and my advice. I'm fed up with promoting South Tyrol abroad and then being made a fool of at home.

ff: But you have a political mandate from this region that you're obliged to fulfil.

RM: I had a European mandate, I'm not a South Tyrolean or an Italian politician. I don't know who voted for me. I mean, who does know? I have never taken my mandate for the European Parliament to mean that I am obliged to obtain money, or whatever, for South Tyrol. I'm aware that most people might see it that way, but this is precisely why Europe and the European Parliament is what it is. Namely, a marketplace for individual interests and a sterile debating society.

ff: You're not exactly overzealous when it comes to your participation in the European Parliament.

RM: I don't waste my time on parliamentary chatter and gossip. I raise awareness of issues outside it. Michl Ebner can make as much fuss as he wants. I concede that he is very hardworking, just like most other colleagues in the European Parliament. They sit there from six in the morning until eleven at night. They produce a lot of paperwork. . . .

ff: Do you feel like you're wasting your time?

RM: No, I'm learning, but I get annoyed. It drives me crazy, when these people talk for five hours on end and say things like: "traffic must be transferred from road to rail." We all agree, but it's nothing but a talking shop. In fact, heavy traffic on the roads is increasing.

ff: You say that you don't want to be South Tyrolean anymore?

RM: I am and will remain a South Tyrolean, a child of Optants. I'm even an angry farmer. I have two farms, as if one alone wouldn't be enough to make me South Tyrolean. A farm is a perpetual source of worry and ultimately brings a very poor return. But that's the way we are. Like most South Tyroleans, I want to be a farmer, to feel rooted, to belong. A farm is the best retirement provision there is. Yet at the same time, it's a prison.

ff: But there is a section, let's call it the enlightened one, of South Tyrol that appreciates the value of Reinhold Messner for South Tyrol.

RM: They appreciate Messner as a product. It's a product they've had for free. When I was abroad, I always defended South Tyrol. Back home though, I've always aggravated things. . . . If people here say that Messner is worth nothing, then let South Tyrol pay for its own self-promotion.

ff: Do you want to punish South Tyrol?

RM: No, I don't want to harm South Tyrol. But I'm no longer concerned about our future. And that's an end to it.

Around this same time, I wrote a piece for the *Tiroler Tageszeitung*:

> I returned from Nanga Parbat in August. At home in South Tyrol, our small province often feels strangely cramped. And yet the distance between people seems much greater here than elsewhere and the behavior strangely irrational and uncomprehending. Hardly anyone seems to have the courage

to express their own opinion. It feels like this ignorance has increased since I've been away. I've noticed higher levels of distrust and nebulous fears than even a few months earlier. Time on the other hand, seems fragmented. Are the intervals between moments shorter here than they are in the Himalaya?

It's as if there were only individuals, each standing alone, and above them a voice with which one either identifies or comes to terms with, yet which everyone fears at the same time. I suddenly find myself somewhere in between different worlds again here at home. The discrepancy that also existed between other South Tyroleans and those who speak for them, left me feeling at first dumbfounded, then angry, and ultimately sad. I wasn't ready for that and felt out of place under South Tyrolean skies. My state of mind made me uneasy.

Not because people in South Tyrol are somehow strange, living on the slopes of their mountains or in their deep, dark valleys. Nor because of the often-incomprehensible dialect, the language that they speak. I feel like an outsider, like I'm not part of the majority. I'm the one that some refer to as the *Nestbeschmutzer* (a traitor to their own country), who they tolerate as some kind of foreign body.

Do we all really have to bend over backward to claim special rights for South Tyrol—to have autonomy? This autonomy might guarantee protection for minorities—i.e., the right to a homeland and prosperity for all. However, it does nothing for solidarity, togetherness, or humanity. On the contrary, it creates more envy, more hostility, more resentment. And above all more distrust. It's almost as if the special status that we South Tyroleans now enjoy makes people more selfish. Despite the fact that time and people have stood still here for centuries. In so many different ways. Perhaps it's only the minorities in the "minority" who feel this way—Italian-speaking South Tyroleans, a few Ladins, and a handful of nonconformists with no one to lobby for them—especially those who are publicly denied any right to a *Heimat*.

There are the sons of rich citizens who want to keep South Tyrol for themselves. They're not interested in changing the status quo. Or, a more extreme faction, the young men who show what they're made of and boast to their friends by racing through the village streets in their fathers' big cars on Friday nights. Independence that's abused casts a long shadow.

Yet in spite of everything, this desire for autonomy has not been worn out. Not yet. Because *Heimat* still forms the emotional, ideological, and, yes, even political heart of the autonomous community. These days, it might no longer be a "*Heimat* created by God's hand," or a *Heimat* held together by *Wirgefühl* (a sense of togetherness and unity). This notion of *Heimat* is the source of all legitimacy in South Tyrol and it's frequently invoked by "the party" and "the newspaper" (the *Dolomiten*—South Tyrol's oldest and most important German-language newspaper). *Heimat* is what influences everything else in the system.

For half a century this province has been ruled de facto, as perhaps the Kaiser used to, by just one party—the South Tyrolean People's Party (*Südtiroler Volkspartei, SVP*). The *Heimat* "belongs" to them, and them alone. Don't get me wrong. We don't have to pay a tithe. Instead, we pay our taxes to Rome, and receive our subsidies in return. Which also helps underline how benevolent our provincial fathers are.

The carefully guarded information monopoly is the second pillar of this system. For generations, one publishing house alone has determined what's right and what's wrong. To criticize its notion of *Heimat*—Tyrol's unity, the importance of the church, our own home—meant the end of your career. Silenced, slandered, ostracized. Dissenters disappear from the newspapers. Your credibility is destroyed, and your strength is sapped. The press enforces what party propaganda and subsidies cannot. It creates a climate that paralyzes you and thousands of other minorities like you. That's the tragedy of the whole thing.

Which explains my unease, my despair. The autonomy system has become a trap. You'd better watch out if you don't belong to it.

To understand my state of mind, it's important to know that with each of my expeditions, I effectively leave the world behind. But every time I come back, returning becomes more difficult—as I get older—and at the same time more revealing. Maybe this is just a hunch, or is there more to it? At night I'm plagued by nightmares. During the day I sense the questions that are never raised, the aggression, and a feeling of hopelessness. At times like these, I think I know where all this unease comes from. Time and again, I ask myself what the cure could be.

What I miss most in today's South Tyrol are competing ideas. Without competition there can be no real change or chance of renewal. Is there no hope? Not at the moment. In a world in which contracts, recognition, and subsidies only go to those who conform—and the *Dolomiten* newspaper only echoes the same old prejudices—nothing changes. Judgments can be refuted. The same doesn't apply to prejudices.

I tried so many times to find a way to make it bearable for me to stay and to take part. But every time I've tried to approach people, the media monopoly has turned them against me. It's something I don't understand. Why all the disinformation? The ostracism and malice? I have had either to suppress what I felt, or to remain an outsider. Maybe the answers to these questions lie just beyond my reach. Or perhaps the things I've always wanted most to discuss were just never supposed to be mentioned. Every year it's gotten worse until I now find it unbearable. The meanness of our opinion leaders can reach such heights that it becomes omnipresent. It's so terrible, that to me everything else falls silent in horror. Yet I refuse to remain silent in the face of so much injustice. Even if our hardworking provincial governor labels my protest as my "complex."

Next year, I will be another year older, again. And not understood, again. Neither accepted, nor integrated—yet again. Am I being exploited? Perhaps I serve as a cover for the "openness" of a system that is in reality closed. Free spirits are seen as "politically incapable," "deceitful," and "ridiculous." Unable to set an example himself, the most powerful opinion maker in the country only trots out empty phrases; but very few dare to contradict someone who is omnipresent. Is this cowardice? Yes, but there's also more to it. To be so submissive requires a kind of courage, the courage to sacrifice oneself. This is where I run out of patience. Because this is my life—and not some joke to be laughed at while people sit around a table playing cards. I might not be able to change the situation, but at least I can try to describe it.

I have had twenty years as a young person, twenty years as a warrior, and nearly twenty years under my belt as a family man in South Tyrol. I would have preferred to spend the final twenty years of my life cultivating our spiritual heritage. But the yes-men and false historians have long since divided it among themselves. Where the "party" (the *Südtiroler Volkspartei*) ends, there is nothing but desert. You can enter it, but you won't make it back. Where is the much-vaunted multiculturalism, after we got a first taste of it under Luis Durnwalder as provincial governor?

There's still too much emphasis on belonging to individual language groups instead of general bilingualism. There's still way too much reasoning and rationality, know-it-all mentality, and *Meinungsdiktatur* (dictatorship when it comes to different opinions).

Otherwise, I barely recognize the South Tyrol that I grew up in. The villages, orchards, and vineyards, the fire stations and municipal theatres have all grown big. It's become a region of milk and honey. It has an abundance of everything, except knowledge, self-criticism, and the ability to change. Everyone for themselves and the EU against all. As if it wasn't just about our rights in Rome. What about our autonomy as individuals?

Is it only me who hears this screaming silence, underground, in the night? There is so much uncertainty hushed up. There are so many ideas shot down. There are so many great ideas and visions that get nipped in the bud! Why are alternative voices in this country so cautious? Why is our South Tyrolean image so full of clichés?

South Tyrol is still associated with the myth of peaceful coexistence, honesty, the ability to suffer, and strength of character. Yet the law is broken time and time again, there's character assassination and cheating—all in the name of our *Heimat*. Especially by those who would sell off their "beloved *Heimat*, this land of ours" to the highest bidder. And when it comes to God, who the vast majority have always prayed to, it's the same as with the party. Somehow you know God is going to fix everything, even if you don't believe in him.

Fortunately, it's all downhill for me now and I can live with it. I feel tired, my feet hurt, sometimes I'm exhausted as I try to find the way back on my long journey home. I still look out for kindred spirits, helpful landmarks, bridges, and crossings. Without finding them. No, as long as people continue to only talk about bridges, bridges between cultures, bridges between generations, bridges between ecology and the economy, then I will still have to find my way home.

If we're not fit for the future, I'll keep searching for my way back. Back to a new beginning. When will the people's party (the *SVP*, which aims to represent South Tyrol's German-speaking population and Ladin speakers) become the autonomy party, where all three language groups have influence?

Why is this tragedy played as a comedy in this beautiful setting? Despite the famous mountain scenery, I hear a deep sadness that howls at me from everywhere.

It's as if South Tyrol has to weep for itself.

The suffering of those who have been marginalized is an integral part of who we are. And it's hardly been mentioned for centuries. There are no complaints, and no answers.

South Tyrol has some of the world's most beautiful landscapes. If you come here only to be on holiday, then it's the perfect place to enjoy life, relax, and be spoiled. Yes, we're great hosts.

Sometimes this world also appears to me to be quiet and peaceful too, as if it were a painting, or printed on a postcard or advertising promotions. Yet it seems to me that for ten years now, I haven't moved a single step forward. Nothing changes. We all just stand here with our assumptions, our prejudices, and our loneliness. South Tyrol is a small, yet mute, place.

This is a "somewhere" with distinct seasons, where a handshake is tantamount to a contract and where loving your *Heimat* is considered the highest virtue. Where honesty is a given, like the wind and the weather. We're always doing the right thing, just like everyone else. But almost everything is sacrificed for profit, including the ability to be yourself.

No, the party has no answers to the important questions. And most of what we read in our newspaper is manipulated and biased. That's why I want to get out of here. Up and away. I've been trying to join in for too long. Because I refuse to abandon my opinions, I am slandered, deliberately misinterpreted, ridiculed, and remain condemned forever. I've never gotten used to living as the "accused party."

To be condemned by henchmen of the real criminals is not as bad as it might seem, however, because once you've been labeled a criminal, you're free as a bird—although perhaps you are no longer carrying the self-image of the "unspoiled and genuine" South Tyrolean.

When you have nothing left to lose that hasn't already been lost, you go into exile voluntarily. You withdraw into your inner desert—where all signs of human existence are confusing, but nevertheless pleasing.

Still, I refuse to give up. I will go down fighting. Aren't there thousands of curious young people out there hoping for a very different kind of South Tyrol? It's not in my nature to hope without any kind of vision for the future. But for the time being, leaving is the only alternative. South Tyrol remains an eternal challenge. I can't help myself.

30

WHITE WILDERNESS

Does man make time or does time make man?
Is the human spirit really free, or is it bound to time and place?
When a person goes beyond the limits of his time, they will not be recognized, or they might even be declared crazy.
I spin myself into a chrysalis and leave it to time to see what will come out of this woven cocoon, be it maggot or butterfly.

—artist Caspar David Friedrich

Who needs wilderness? What purpose does it serve? In the era of the global village, the internet, and satellite navigation, it might seem old-fashioned to consider these kinds of questions.

The wilderness, although seemingly worthless, is a treasure that transcends human time. We all need the wilderness, even if not directly. It's where we evolved into the people we are today. Without it, our powers of imagination would be so much poorer. The more crowded we become, the more we need the wilderness, an isolated world that stirs us humans with its secrets, its dangers, its grandeur, just as it stirred us thousands of years ago. This doesn't mean that we should all just jump over our garden fences and head into the wilderness. That's not what I mean. But if there were no wilderness, we would all be so much poorer. Wild areas belong to everyone, even the people who prefer to avoid them. And to those who profess to love the wilderness, I advise them to travel there as simply as possible, to get to know the wildlands this way. Because otherwise people can quickly start to destroy the very things that make the wilderness so exceptional—its silence, vastness, and unrushed spirit.

For a long time, here in Europe we attached little value to wilderness. Then, we declared it something to be conquered—the North Pole, the Antarctic, the Greenland ice sheet, Changtang Nature Reserve in Tibet. What would these areas be like if we were to ignore exploiting the potential oil, gold, and uranium reserves to be found there? Would wild areas be just a vanishing point for human vanity, or something more? We make sense of the world

through our subjective experience of it, unlike science, which learns through objective problem-solving and trial and error. Old ideas about the world are continually superseded by new understanding. In this respect, the wilderness takes on a whole new significance. Reversing our conquest mentality leads to the notion of a "white wilderness" where values such as silence, infinity, and slowing down become important again. Providing we don't first carve up, divide, and conquer these wild areas. For thousands of years, humankind held special places as sacred and holy. They were thought to be where the gods lived, where there was nothingness, or where knowledge and revelations were stored; they were often made accessible only to the chosen. By the beginning of the last century, mankind was exploring every last wilderness on this planet. The white or empty spots on the map of the world were there to be explored and filled in.

Thanks to the unlimited possibilities afforded by modern technology, people today can travel to just about anywhere to access these sacred places.

They can see them using satellite imagery and aerial photography, driving out the spirit of these places in the process. This destroys their most important characteristic—their otherworldly nature.

There is no point in being a "conquistador of the useless," as Lionel Terray called it. It's only when we renounce the ideas of conquest and development and embrace the preservation of "useless" wilderness that the wilderness becomes the key to the universe and to ourselves. Viewed in this way, research and experience become mutually exclusive activities. The more we know about the world, the less curious we become about it and ourselves.

This is why we need unexplored wilderness. Alongside fire, air, earth, and water, these wild areas are also the basis of our existence.

The wilderness has tremendous value for recreation and insight. No matter how absurd traveling or exploring a wilderness might seem, it can be highly beneficial. Each time we hit the road, we're confronted with a unique, true image of the world. It gives us the opportunity to take stock. And it inspires us to dream. Silence, peace, and tranquillity are only conceivable if there are places where they actually exist. Even if no one has ever been there.

By white wilderness, I'm referring to the white spots on the map—mountains where there are no cable cars or waymarks, deserts and jungles where there are no roads, the distant poles of Earth.

These should all be sacred to us, because white wilderness offers us revelation. In the long term, we will only be able to continue exploring the natural world with all its vastness, limits, peacefulness, cruelty, and rules if we can encounter these parts of the world as human beings and not human machines. Or, to protect it as a primeval landscape for the next generation, we could avoid it entirely.

In 2000, I proposed a wilderness theory, and with other adventurers, I suggested starting a movement to protect our remaining wildernesses. My original White Wilderness concept soon transformed into the Mountain Wilderness. In Italy, the idea started to gain support. I became involved in a few of the initiatives and was pleased to find others who were also prepared to defend these last wilderness areas. For example, we demonstrated against a new ski lift on Mont Blanc and collected litter on the Marmolada.

During the international year of the mountains in 2002, as a member of the European Parliament, I compiled an agenda to protect the mountains. One of the projects involved an old fort from World War I on Monte Rite, between Pieve di Cadore and Cortina d'Ampezzo, in the heart of the Dolomites. I'd turned it into a mountain museum to tell the story of the development of climbing in the Dolomites. However, one of the younger leaders of the movement turned against me. Maybe he just wanted to raise his profile for an upcoming election? The project, which I had spent three years working on, was criticized as being bad for the environment, and I was accused of being a hypocrite. And yet, working with the municipality of Cibiana di Cadore and the Veneto region, I had managed to create a sustainable museum. We reused the existing structure, though we had struggled with the huge converter for television and electricity that had stood there for years.

What was the best way to respond to the accusations?

I decided not to do so in public. I left the Mountain Wilderness organization but carried on fighting for the wilderness.

In 1998, I had outlined my position in *Baumeister*, a German magazine for architects:

> Maybe it's already too late, but I feel we should be looking more closely at what really happens when we encounter natural mountain landscapes. The way I see it, alpinism has two options. Either alpinists distance themselves from nature—from both mountain nature and human nature—or they stand up to defend timeless mountain values.
>
> The majority of outdoor consumers want nature to be nicely prepared for their mountain holidays. You see the results of this everywhere—carefully managed paths and trails, including right up to the summit of Mount Everest. It's almost as if Europe sees its wilderness as something out of date, that needs to be made ready for a leisure-seeking society that views concepts such as "risk can discipline you" or "fear as a regulator in high mountains" as old-fashioned. All this is perfectly understandable. Nevertheless, I feel that it's important to defend the remaining wilderness.
>
> The twentieth century, with its multiplex cinemas, amusement parks, and water park destinations, doesn't need the Alps and the remaining mountain wilderness areas. It has enough mega arenas. Consumers already find ample opportunities in urban areas. Why don't we just leave wild mountain areas as they are? This is the only way to ensure that we will continue to experience something special and mighty when we climb them.
>
> The only truly evolved form of alpinism is alpinism without the incessant development of mountain areas. We humans are inadequate beings who

don't belong in the high mountains, at least not permanently. For wannabes who need to flex their physical or mental muscles out of sheer "fear of missing out" or boredom, there are ample en masse experiences to be found in big amusement parks and cyberspace.

But we shouldn't be pimping the mountains to turn them into artificial worlds. If we want to save mountaineering, then we need to save the mountains from too many mountaineers. And not through bans and prohibitions, but by fostering the values that make mountains what they are in the first place. The values that also serve as a filter that allows people to go only as far as their endurance, skills, and ability to face fears will let them. Some alpinists love mountains and alpine streams so much that they re-create them in front of their little houses in the countryside, next to their garden gnomes. These people need to understand that the real benefits of wilderness are quickly sold out by the continued "conquest of the useless." It's as a place of risk and danger that the mountains have lasting value. And the mountains must be protected; not only for the several million mountain hikers and climbers, but for everyone, even those who will never climb them.

Unlike agricultural and commercial landscapes, where man dominates nature, mountain wilderness areas should be understood as spaces where human beings dispense with development. A space where people don't remain, and they don't live permanently. All technical infrastructure and installations, whether cable cars, roads, telephone poles, power cables, or climbing bolts, must be avoided.

The real value of the wilderness—which is also linked to its long-term commercial value—is inversely proportional to the degree to which it is developed.

I'm not saying that we should stop people from going to the mountains. Ultimately though, the mountains will only remain accessible to everyone if we stop any more development. And this applies to major interventions such as excavating and drilling, as well as to signposting and route descriptions.

31
THE BATTLE FOR SIGMUNDSKRON CASTLE

Our Heimat *custodians sometimes act like terrorist cells.*

—folklorist Elsbeth Wallnöfer

When Luis Durnwalder, the governor of the autonomous province of South Tyrol, offered to let me use the Sigmundskron Castle ruins for a museum in the form of a loan agreement in 2001, it felt like a great leap of faith. At the same time, however, a group of opponents started organizing a major campaign to prevent it. South Tyrol's main daily newspaper called on politicians, decision-makers, and association board members to oppose the project. The newspaper covered the issue on a daily basis. In the end, there was so much pressure that the provincial governor was forced to cancel the agreement. Instead, the opponents demanded a European-wide bidding process for the use of Sigmundskron Castle.

I was devastated, having invested so much time and energy in the project—it was the biggest I had ever launched. I felt paralyzed. That was the final straw. I handed the keys back and started new negotiations with the governor of North Tyrol and the governor of Trentino. Maybe they could offer another site where I could accommodate my ideas and display my growing art collection. If, as the press claimed, the majority of people were opposed to a mountain museum in Sigmundskron Castle, then I had failed.

A dozen or so South Tyrolean decision-makers were in favor of my idea, but the media pressure increased week by week. Conspiracy theories and twisted facts abounded. Warfare was waged with highly contemporary weapons. There was little I could do in the face of so much disinformation.

Hans Karl Peterlini, editor-in-chief of *ff* magazine, described the pressure in his article entitled "Terror of Opinions against Messner":

> Reinhold Messner and Sigmundskron Castle are currently the subject of a witch hunt.

Sigmundskron Castle near Bolzano

If the aim is to get rid of him once and for all, then they're going about it the right way.

At present, there is a concerted effort to effectively destroy Reinhold Messner's dream, and make it clear to him that he should leave South Tyrol altogether.

This is how far it's gone. And yet, this should not be allowed to keep happening. People in South Tyrol are given a roasting until they either fall into line or give up completely.

The disagreement might have started out in good faith. Many certainly felt that it was a fair fight for a just cause. But the scale of escalation we are seeing in the fight against the proposed Messner museum at Sigmundskron Castle is completely out of proportion and has little to do with the original aims. It's become a clever and cynical campaign and an exercise in targeted manipulation.

By now the slogans are well known, calling the project "Disneyland," the "Messner show," the "ruin of an ensemble," "destruction of a historical site," "desecration of the most sacred site in South Tyrolean politics—Sigmundskron Castle." All of these claims are nothing but propaganda. And those behind it surely don't even believe in it themselves.

They certainly can't feign innocence now that they've allowed manipulation by the *Dolomiten* newspaper, story after story, for a political crusade. It must make every democrat's stomach turn to see all fair play go out the window in the fight over Sigmundskron Castle. The *Heimat* custodians' association is dodging any discussion with Messner. The *Dolomiten* newspaper *has never properly given* Messner an opportunity to explain what his project is about. Anyone who isn't opposed to the project, or at least not against it for purely objective reasons, is publicly pilloried. This applies among others to the departmental director of the Cultural Provincial Council, the otherwise highly-respected Office for Landscape Conservation Commission, the provincial governor, and the Environmental Provincial Council. When historian Hans Heiss suggests that Messner could expand his museum to include the mountains, masculinity, and shooting—then the *Dolomiten* trumpets the headline: "Shooting Museum, Not Mountain Museum." It would appear that the *Dolomiten*'s credo that the Messner museum must be stopped leaves no room for doubt or argument.

What was so bad about the idea? Sigmundskron Castle had been neglected by politicians for decades. It was left to the tenants to decide how to run its restaurant, cope with the local drug dealers, the wild camping, and the stench from the refuse heap. The province only really started thinking about the castle when a potential South Tyrolean Italian (!) buyer started making enquiries. And even then, they weren't sure what to do with it.

What could be better than to let Messner open a museum right here? A museum dedicated to one of the core themes of South Tyrol. South Tyrol has museums for all kinds of nonsense. And most of them cost more than Sigmundskron. Every region in Germany, North Tyrol, or Trentino would jump at the chance if Messner were to offer to set up a museum and pay for it with his own money—and restore an old castle in the process.

You don't even have to like Messner. Granted, you might resent him using his name. But who else do you name a mountain museum in South Tyrol after if not the best-known mountaineer from the place? How can it be that Messner's name is touted at tourist trade fairs and yet treated like dirt at home?

The pressure to prevent the Messner Museum by any means comes from the press. And this has little to do with the Kaiserberg, where Sigmundskron

> sits above Bolzano, and more to do with what is still possible in South Tyrol without the approval of Mr. Ebner.

Michel Ebner was an influential media mogul and European member of Parliament at the time. This opinion piece in the *ff* neatly summarizes the mood that was against me in South Tyrol that proclaimed "Messner for himself, and everyone else against his Sigmundskron project."

The second, smaller newspaper in South Tyrol, the *Neue Südtiroler Tageszeitung*, published an interview that Christoph Franceschini conducted with me entitled "A Lesson in Media Dictatorship":

> **CF:** The paper's message is clear. South Tyrol is in danger of being spoiled by madman Reinhold Messner. . . .
>
> **RM:** This is a campaign orchestrated by the "Christian brothers." They control the media. This just shows exactly what I've been going on about for years in South Tyrol. Namely, that one newspaper influences everything. It's gotten so blatant that more and more people see that it's not about the issues, but about putting someone in their place. I've never received as much support and encouragement from others as I have done over the past few weeks.
>
> **CF:** Almost every week, there seems to be a new dispute. The latest one is about the car park. . . .
>
> **RM:** This story about the car park comes from the "Christian brothers" too. It's a farce. Long before I came to Sigmundskron, there were plans to build a car park next to the landfill site, for a local recreation area. Nobody was that bothered about it. It was only when someone noticed that the castle could also use the car park that all the stops were pulled out to prevent the car park from being built.
>
> **CF:** Instead, there was a proposal to build a car park at the foot of the hill on which the castle was located.
>
> **RM:** Bolzano city council was considering building it at the bottom. The idea had regional backing. But then the project was blown right out of the water during the decision-making process, even though it was the best solution. It was stopped by a disinformation campaign. The "Christian brothers" are experts when it comes to that. Now the plan

is to go back to the original (four-year-old) idea again and build the car park up on the hill. But they're trying to stop this too.

CF: The campaign is already up and running. . . .

RM: It makes me wonder who actually makes the decisions in South Tyrol? Are they made by elected representatives? Or by the people who control eighty percent of the German-language media in South Tyrol?

CF: What do you want to prove with Sigmundskron?

RM: It's important to me to get this museum set up, to make sure that it's good. There's plenty of competition from other museums. These days, Sigmundskron is basically an eyesore. However, I believe it could encourage high-quality tourism in South Tyrol. The plan is to develop the mountain theme, our mountaineering legacy, and to show people all over the world what happens when man encounters mountains. It's not going to be another Disneyland, as the "Christian brothers" would have it.

CF: Everyone agrees that an alpine museum could be a real tourist magnet. Why has no tourist board taken a clear position on the matter?

RM: Now we're getting to the heart of the matter. This is about much more than just my museum. South Tyrol is basically under a media dictatorship. We live in a place where many people are afraid—whether they're company owners, employees, or in the public sector. They're fearful of being punished by the newspaper. This is why no one dares to come out openly in favor of the mountain museum. The problem in South Tyrol is not that one party has been in charge for fifty years. The problem is the interaction between the media and the party. And the insolence, above all. It's led to this belief that they can bulldoze anyone out of their way, even when it comes to political decision-making. Our problem is that our media is autocratic. This campaign—it's certainly not a debate—by the "Christian brothers" against Sigmundskron is a lesson in ostracization and media dictatorship.

CF: Aren't you afraid that the "Christian brothers" might win their campaign?

RM: No. I'm confident they won't win. If there's one thing I've learned in life, it's that the greater the resistance beforehand, the greater the success afterward. All my successes have been in spite of considerable headwinds.

32
THE TENDER

Beating someone up in an argument isn't the same as outclassing them.

—Tim Kreider, writer and cartoonist

The Europe-wide tender (a bidding process to submit proposals) for using Sigmundskron Castle as a museum should have been unnecessary. Once it was issued, that was it. The rendering of a tender created an obligation that Sigmundskron be funded privately and operated for thirty years without subsidies. Because, ultimately, nobody wanted to take on the responsibility, I had the chance to take part in the tender. As announced, I would have been happy to dispense with the idea if another project had been submitted.

The tender ramped up the pressure even further. The former provincial governor Silvius Magnago was called upon to oppose my project, and the South Tyrolean Provincial Association for the Preservation of Local Heritage opened a special donation account to finance its own entry for a high-quality project.

The controversy surrounding my museum project dragged on for years. I still don't know why so much vitriol and energy was expended on preventing someone else from doing something that they wanted to do themselves. Despite the fact that they weren't able to manage it. An advertisement appealing for donations "to stop a mountain museum on Sigmundskron" was a final attempt to stop me in my tracks:

> Sigmundskron near Bolzano is not only the oldest documented castle in Tyrol, but the largest and most unusual in terms of its architectural design. Signs that people settled there can be traced back over several millennia, from the Stone Age to the present day. Sigmundskron is also the castle symbolizing South Tyrolean autonomy. After the Second World War, the inner courtyards were twice the venue for landmark political rallies. On May 5, 1946, South Tyroleans demonstrated for the right to autonomy here. On November 17, 1957, around 30,000 people demanded genuine autonomy under the popular slogan of *Los von Trient* (Away from Trento).

> Due to its central location, Sigmundskron lies right at the very heart of South Tyrol.
>
> The province of South Tyrol has recently acquired Sigmundskron. Refurbishment and building maintenance are to be carried out in the near future. The provincial government and municipality of Bolzano have already approved Reinhold Messner's plan to build a mountain museum on Sigmundskron. Under pressure, a competition for ideas about the future usage of the castle was put out to tender only recently.
>
> What does a medieval castle have to do with a mountain museum?

All in all, the museum project at Sigmundskron cost ten years of my life and a lot of my own money. So, it's no wonder that nobody else entered the competition in the end. On my eightieth birthday, I want to complete the Messner Mountain Heritage project with its Messner Mountain Museum and satellite museums. I've devoted half of my life to it. How lucky I've been to grow as a person by overcoming problems, opposition, and animosity. To have had the chance to experience so much of my life that went right.

The *ff* reported briefly, but objectively, on the "victory." Because of my opponents' mean-spirited and miserly conduct, I'd managed to reach the figurative summit after all.

> After a year of fierce polemics and skillful maneuvering by the *Dolomiten* newspaper and the local heritage association, and members of the provincial government being put under enormous pressure, the provincial government has backed down. The invitation to bid for the project was issued. And now, Reinhold Messner is now back where he wanted to be. After clearing up the remaining issues, the commission awarded him, as the only applicant, the contract to set up a museum at Sigmundskron Castle.

33

THE ONLY WITNESS

Using targeted character assassination to tear our family apart is a crime committed by those seeking revenge and destruction.

—Reinhold Messner

There have been hundreds of articles and thousands of pages written about the death of my brother. Over the years I've responded to some of them. But the doubts and lies spread by my expedition teammates remain. Even the widely respected *Süddeutsche Zeitung* had their reporter Achim Zons gunning for me. I've great respect for the paper, but quoted here is an excerpt from an interview that doesn't do it any credit. It's with *SZ* department head Hans-Jürgen Jakobs and Achim Zons on July 2, 2003.

Mountaineer Reinhold Messner on the media, the death of his brother, scandals, and a cinema project.

SZ: Mr. Messner, for many years you were the mountain hero in the media. Now there are doubts rising again. Your former expedition teammates accuse you of leaving your brother Günther to die on Nanga Parbat in 1970. It's in all the papers.

RM: I've no desire to be a hero. And this "scandal" is nothing new. The first derogatory stories about this tragedy appeared in 1970. They were based on the same claims as those made today. All very negative. This time, though, the allegations are more clearly formulated. Last year *Der Spiegel* and *Profil* magazine started pushing the story. At first, they were very careful about how they went about it. The attacks have now become character assassination. This is why I'm involving a lawyer.

SZ: In 1970, Karl Maria Herrligkoffer, your expedition leader, was the main Messner critic. Now, both Hans Saler and Max von Kienlin have written a book on the subject. Their reports contradict your version of the story, the one that you describe in *Die weiße Einsamkeit* (Naked Mountain: Nanga Parbat, Brother, Death, Solitude).

RM: They're playing to credulous journalists. They flatter magazines, like *Der Spiegel* and others, to make themselves feel good. This is something I never do. I've always tried to tell it straight.

SZ: It sounds like you're separating the media into good and bad, based on whether they report in a friendly or critical manner.

RM: No, this is not what I'm doing. That's exactly what the others are doing, the do-gooders. I've great respect for well-researched, high-quality journalism.

SZ: Some say that you are being oversensitive, because you're losing support in the media.

RM: Rubbish. I just want to see fair play. My books are successful because they're well written. This has little to do with help from others. And naturally, I've used the media too.

SZ: At any rate, you're critical of the media. Surely, journalists are supposed to report on controversial topics and present the arguments to the public?

RM: When it comes to this story, it's important that they look behind the scenes. If my teammates were claiming, for example, that I didn't help with preparations on the mountain or that I was lazy, then I wouldn't be bothered. But if they claim that I abandoned my brother at the summit of Nanga Parbat because I was determined to traverse the mountain on my own, then I want to know what gave them this idea? Have they got any evidence to prove it? Do they have a map or a plan? The teammates in question weren't at the summit. Did they have the ability to quickly fly up and see what I was doing there? Von Kienlin and Saler now have to sign an affidavit to swear that I sent my brother back alone—otherwise their books will be withdrawn. I know that I did not betray my brother. Unfortunately, I'm the only witness. Does this therefore mean that we should believe others? And not me? Why might they hold these prejudices against me?

SZ: At one decisive point though, you were not the only witness. When your two teammates Kuen and Scholz saw you and your brother on the face. Why did you say at that moment that "everything's okay"? Why didn't you call for help?

RM: Of course I called for help! But when I saw that they couldn't help us, I waved them away—so as not to endanger them. My position is the same as it's always been. You can either choose to believe me or not. But the story told by the others is an invented conspiracy, for whatever reason. Maybe at some point, someone will find out that von Kienlin wrote his diary after the events. He only found it later on. Someone should check the entry of July 4, 1970. You could do it. That's what journalists are for.

SZ: You can't criticize journalists just for reporting indications and plausible explanations that contradict your story. For example, von Kienlin says that when you all met after the summit tragedy, six days later, the first thing you asked was: "Where's Günther?" Who else could have known but you?

RM: I describe in detail how I searched for my brother and could not find him. During the descent, I was convinced that he was right behind me. I stumbled around calling for my dead brother for days. It was a completely exceptional situation. You journalists should read my books. Von Kienlin was a pompous "out-of-Africa" explorer type, he was no climber, he was invited to join the expedition as a guest—

SZ: And he used to be your good friend. When journalists want to find out something, they investigate both sides of the argument.

RM: But we're talking here about the difference between events that have actually been experienced and theories that are invented speculation! I guided my brother back down the mountain. It was the natural thing for me to do. You can choose not to believe me, but then you need to find witnesses to prove that the opposite is somehow true. It's not sufficient to base such serious accusations on just rumors.

SZ: Many big stories started out as just rumors.

RM: But when journalists start reporting rumors as facts, that's character assassination. Listen, I stood my ground. I didn't disappear off to Venice or Greece. I wrote a book where I answered all the accusations. Nevertheless, this Nanga Parbat story has damaged my reputation, and I need to win back credibility. But the media will never help me in this. This is why I intend to find my dead brother there where I lost him—on a glacier on the Diamir side. If I succeed and my version of events is proved true, then I'll sue everyone who said that I left my brother to die.

SZ: Are you considering doing a series with the German talk show host Michel Friedman? There have been lots of rumors.

RM: No. Friedman is someone I have great respect for, but he deals in moral issues that can either be faced or not. I'm no moralist. Whenever someone does something outstanding, small-minded traditionalists come wading in with their morals—that's just the way it is. I'm primarily interested in the facts. Morals are weaker than human nature. It's human nature that conditions us to behave in a particular way, to act to save ourselves or the lives of our partners—as long as there is a glimmer of hope. To abandon my brother would be contrary to natural human instincts.

SZ: Do you feel that journalists want to dismantle the Reinhold Messner mountaineering legend?

RM: Yes. It makes perfect sense. Because it sells newspapers and feeds feelings of envy. *Der Spiegel* magazine says that it works with "facts and figures." In reality, it's often more like "fiction and figures." Last autumn, I gave an interview to *Stern* magazine and talked about the "Austrian *Spiegel* and its character assassins"—there was no lawsuit.

SZ: On the other hand, you do benefit from your constant media presence. Saler and Kienlin have also written books, but they're not going to make the bestseller lists, while your latest book is already at number forty-three.

RM: If it were not for this campaign against me, maybe my book would even be at number twenty? The others are pushing their narrow-minded psychology—devoid of all facts. They're cashing in on my reputation.

SZ: So now you intend to attempt to find conclusive proof to support your opinion. Do you want the media to accompany you on the search for your dead brother?

RM: Opinion? Why should I allow myself to be bullied?

SZ: To have witnesses.

RM: The search expedition is going to be a highly complex undertaking. We have a huge area to cover, something like thirty square meters. It will be very dangerous. I won't be able to take reporters into an avalanche zone. There will be plenty of other witnesses.

SZ: And at some point, the whole story will be filmed—the high point of any career in the media.

RM: There has never been a cinema film about my experiences. You've given me a good idea. Maybe, after the search. If it's successful.

Old man finds remains of brother thirty-five or thirty-seven years after his death and proves his innocence. That's some script. It's a story that goes way beyond just mountaineering.

SZ: But for now, you still have to live with the doubts.

RM: Even the *Süddeutsche Zeitung* made a fool of itself with the flippant comment that Messner should finally give in and admit that it is as Saler claims, then he would have climbed his first nine-thousander. I cannot and will not concede to other people's lies. Not even after the psychological torture of these past weeks.

SZ: Your former expedition teammates have not made all this up.

RM: Not all of it, but much of it. I have no desire to discuss psychological aspects. By attacking and dismantling Reinhold Messner, Saler and von Kienlin have succeeded in interesting publishers and attracting attention. In economic terms, they're free-riders and hangers-on. I've contributed a lot with my books. *Die weiße Einsamkeit* (Naked Mountain: Nanga Parbat, Brother, Death, Solitude) is something like my forty-first or forty-second book.

The *Süddeutsche Zeitung* followed up this interview with a further article: "Interim Victory in Messner Dispute—Court Issues Temporary Injunctions":

> In the dispute regarding the death of his brother thirty-three years ago on Nanga Parbat, Reinhold Messner has had the further distribution of two books banned for the time being. Messner's lawyer from Hamburg law firm Prinz said on Wednesday that the Hamburg district court had issued temporary injunctions against two Munich publishers and their authors, who say that Messner is responsible for the death.

A bone found in 2000 and Günther's remains, which were found in 2005, unequivocally show that my brother died on Nanga Parbat's Diamir Face. What's more, he was found at the bottom of the glacier that had carried his body 3.5 kilometers on toward the valley. In the meantime, my brother's second boot was also found lower down.

This all proves that the statements by my teammates, who claimed that I had sent my brother back to the Rupal Face, were based on lies. Their concerted actions were intended to distract from the fact that none of them had come to look for us in the Diamir Valley.

Although it should have been clear to them, if they had known where we were descending, the rested members of the team could have switched to the Diamir Valley to come and look for us. However, they obviously did not know, and it wasn't clear to them where we might be, so in this case no one could blame them for not looking for us. Their lack of knowledge about our descent route and the fact that they didn't mount a search party are mutually exclusive.

Herrligkoffer, the expedition leader, had the team scan the southwest face of the mountain with a telescope,. where he thought we might have tried to find a way down. We wouldn't have found a descent route there. Nevertheless, it shows that after our disappearance, back at base camp, they did not assume that we had planned to descend via the Diamir Face.

In an interview with Josef Seitz for *Focus* magazine in 2003, entitled "Death, Guilt, and Smoothing Over the Truth," I discussed the issue:

F: Mr. Messner, are you a liar?

RM: No. My teammates, who are now pedaling their lies, are talking about events that they did not experience themselves. I know what I'm talking about because I experienced it directly. I'm prepared to make a sworn statement that I descended via the opposite side of Nanga Parbat—with my brother. If the others want to declare under oath that I sent my brother away or left him behind at the top, they will have to answer for perjury. My brother's body will provide the proof. If it is found where I say it is, on the Diamir side of Nanga Parbat.

F: So is your expedition teammate Max von Kienlin, who is now publishing his diary, a liar?

RM: His diary falsifies the truth. At least, it does when it comes to this point.

F: Von Kienlin claims to have invented the story, together, with you, of your brother Günther's death to provide to the world, and in particular your parents, a plausible account. Von Kienlin says that after you traversed Nanga Parbat, you had no idea where your brother died. He says that it was only later on that you developed the story that your brother traversed the mountain with you, and was buried by an ice avalanche in relatively safe terrain. Did von Kienlin, who was your friend at the time, help you lie to the world? He accuses you of planning the traverse, which turned out to be fatal for your brother, and not—as you say—trying to find a way down to escape from mortal danger.

RM: Whoever says that I planned the traverse, must have known about a plan. But there was no plan. I did talk enthusiastically about a traverse; I don't deny it. But I only went to Nanga Parbat to make the first ascent of the Rupal Face, the highest face on the planet, 4,500 meters of rock and ice. Yes, it was an ambitious goal. I was ambitious.

F: Are you pathologically ambitious?

RM: I would say that I have a healthy sense of ambition. I've been on over one hundred expeditions. And I have survived them all.

F: Your brother didn't survive. Do you feel guilty for his death?

RM: Yes. I've felt guilty for thirty-three years now that I survived and he did not. A few of my old climbing teammates seem to struggle with the fact that I'm still here and they keep on inventing new accusations that I sacrificed my brother for fame. It's psychological torture. They want to put me under pressure and make me look like a fool. No, I refuse to stoop to their level.

F: And yet you have every new book that criticizes you threatened by the law firm Prinz.

RM: These books are not criticism. They are character assassination. My warning to them to stick to the facts was in vain. When my brother is found, then I'll react. Then this character assassination campaign will have legal consequences. And I will have to claim damages from the publishers. These are unprecedented injuries that have been inflicted on me.

F: You're the only witness to a lot that happened on that mountain. This gives you a monopoly on the truth.

RM: Yes, but this does not give others the right to conjure up some other version of the "truth" based on rumors, where there is no evidence. I'm the only one able to report on the death of my brother. You can either choose to believe me or not. All other statements are just speculation. I'm the only one who knows what happened up there.

F: There's one other point with two further witnesses. On June 2, 1970, at 10 a.m. it's said that you spent three hours calling for help because your brother was too weak to climb back down. When Felix Kuen and Peter Scholz, two other expedition members on the way to the summit, came within calling distance, you sent them away with the words, everything was OK. This makes everything else you say difficult to believe.

RM: I started calling for help over the edge. It was pretty naive. There was little hope, it was virtually unthinkable that anyone would come. Then, suddenly I see someone. And I think: They're coming to help, to rescue us, they've heard me.

F: You were calling for help, but without hope? Were you panicking?

RM: I was not panicking. There are some things on Nanga Parbat that I can't give a rational explanation for. When Kuen and Scholz arrive, I try to make it clear to them that they have to climb up to us. They've got a rope with them. Günther and I need a rope to abseil. When they don't climb up, it becomes clear that they can't reach us. The terrain between us is too steep and the rock is too brittle. I don't feel that I can downclimb to them either. I can't ask the lead climber Kuen to risk too much. So, I said that everything was OK with us.

F: Do morals change the higher you go?

RM: At 8,000 meters, you judge things differently than you would back down in the valley. If I'm moving in an environment where everyday rules are no longer valid, then human nature applies, and not human morals. In borderline situations people behave one way or another, because they can't help it. If you look back through history, you'll find few examples of a brother killing another brother.

F: Romulus killed Remus after his brother jumped over the wall of Rome to insult its construction.

RM: That's a legend, not a fact!

F: Cain kills Abel and says that he is not his brother's keeper.

RM: On the mountain, you do your best to keep anyone alive, especially your brother, for as long as you can. Your partner is your most important source of help. It was only natural that I tried to lead my brother down off Nanga Parbat. For two days and two nights.

F: Were you your brother's keeper?

RM: Yes. I was my brother's keeper. And I lost him. It was my fault. And I shall carry this burden for the rest of my life.

34

HANS SALER'S LETTER

"Happy" people secretly and hypocritically demand to be manipulated for their own good. Truth and happiness don't go together. Truth hurts; it brings instability; it ruins the smooth flow of our daily lives. The choice is ours: do we want to be happily manipulated or expose ourselves to the risks of authentic creativity?

—philosopher Slavoj Žižek

At the end of 1998, Hans Saler asked me to write a foreword to his book *Ein Winternachtstraum* (A Winter Night's Dream). Saler, who was on the Nanga Parbat expedition in 1970, now lived in South America and I was glad to hear from him. Naturally, I was happy to contribute to his book.

As a young rock climber, Hans was active in Austria's Kaisergebirge. On Nanga Parbat he showed talent and commitment. When the team had given up on Günther and me as lost, he stuck it out high up on the Rupal Face—together with Gert Mändl—in the hope that we might still be up there.

Years later, when it was claimed that I had been planning to traverse Nanga Parbat all along and that I had told the team of this, it was Hans Saler who led the accusations. He was the one who coined the expression "sacrificed his brother to his own ambition." The accusation was intended to expose a crime, a crime against the expedition team. I put a question back to him at the time: Why did no one come to search for Günther and me in the Diamir Valley if all of you supposedly knew that this was what we were planning and that was the only place we would descend? Saler couldn't have joined the search party himself, because he was still holding out high up on the Rupal Face.

So why did he turn the notion of camaraderie among climbers as a weapon against me? Had he experienced a similar tragedy? Had he also lost a climbing partner? Was he somehow projecting this back on me with his repeated accusations? Achim Zons, the *Süddeutsche Zeitung* journalist I mentioned earlier, revealed a lot about his and Saler's state of mind during the campaign that he, Zons, conducted for years against me.

On November 1, 2005—after Günther's body had been found—someone dared to respond to Achim Zons's articles in the *Süddeutsche Zeitung*. This is the final paragraph of the reader's letter printed in the paper:

> These articles show me much more. With almost X-ray-like detail, they show me exactly what kind of person wrote these articles. They show the patterns of thought and behavior in which he's trapped. How he probably lives his own life. How he thinks about himself and others. They say more about the author than they do about the person actually being discussed. It might be the latter who is being pointed at, but ultimately the image that appears is of he who is pointing the finger by writing these articles.

In May of 2007, I wrote a final piece on the issue—in third person—under the title "Naked Character Assassination." Because I felt like I was both a participant and an observer on Nanga Parbat in 1970:

> On June 28, 1970, the two Messner brothers disappear in the summit area of Nanga Parbat. The following day, expedition leader Herrligkoffer learns of this at base camp. While Reinhold Messner attempts to guide his brother, who was suffering from altitude sickness, down the flatter, Diamir side of the mountain into the valley, his teammates wait on the Rupal side. On July 3, the expedition, convinced that the Messners could not have survived, leaves to start the journey home.
>
> When Reinhold Messner unexpectedly reappears, expedition leader Herrligkoffer states that the possibility of traversing Nanga Parbat and the effects of doing so are something Messner must have been aware of beforehand. Moreover, he justifies his comments by claiming that Messner carried out a preconceived plan, without which he could not have survived, and that he left his brother at the summit. According to Herrligkoffer, counterarguments only further prove Messner's guilt.
>
> Thirty years later, other former expedition teammates claim that Messner, out of pure ambition and in complete disregard of mountain camaraderie, sent his brother back over the Rupal Face to his death. And yet, each of these scenarios, not just the Messner brothers separating, are conjecture and speculation. Since then, even more serious than the lies at the time are the ways that statements and facts have been distorted, diaries rewritten, and documents

manipulated. This is character assassination in the name of "camaraderie." Their verdict: What could be worse than abandoning your own brother?

In the meantime, all the main claims have been refuted. The discovery of Günther Messner's body in 2005 validated Reinhold Messner's account of the tragedy in 1970. He is still waiting for an apology from the character assassins and their associates.

The teammates were unable to admit that they had blindly followed the simplistic logic of their expedition leader. And this forced them to invent

> more and more excuses. Messner had survived what could not be survived, they thought. Because nobody believed it was possible to descend the mountain via an unknown route. Nobody believed that it was possible to traverse Nanga Parbat without bivouac and climbing equipment—even with advanced planning.

So—fifty years later—the idea that Reinhold Messner sacrificed his own brother to his ambition remains more comforting than the fact that it made no sense for the rest of the expedition members not to search for the missing persons.

This is an observation, not an accusation. Nobody could have expected us to find our way down off the mountain in 1970. So why should anyone have come to look for us on the Diamir side?

The fact remains, though, that after we descended on our own, no one came to look for us in the Diamir Valley. However, even though they were all proved wrong in the end, the television films about the tragedy on Nanga Parbat had long since been broadcast, and the books and newspapers sold by the millions. My conclusion is this: their lies might have been invented at first to excuse and justify; but to intentionally obscure the facts was, and remains, naked character assassination.

Walter Bonatti suffered a similar fate after he helped to achieve the first ascent of K2 in 1954. It was falsely claimed that he had used up bottled oxygen intended for the summit team, resulting in the team running out of oxygen in the death zone during the successful summit attempt.

That was a character assassination that Walter Bonatti had to suffer for five decades—despite the fact that he was ultimately fully vindicated in court.

35
BLOCKHEADS

The best way to answer anger is with silence.

—Confucius

After the remains of my brother's body were found, it was clear to everyone that Günther had made it to the lower part of the Diamir Face. My expedition teammates from the time had to keep coming up with new scenarios to explain his death, to avoid being convicted of deliberately making false statements. In particular, Max von Kienlin's defence sounded strange, maybe because he knew comparatively little about mountaineering. The "baron's revenge" seemed to know no bounds and von Keinlin regularly found an audience with journalists who believed his story. Noblesse oblige. The other expedition members were quick to support him, and he did the same for them in return. In an interview with the Swiss magazine *Weltwoche* at the end of 2005, I attempted to explain why the argument was going to continue. Basically, the more famous I became, the more profitable it became to publish counterarguments against me. That's the price of fame. It's easily misused by others.

W: Mr. Messner, this summer your brother's body was found after thirty-five years. What do you feel? Grief? Anger? Satisfaction?

RM: It came as no surprise to me that my brother was found on the Diamir side of Nanga Parbat, where we descended together in 1970. I want to say that first. But to answer your question, I felt relieved to find my brother after so many years. And yes, I felt a sense of satisfaction to prove wrong everyone who claimed that I had abandoned him on the other side of the mountain. At least for my family—for me, my brothers and sister, my parents—we now have a sense of closure. Günther was twenty-four years old when he climbed Nanga Parbat with me in Pakistan and was killed during the descent. It's difficult to accept that your dead son or brother is lying somewhere out there in the snow and ice without being able to take leave of him.

W: Your brother's head was never found, nevertheless, you were sure right from the start that it was Günther. Why was that?

RM: The body parts were spread over an area of about eight square kilometers. There were only bones left. His head must have been torn off in the glacier beforehand. There are powerful forces at work. Down inside the ice, there are holes and streams, maybe it got carried away. It was lucky that Günther's foot was still in his boot that came out of the glacier. A small piece of tissue was enough for DNA analysis. But even without the test I knew that it was my brother. In the 1970s we were wearing these special three-layer boots. No one else had them, only the climbers on the Herrligkoffer expedition. In addition, the boot had a special loop on it to prevent the crampon from coming loose—and it was exactly as Günther had tied it.

W: The DNA test done last October proved that it was Günther. And yet the dispute with your former teammates continues. Why is this?

RM: No, the dispute is not going to continue. Because I've stopped responding to lies dressed up as new accusations. The central question was always, which side of the mountain did my brother go missing on. And I've always said that I brought Günther nearly all the way down. After reaching the summit of Nanga Parbat, we came down the other side together, the Diamir side. My critics maintained that I left Günther behind and told him to go back down the way we had come up, and that he had fallen off. They said that if Günther's body was ever found on the Diamir side, then they should all be considered "blockheads." My brother has now been found in the Diamir Valley on the western side of the mountain.

W: So now we can call certain experts blockheads, with impunity.

RM: Exactly. They're blockheads, all of them. Including those who parroted the lies.

W: Nanga Parbat, 8,126 meters high. It's where your international career started. At the same time, the mountain is responsible for your greatest tragedy. Did you ever regret taking part in the expedition?

RM: First, it's not true that my international career started there. . . . It wasn't till a few years later that I got international recognition for the ascent of Mount Everest without bottled oxygen. Second, the mountain itself is never responsible for a tragedy. Do I regret the expedition? If I had known what was going to happen, I would not have gone. But I don't think about these things. You never know what might happen when you go on an expedition of this size. There's no point going on about it afterward. No, I'm no victim.

W: Some people say that extreme mountaineering is all about resentment, envy, and hatred. Is this true?

RM: The emotions you experience on the eight-thousanders are definitively very strong, but not only in a negative sense. The fact is that in extreme situations, it's ultimately always down to you. To put it simply, being a successful mountaineer means knowing how to stay alive. You're only successful if you survive. The things that others make up about it afterward are usually ridiculous.

W: Walter Bonatti, who was involved in the K2 expedition over fifty years ago, is still fighting for respect and recognition today.

RM: Without Walter Bonatti, the Italian 1954 K2 expedition would have failed. He risked his life to help his teammates. He was abandoned and had to survive a night without protection at 8,100 meters. It's amazing that he survived at all. The truth always prevails in the end. This applies to Bonatti, to me, and to others as well.

Monika Lerch (on behalf of *CliniCum* magazine) witnessed how I have tried, after the discovery of my dead brother's bones, to come to terms with the years of accusations. She reported on the science that helped me to do so:

> In the summer of 2005, at the foot of the Diamir Face on Nanga Parbat, a mountaineering boot and bone remains were found, which Reinhold Messner thought belonged to his missing brother. He delivered a toe bone from the boot to our institute in September so that it could be investigated.
>
> Professor Richard Scheithauer, head of the Institute of Forensic Medicine in Innsbruck, opened the final chapter in the tragedy of Messner's brother who died 35 years ago during a mountaineering expedition. The circumstances of his death have been a source of speculation ever since.
>
> For over a third of his life, Reinhold Messner has been accused of abandoning his brother in the snow and ice. Messner has always maintained that he and Günther climbed Nanga Parbat via the Rupal Face, making the first ascent, and then descended via the Diamir Face where

Günther was caught in an avalanche. He had no proof of this. It was his word against the word of his teammates. There were many questions. It was not possible to unequivocally determine what really happened on June 29, 1970. Nevertheless, for years the press leveled accusations at Messner about this unresolved past. Messner said "the worst lies" came from *Der Spiegel* magazine. During a press conference, he also added: "My story has taught me that *Der Spiegel* magazine does not report facts, but figures and fiction."

Whatever emotions Messner triggered among supporters and opponents, reactions to him were never mediocre. Messner polarizes not because he's extreme, but because he's an extremist. This is a man who is proud of his rough and rugged edges, but who also knows that the media looks for his weaknesses and enlarges them, as if they were using a magnifying glass. Over the years, he lost his desire to take part in discussions and interviews. Finding Günther's body seemed to be the only chance of clearing his name. The location of the body would confirm his version of the story. He spent more than 100,000 euros trying to find it.

On July 17, 2005, his search was over. A melting glacier revealed human remains at 4,300 meters under the Diamir Face. The body was wearing Günther Messner's boot. Reinhold Messner left immediately for the Himalaya. He was accompanied to the site by Dr. Rudolf Hipp, who removed five bone samples from the corpse and stored them in sterile containers. The team carefully divided the sample between four rucksacks, and then made their way back to Europe. Messner had the final remains of the brother cremated in Pakistan with permission from his family.

Who was the dead man? The Institute of Forensic Medicine in Innsbruck has now dispelled any doubts by confirming the identity. It was Günther Messner, the missing brother.

"The probability that the bone comes from a brother of Reinhold and Hubert Messner is 17.8 million times higher than the probability that it comes from a stranger," explained Professor Walter Parson, department head at the Institute of Forensic Medicine. He went on to describe how the mitochondrial DNA profile is typical for western Eurasia, and detailed the extremely rare individual characteristics of the Messner family in positions 16233 and 16355 and also pointed out to the assembled journalists that the Y-chromosomal DNA also matched that of the living brother.

Professor Parson speaks of the Y Chromosome Haplotype Reference Database, scientific developments, and the Institute's experience gained through analyzing tsunami victims from Sri Lanka and the resulting improvements in biostatistics.

Messner can hardly wait for him to finish. He sits nervously on the edge of his chair. In a slightly shaky voice, he reiterates his version of events, once again. That he had wanted to climb the then still unconquered Rupal Face alone. And that his brother Günther and the cameraman Gerhard Baur were to secure the descent route, as agreed with the expedition leader Karl Herrligkoffer. Messner's forehead creases as he recalls how his brother decided to follow him on his own initiative, without consultation. He didn't ask Günther why he had climbed after him. He didn't send him back on his own. They had been climbing mountains as a close-knit team for fifteen years. It was obvious that they would go on together.

Messner does not mention how they stood together at the summit. How that must have felt for them. He talks about Günther's deteriorating condition, that it was important for them to get down fast. The two brothers therefore chose to descend via the Diamir Face, something no one had dared to do before them.

As if he had been waiting for his turn, a *Spiegel* reporter confronts Messner with the first unpleasant question. He immediately goes into detail, asking technical mountaineering questions. Why had Messner gone on ahead when his brother was in a poor physical condition? Messner explains that it's standard practice among mountaineers for the partner who is feeling fitter to go first to find the best way down through crevasses. In the audience, two rows behind the *Spiegel* reporter, two other mountaineers nod their heads in agreement with Messner.

Wolfgang Nairz and Professor Dr. Gerd Judmaier have climbed many tours together with Reinhold Messner. Messner would never have abandoned a climbing partner just to attempt to set a record—not even in an extreme situation. Judmaier certainly knows what he's talking about. He was nearly killed in an accident himself, shortly before the tragedy on Nanga Parbat, and was rescued only thanks to his family and the mountain rescue team. He shared a hospital room with Messner on his return from Nanga Parbat. "I'm one hundred percent convinced of his version of the story," he says. "The place where the body was found and the glaciological date are proof," adds Wolfgang Nairz. However the *Spiegel* reporter continues to question everything.

An argument starts in the press conference. Messner suddenly gets very emotional. It seems that he feels he has to shout down contradictions arising from the polarization. And in turn, he opens up further contradictions. He's not at all diplomatic. He makes no apology for his emotional outbursts, but asks for understanding. The results of the DNA analysis are indisputable, and yet Messner has to face accusations of body snatching, theft, and smuggling because he had no export license to take his brother's bone samples out of the country. It turns out that there is no standard procedure for this kind of case. Messner should have requested permission from the Pakistani government, his critics say. He himself felt he had done his duty as he had acted with the approval of two regional mayors. The forensic experts agree with Messner's approach. They explain that for a proper DNA analysis it's important to secure samples as quickly and as professionally as possible. The reporter shrugs his shoulders, pockets his notebook, and leaves.

Shortly afterward, *Der Spiegel* magazine reports that "After the body of his brother found on Nanga Parbat was identified, Reinhold Messner considered his name cleared. But his critics continue to have their doubts."

"My opponents," Messner demanded, "should finally be silent." The bone samples taken from his brother were buried in the family grave.

36

EXCLUDED

If critics were only to talk about the things they understood,
the world would soon become a much quieter place.

—Reinhold Messner

For many decades, I had a generally positive and stimulating relationship with the Deutscher Alpenverein (DAV—German Alpine Club), the world's largest mountaineering club.

This all changed in 2003. A deliberate and sustained effort to damage my reputation and credibility was allowed to take place at the DAV headquarters on the Praterinsel in Munich—without any form of debate. I wrote to complain to the DAV management in a letter dated November 24, 2005. After the discovery of part of my brother's body, which confirmed my account of the Nanga Parbat tragedy, I expected an apology.

> Reading a press release issued by the DAV, I gather that the DAV will not allow itself to be instrumentalized. Unfortunately, this decision comes a little late. This dispute has already exploded due to the backing of the DAV (Praterinsel 2003). I was aware of the matter at the time and, expecting a character assassination campaign, I contacted both Friederike Kaiser from the DAV museum and Josef Klenner, DAV chairman, personally and in advance. The subsequent game of hide-and-seek is as embarrassing as previous exclusion campaigns, and is precisely what is happening here.
>
> DAV publications have published incorrect facts by certain 1970 expedition teammates without checking the statements or correcting them afterward. Therefore this falls under the DAV's scope.
>
> It might be the case that the DAV has a new chairman, who has no knowledge of the affair. It might also be the case that the DAV lacks the expertise to act on such a distant matter.
>
> But when you clear away the smoke and mirrors, someone still has to take responsibility. Including at the DAV.

> It's true that this debate is damaging for everyone. But to tacitly cover up a "monstrosity" (Professor Hörmann, Bad Boll, 1970), intended solely to discredit a self-determined mountaineer?
>
> The DAV, with almost 700,000 members can surely digest this too [Today the club has more than double this figure]. Nevertheless, I will not allow my right to take a stand to be suppressed.
>
> I find it hard to understand how the DAV naively allowed itself to be used in this matter, unlike the OEVA [Austrian Alpine Club] and the AVS [South Tyrol Alpine Club]. All because a handful of people wanted to pursue their "own political agenda" within the DAV? Time will tell. One thing is certain, even if these people no longer hold their positions, the responsibility remains—with the DAV.

Despite repeated discussions, the matter was not clarified. Finally, on May 8, 2009, I was formally excluded from the DAV:

> Reinhold Messner has repeatedly and massively attacked the German Alpine Club and its voluntary and full-time representatives in recent years. His statements culminated in very personal attacks on individual DAV representatives. His comparisons of the current DAV committee and management to the National Socialists in the 1930s and 1940s are completely unacceptable.
>
> In recent years, both the DAV committee and DAV president have sought to talk to Mr. Messner on several occasions in an attempt to resolve the dissonance and restore a spirit of camaraderie.
>
> Despite some very positive statements, we unfortunately had to accept time and again that our efforts did nothing to change Mr. Messner's fundamental attitude toward the entire DAV.
>
> Due to further recent attacks in the media, the DAV Executive Committee has had to reconsider the relationship between Reinhold Messner and the German Alpine Club. The reason for the renewed discussion was the article by Reinhold Messner in *Bergsteiger* magazine (March 2009). After extensive discussion, the Executive Committee has reached the following decision:
>
> "The Executive Committee has decided that Messner will no longer be offered a platform within the DAV main association or in the DAV Summit Club. Furthermore, we are contacting all sections to request that they also carry this out at a local level.

The *Süddeutsche Zeitung* of 13/14 June 2009 reported on the dispute between Heinz Röhle, the new president of the German Alpine Club at the time, and me.

SZ: "You have to steer the lead sheep in the right direction, and the herd will follow." These words were printed in the German Alpine Club's 2009 yearbook. The sentence features in an essay on environmental education in the DAV and how top alpinists act as a role model. In *Bergsteiger* magazine, Reinhold Messner reproached the Alpine Club that it had "outed itself as what it had always wanted to be: the avant-garde of yesteryear." Are you, Mr. Röhle, happy with the leading sheep metaphor?

HR: The authors could certainly have chosen their words more diplomatically. But what the article actually talks about is the fact that we have been working closely with top alpinists for years. People like Hans Kammerlander set an example. In this context, the term "lead sheep" is not meant to be derogatory.

SZ: Mr. Messner, in your article, you talk of the "young heirs of a totalitarian understanding of the association." Are you saying that there are still fascist ideas in the DAV?

RM: No, that's not what I was trying to say. However, the line about the "lead sheep" is an insult to Hans Kammerlander and the 800,000 association members, who are being labeled as sheep here. Moreover, this is the language of the 1930s. I only asked, what does this sentence mean? Basically, I wanted to defend people like Hans Kammerlander. They're not lead sheep, but self-determined individuals. I hope that the Alpine Club has members who think for themselves, and who don't just follow others in a herd.

SZ: And yet, you're not exactly known for being careful about your choice of words yourself. In your reaction to the yearbook article, you talk of the "avant-garde of yesteryear," of "self-proclaimed blockheads," and "herds."

RM: Only the "avant-garde of yesteryear" uses such language. It wasn't old, non-active members but younger members who used the term "lead sheep." And the current management committee backed them. If I see a sentence like that, then I hope I can give it proper consideration—if I take the DAV seriously. Next issue!

SZ: The "self-proclaimed blockheads."

RM: Those who were there at the DAV headquarters on the Praterinsel in Munich in 2003 who attacked me and sought to dismantle me—they are the "self-proclaimed blockheads." Because that's where the usage was coined. In front of 200 people, mainly DAV members, it was said: "If Messner's brother's body is found on the west side of Nanga Parbat, then we're all blockheads." At the time, it was claimed that the body must be somewhere on the south face. [Editor's note: bones from a mountaineer's body were found on the west face; a DNA analysis proved that it was Günther Messner.] Now that the proof is there, I feel entitled to use the term "self-proclaimed blockheads." After all, it's what they called themselves. I have never used the term before this point. However, since 2003 it became clear to me that the DAV stands in a tradition of excluding others.

SZ: Mr. Röhle, if you're now recommending that DAV associations no longer invite Mr. Messner to speak, don't you think that he has a point here?

HR: Mr. Messner, the German Alpine Club has no desire to "dismantle" you! You continue to repeat this assertion, but that doesn't make it right. Hans Saler and Max von Kienlin were invited to present their book on the Praterinsel because the Alpine Museum in Munich is a platform for discussing topics relevant to mountaineering history.

RM: So, anyone can turn up there and conduct what is a character assassination?

HR: No. We said very clearly that we do not support any particular position. We even let you restate your position once again in the 2005 yearbook. And Mr. Messner, you're also aware that Kienlin wanted to write a further contribution in response to your article in the following yearbook. I made sure that it was not published, because I felt that the dispute should have a line drawn under it.

RM: In 2003, when this whole campaign started, I warned the Alpine Club—not you, but your predecessor—and predicted that it would turn into a character assassination campaign. And that if the DAV did it without inviting me, it would end up as an accomplice. At the time, I was on Franz Josef Land in the Arctic Ocean. The whole thing had been arranged so that I couldn't take part. Why should I have to put up with this? It has been legally proven that this character assassination campaign was being conducted for solely private reasons. It was not about Nanga Parbat. Was the Alpine Club happy to support this?

HR: That's a serious insinuation!

RM: If you have no guilty conscience—not for yourself, but on behalf of the association—then you've not understood anything.

HR: If that were the case, then I would not have come to visit you at Juval Castle in 2006. I brought you a bottle of wine, you presented me with a bottle of your wine, we had a constructive three-hour conversation. We agreed to write a text together—

RM: Correct.

HR: —where we would outline our different viewpoints. The whole thing was coming along nicely. And then there was the *Alpintag Köln* (DAV Alpine Day in Cologne). You attacked our Vice President Ludwig Wucherpfennig there, in front of the whole team, and again accused the Alpine Club of being close to fascist ideas. It's no surprise that I was unable to get a majority on the Executive Committee to agree to a goodwill initiative between you and us after that.

SZ: Mr. Messner, what would it take?

RM: I told Mr. Röhle in Juval: All it would take is a few words. Is it really not possible to say just this one sentence? The sentence is: We distance ourselves from the claim made in 2003 on the Praterinsel that Messner abandoned his brother.

SZ: Herr Röhle, was it a wise decision to recommend to your local associations that they no longer invite Messner to speak?

HR: We're not in a position to dictate anything to our 354 local associations, because they're legally independent. But you can imagine that after your *Bergsteiger* magazine article we realized that there was a lot of anger in the local associations and at a national level. We felt that it no longer made sense to continue to give you, Mr. Messner, a platform within the Alpine Club. In future, you are more than welcome to come to our press conferences, to visit our exhibitions, and to stay at our huts—

RM: I don't need your huts, I'll bring a tent with me in future. (Laughs)

HR: —but we do not intend to invite you as a speaker. This is a perfectly normal reaction. I don't invite guests to my home if I know that they are going to insult me.

In his speech at the *Edelweißfest 2009* at the DAV Eichstätt association in Bavaria, the chairman Gerhard Seibold, an active mountaineer and man of culture, talked about the DAV exclusion campaign:

> I would like to attempt to address a very difficult and controversial issue, "Messner vs the DAV." Earlier this year, in May, all 354 DAV local associations received a letter from the Executive Committee asking them not to give Reinhold Messner any platform or invite him to speak.
>
> What were the reasons for this? The decisive factor was ultimately the article Reinhold Messner wrote in *Bergsteiger* magazine (March 2009), where he said, among other things: "It's not Reinhold Messner, but the world's largest mountaineering association with 815,000 members that's responsible for the dispute."
>
> When a club decides to exclude a certain climber, the facts speak for themselves. The German Alpine Club has a tradition of exclusion. In the 1920s and 1930s it excluded Jews and nature lovers. At the time, the main body of the association was sympathetic to National Socialist sentiments.
>
> The Alpine Club made big mistakes during this period and brought heavy guilt upon itself. Our local association was also affected by this. This is why there is a memorial stone against hatred and intolerance in front of the Glorer mountain hut.

Manfred Sturm, who took over the legacy of Karl Herrligkoffer, tried for a long time for reconciliation. But it was in vain.

My letter from October 25, 2023, explains why it was not possible:

> Dr. Herrligkoffer is dead and therefore unable to correct his false statements. His son is not to blame. The Herrligkoffer Foundation, though, has become part of the DAV, and the DAV does carry a responsibility for the reporting on (but not for what happened on) Nanga Parbat in 1970. Until Günther's body was found in 2005, I was lenient. Since everything has now been proven, the DAV, without which the campaign would not have been possible, shares responsibility. It was mainly DAV functionaries and DAV members who were involved in the original "witch hunt" at the DAV premises (in Praterinsel, 2003). This was then later expressed in more concrete terms in my exclusion.

Why did the DAV never distance itself from the lies? Why should I have had to listen to the same outrageous accusations that Herrligkoffer first made in Bad Boll in 1970 (December 13, 1970), which reached criminal proportions in 2003? Because I have defended myself, I am being deprived of "any platform." Even within the Summit Club, where I had led some of the "boldest trips."

Today I am convinced that the DAV had as little idea of what it should be responsible for in my case, as the club did in 1924 when it excluded the Donauland section with its Jewish alpinists and supporters.

It was not me who started the argument. Not in 1970, and not in 2003. I was only responding to Herrligkoffer's deceits and conspiracy theories that were set off like an avalanche at the DAV headquarters in Munich.

By remaining silent on the issue, the DAV (which represents a membership of more than a million) with its public dissociation (not as it should be, from the lies of some of its members, but instead from Reinhold Messner) has ultimately helped perpetuate the Nanga Parbat falsehood. As such, the DAV should feel responsible—though not guilty—for the character assassination campaign against me. And it should stand by this responsibility. The lies and the fabricated accounts of separate descents, Günther's and mine, from the summit of Nanga Parbat severely damaged my credibility. I have managed to restore it. Yet the DAV continues to hide behind its many "good old boys."

37

NANGA PARBAT, THE FILM

A journey of a thousand miles begins with a single step.

—Laozi, founder of Taoism

Joseph Vilsmaier's film about the Nanga Parbat 1970 tragedy received a lot of criticism, in many respects justified. Maybe trying to tell the story by sticking closely to the facts was the wrong approach. A bolder feature film would have allowed more emotion, more character, and more drama.

I was often present during the filming, in Villnöss, in Munich, and in Pakistan. In our fact-based approach, Vilsmaier and I may have failed to profoundly capture the feel of the life and death moments. We didn't do them justice.

Other 1970 expedition members disapproved of the film. They complained that it was too much of a feature film to document the expedition faithfully. They also complained because they were not involved in the project.

Thomas Huber senior, father of the famous "Huberbuam" (the Huber brothers, rock climbers and mountaineers) and also an extreme mountaineer himself, felt that the film was an authentic portrayal:

> I don't agree with the criticism of the film *Nanga Parbat* in the *Anzeiger* newspaper and other media. It's an authentic and skillfully filmed portrayal of a dramatic episode in mountaineering history. It would be fair to compare it to Jacques Ertaud and Marcel Ichac's unforgettable film *Les étoiles de midi* (Stars at noon).
>
> If Nanga Parbat was not connected to Messner's story, it would have received unanimous praise. Instead, it's criticized wherever possible. Was this the same with *Nordwand* (North Face)? The 2008 German historical fiction film, directed by Philipp Stölzl and based on the famous 1936 attempt on the Eiger north face, was probably the worst ever so-called *Bergfilm* (mountain

film). It was poor right down to the smallest details. Nevertheless, it was awarded first prize at the Tegernsee International Mountain Film Festival. It was just that it was not a film about Reinhold Messner.

I got to know Reinhold and Günther in their youth, knew Herrligkoffer too, and had also met Felix Kuen in the mountains. Herrligkoffer's character is accurately portrayed in the film, right down to his gestures. It seems pointless to say a word of criticism. He was an effective organizer, but also something of a dictator, when it came to his Nanga Parbat. It would have been a shame if the request for an "explanatory" preamble had been granted.

It goes without saying that Reinhold Messner is a thorn in the side for many people, due to his verbal attacks. But he has achieved so much. If there were more people like Messner, maybe we could have prevented the Wilder Kaiser mountains from being turned into an alpine *Klettergarten* (bolted climbing park). Where does the truth lie when it comes to the story of the drama on Nanga Parbat? Isn't it normal for every mountaineer to dream of new and different routes and to share this dream with his teammates, as Messner probably did? Reinhold had no idea that this dream would turn into such a catastrophic reality. There have been many equivalent or similar situations in the history of mountaineering. But where were the critics when Riccardo Cassin lost two members of his party on the northeast face of the Badile? He too will have to live with this for the rest of his life. However, there were no critics. There was only sympathy from all sides.

Even without going into the details of the history of the Nanga Parbat drama, there are still so many questions. Why don't Gerhard Baur and Jürgen Winkler, both of whom I hold in high esteem, tell us what actually happened when Felix Kuen and Peter Scholz returned from the summit? Why was there no discussion of immediately organizing a rescue operation to the Diamir side, which Reinhold had talked about when he shared his dream of a Nanga Parbat traverse? Didn't Kuen and Scholz talk freely of their own accord how the Messner brothers reached the summit before them? I'm sure that part of the team wanted to do something immediately, but couldn't go against Herrligkoffer. Why was the issue of his completely traumatized fight for survival ("Where is Günther?") played up so much after his rescue? There are so many questions. At any rate, this film is a

> rich and positive contribution to the *Bergfilm* genre. It would be a shame if its critics continue to put it down in a non-objective manner, just because it's the story of Reinhold Messner.

I have always tried to learn from criticism. Over the years, I've answered a thousand and more letters and thanked people for their critical objections. This way, I have learned a lot. In the age of digital communication, however, it has become harder to stay in touch with each other. Anonymous insults, threats, and mockery are quickly posted and then remain online. Forever.

38

SELF-EMPOWERMENT AND FREEDOM

As soon as you master one thing, you should become a student in another.

—writer Gerhart Hauptmann

I have had to overcome many different types of obstacles in the natural world. From the north face of the Furchetta in the Geisler group to the 4,500-meter Rupal face of Nanga Parbat to the Arctic Ocean—I faced them and I survived. I failed many times too—but it's better to try and to fail than to die trying.

I encountered obstacles of a different kind back in civilization. They were not deadly, and I didn't always have to take them on. Still, in the wilderness I was able to make good use of my audacious nature; away from the mountains it was often no help. I was angry, and I fought—often without getting anywhere. Wilderness has no intentions; humans do, and human intentions are diverse and not always driven by empathy. I had the good fortune not to have inherited anything. I was skeptical about conventional ways of doing things. Before I'd even finished my degree I'd decided not to pursue a career. It's not that I didn't want to do anything. But I was open to everything, even the unthinkable.

As such, life became one big learning process, much to my delight. I'm still learning now. No one has ever tied me down. Neither religion, morals, nor other ties. This didn't come easy. In the beginning I led a kind of double life, a bourgeois home life and an anarchic climbing life. I discovered how to live a more self-determined life later on. I didn't plan it, it just happened.

Each obstacle faced was a challenge, each allowed me to grow. I am still following my heart and exploring possibilities.

At the edges of the Earth, however, even the loner is confronted with his loneliness. Left on his own, everything becomes absurd. In the death zone, there are many constraints. There at the threshold between life and death, it's not our will that ultimately decides, but our instincts that take over. So, my freedom has always been relative. It's self-preservation that determines our actions, not our love of freedom.

I have started over again from scratch five times in my life. Each time, I pushed myself to the limits. I devoted all my time, resources, and enthusiasm to reach my goal. Nevertheless, I could have failed each time—and I often did fail too. But then I tried again and again, and, in the end, I succeeded in realizing my visions. First as a rock climber then as a high-altitude mountaineer, an explorer of limits crossing deserts and pack ice, a myth researcher, and now a museum designer and filmmaker.

When I was twenty, I made my first ascents in the Dolomites, but wanted to climb without placing bolts and so climbed ever-steeper routes. I didn't want to change the rock or the mountains, instead I wanted to improve my ability. I achieved this through training, commitment, and focus. The mountains that had to be moved each time were only things in my mind. It was my mental strength that carried me over all obstacles, right up to Everest, the "peak of hopelessness."

At first it was all about getting to the top; later it became all about making it back down. It was only at the bottom, beyond the glacier, between the first lichen-covered rocks, amid the first insects and the gushing meltwater, that my emotions would burst out, like lava from a volcano. It was surviving that made me strong. It stimulated and inspired me to give my all again and again. To give everything, including my life. To win it.

There is nothing more powerful than regaining your life. That's why I do what I do, again and again.

I was never motivated by duty; I was motivated by commitment. Once I had grown up, it was I who consciously decided what people, things, and tasks to make part of my life. I'm talking about very specific people, very specific things, and very specific tasks that often only made sense to me. Freedom begins with measuring, assessing, and creating meaning.

Anyone who's looked death in the face knows that it is not what we have but what we do that counts. My biography is my life's work—I'm the only one responsible for it. It's all there in my backpack, as it were. I have to carry it; it doesn't carry me. What keeps me going is the same thing that makes me strong, that keeps me creative and young, that makes me cheerful, positive, and, sometimes, even exuberant. Moreover, it's the ideas that I project forward that empower me. When I'm invited to contribute, to express myself, to help shape things, then I can be myself.

If you have an idea of what lies beyond the limits of the possible, it can feel good to settle down. It becomes less important to retrieve some taboo from the roof of the world. Instead, it becomes meaningful to respect the taboo that makes us human in the first place. Namely, our limitations.

39

INTERJECTIONS

If everyone's shaking their heads at your idea, then go for it.

—photographer Remo Neuhaus

In an interview with *ff* magazine in 2007, I talked about my attitude to ageing and calling South Tyrol my home, among other topics.

ff: You're 63 now. Do you have a problem with growing old?

RM: No, but ageing is an enormous challenge. I'll continue to be creative and do what I can, as long as I stay in good shape.

ff: You once said that you could only function if you straddled a state where you were injuring or destroying yourself.

RM: Yes, that's the key to crossing the frontier. When I embark on extreme ventures, the possibility of perishing during the journey is very real. I don't court death, but I do accept that it could happen. Preventing annihilation is paramount. Nevertheless, I still give everything I've got to achieve my goals. Which is why I admit that I oscillate between injuring myself or possibly finishing myself off.

ff: What do your children mean to you?

RM: They are very important to me, but I still live my life. Just because we have children, we're not obliged to simply fetch our pipe and slippers and sit by the fire.

ff: Suppose your Sigmundskron museum flopped, and the local governor offered to help you out financially—would you accept?

RM: First, the governor is not going to come and help me, because he has to comply with contracts that required me to be financially independent for thirty years. And second, because I can if needed withdraw money from other ventures to cushion the impact of any looming bankruptcy. The latest attempt by the management at Weinbergweg—

ff: In other words, the publishing house Athesia.

Translation: Look down there—that's Reinhold Messner on the hill of Sigmundskron Castle. It's the first mountain he might go bust on. (*Die Pleite Geier* means "the vultures are gathering.")

RM: —is still trying to thwart the Sigmundskron project. They've even tried to obstruct parking options for the museum. They clearly want to see my project go to the wall. They won't succeed because we work with international guests and not so much with South Tyroleans.

ff: Do you regret your venture?

RM: I don't want to complain. I've only got myself to blame for the museum. I was allowed to get it up and running and am happy about that. I embarked on the adventure just as I did when I was twenty-five with the Civetta North Face, and as I did on Everest at thirty-five and in Antarctica at forty-five.

ff: What does South Tyrol need to do to position itself culturally?

RM: In the future, we'll only have a chance if we fill niches. South Tyrol is powerful enough to unlock the mountain as a niche market, and the same goes for its culture too. People come here for a holiday in the mountains. We sell apples, wine, wood, and expertise from the mountains. We offer a unique mountain landscape. Where mountains are concerned, we would be well advised to become leaders—worldwide.

I've been doing my utmost to promote mountain tourism culturally since 2006. However, I wonder whether it's clever to discredit here at home an advertising medium that appears abroad for South Tyrol. This is what conservationists, nature lovers, and self-appointed castle keepers are doing in the case of Sigmundskron. It's somewhat two-faced to preside over the decline of the region you come from and yet criticize that decline at the same time.

I'm not just interested in maintaining, preserving, and restoring our cultural landscape, but also in reshaping it—which explains my experiment with the "house in the rock," an apartment cut into the rock to fit in with the surrounding alpine landscape. Architect Werner Tscholl found a solution to building in attractive locations without changing the world externally.

The "house in the rock," designed by architect Werner Tscholl

40

CULTURAL HERITAGE

All areas of culture—traditional alpinism is also one—have their own collective attitude. Some culture bearers provide more ideas, answers, and concepts than others and are often ostracized for it: their approaches differ far too much from the generally accepted ideas of the mainstream.

—Reinhold Messner

I did something of a taking stock during my talk at the South Tyrolean Alpine Association's sixtieth anniversary celebrations at Sigmundskron Castle on June 10, 2006. I have abridged and updated the following text, which is based on parts of it:

> This museum doesn't belong to me. It's a meeting place for everyone who cares about the mountains, the culture behind them, and the heritage of alpinism and who wants to spread the message. Mountaineering is more about emotions than intellect.
>
> I've been endeavoring to incorporate these emotions for years. Our past, alpine history, and mountain literature are magnificent. There are more than 10,000 entertaining publications, and music about mountains—not just in Europe, but worldwide. There are plays about mountains and, above all, there are images. Many great philosophers have bequeathed us mountain metaphors. Most religions involve deities from above who figuratively descend from the mountains. For instance, Moses came down from Mount Sinai with the Ten Commandments. The mountains were viewed as a bridge from Earth to heaven. We should continue to respect them as such. We need to approach the mountain with devotion, indeed respect. As a gateway to the beyond, to a dimension we cannot reach.
>
> Mountaineering isn't a sport. What is it then? I realize this has been debated for over a century. It's neither better, nor worse, than sport; it's something else. We associate sport with measuring performance. However, it's impossible to gauge mountaineering. Mountaineering is more than key

performance or comparative indicators. It isn't about being fit for fun or getting that kick. I know that's how many young people perceive it. But I'd like to remind you that the experts among us always start where the fun stops. Traditional mountaineering isn't just fun.

The German poet Gottfried Benn defined mountaineering as "life provoked by death," as a "longing for life." In other words, death plays a pivotal role in what we do. If the going up's not dangerous, it doesn't stretch us. The goal is to avoid the risks and to remain vigilant. The art of mountaineering is, though it's perilous, to not die in the process. It's hard to explain this contradiction to the average person. That mountaineering with its avalanches, rockfall, lightning, and thunder is dangerous, above all because to err is human. We make mistakes, which (on the mountain) are often fatal. We draw on experience, ability, equipment, and time to reach our goals. And these goals are always ones we've set personally. We know we could get killed. Mountaineering is a unique adventure, a balancing act between injuring and possibly killing yourself. Anyone who has read books, from Emil Zsigmondy to Walter Bonatti, on the subject will find similar sentiments echoed. As human beings, we can tackle self-imposed goals and embark on adventures that appear absurd, adventures where death is considered a possibility. We make useless endeavors meaningful.

Mountaineering is always an end in itself. We're not climbing mountains for a nation or a club or a group, we're doing it for the subjective personal experience.

We alpinists—anarchists on the mountain—make our own rules. We're generators of ideas, actors, and ultimately arbiters of our actions all rolled into one. Traditional mountaineering is about taking responsibility for yourself. It's a privilege to climb areas not made for us humans, where key performance indicators play no role. If we reduce what we experience to numbers, we're not really in a dangerous space. Yet danger is part of nature. If we subtract danger from the mountains, we render them fake and banal. I don't climb to battle prejudices. There would be little attraction in that. I didn't climb the highest mountains on Earth to highlight environmental problems. The purpose of my trek to the South Pole wasn't to demonstrate in favor of a protected World Park Antarctica. I've always been interested in "conquering the useless"—in other words, stretching myself to the full and always going a step further without killing myself.

It's not so much the wild that's undiscovered, but being human. The experience of facing death and surviving allows all our masks to drop, and we learn so much about ourselves in the process, and even about the all-too-human, the true face, the abyss within us. Nevertheless, explorers of limits have a passionate commitment to life. Beginning with the proverbial worldliness of Homer's concept of man: it's an expression of desire, which—heightened by fear—is perceived as meaningful without question.

41

MY LIFE IN SOUTH TYROL

He who is strong, but does not work on himself, will wither.

—Laozi, founder of Taoism

To this day, I still don't know how I have been repeatedly pigeonholed as being left wing. In print, I was often associated with the Lotta Continua, a far-left militant organization in Italy. Fifty years ago, the word "communist" was still one of the worst swear words in South Tyrol. And it was used as a weapon against my friend, the journalist and politician Alexander Langer, and me.

Alexander Langer deserves a great deal of credit for his commitment to minorities in South Tyrol. He has done much to establish peace between the groups who speak different languages by educating people about the background to recent South Tyrolean history. He sat in the provincial parliament in Bolzano and in the European Parliament, and he was instrumental in building the Green Movement in Italy. At his advice, although after his death, I was nominated as a candidate on the Green Party list for the 1999 European elections. All this, without joining the party as a liberal green thinker.

I stayed that way for the five years spent representing the people in Brussels and beyond, as the excerpt from an interview in *ff* from 2012, after I had left office, shows. During the interview, we were talking about media monopolies. The Ebner family already had too much power in South Tyrol at the time, as with Berlusconi in Italy.

ff: You regularly speak your mind about the media. How do you differ from Ebner and Berlusconi?

RM: I have no medium now and no longer have a mandate, just my opinion. Journalists ask me questions and I answer them. I'm at the mercy of the journalists. Ebner and Berlusconi have direct influence over their media channels and often abuse their power. But I also tell people exactly what I think.

ff: Not everyone can do that—you're in a fortunate position perhaps?

RM: I've always spoken my mind, which has never won me a lot of friends. To me, independence is paramount. But one thing I can tell you is that I'll never ingratiate myself with journalists or politicians. It's true that the local governor and I like each other. We trust each other.

ff: Why is that?

RM: Because he does all the deciding. And sometimes, he gives me advice. I also trust him because he keeps his word. If he says he will do something in a particular way, then he does so.

Two years earlier, an interview had appeared in the *Südtiroler Wirtschaftszeitung* newspaper, which once again described my attitude to South Tyroleans as "obstructionists."

SWZ: Reinhold, last week you said that it would be a good idea to build the controversial forest trail in the Antersasc Valley, which is part of the Dolomites World Heritage Site. Coming from a man who fought for decades to protect the mountains from overdevelopment and mass tourism, your opinion could be viewed as surprising perhaps?

RM: No. I've always made a clear distinction between the cultural landscape and the natural landscape. My credo is that we must preserve our cultural landscape for the next generation and minimize our impact on the natural landscape. The Antersasc Alm is a cultural landscape. It has certainly been farmed for over a thousand years—the *Heuweg* (hay path) and *Kalkofen* (lime kiln) are still there today. The hut is located at the only place not at risk of avalanches or rockfall. In my opinion, this alpine pasture is worth protecting. But it's important to mention that to farm the alp—140 hectares of pasture—some kind of makeshift path, at least, is required. We mustn't forget that South Tyrol's farms and mountain pastures are still being cultivated today because they have been developed. Elsewhere, mountain pastures are deserted, meaning a loss of culture.

SWZ: So you give state politics a good report card in terms of the way we treat the mountain landscape?

RM: In terms of preserving the cultural landscape, definitely. In that respect, we're trailblazers in the alpine region. South Tyrol's strength lies precisely in the way cultural and natural landscapes are intermeshed. If people no longer work on our farms and mountain pastures, tourism will suffer. We need to cut the red tape involved when farmers hone and sell their own products so that they can reap more direct benefits from tourism. After all, it's agricultural products—not Coca-Cola and hamburgers—that set us apart from the tourism competition.

SWZ: Which, of course, begs the question—where does the boundary between the natural and cultural landscape lie?

RM: Thousands of years ago, people knew the answer to that question all too well. They didn't interfere with the natural landscape because there was nothing to be gained by doing so. Neither woods nor pasture. Which is why I defended Plan de Corones as a skiing mountain—people used to cut wood there, now another type of business is successful.

SWZ: Are South Tyroleans obstructionists?

RM: They are also that too. There are clubs and politicians who spend their whole time opposing things.

SWZ: What's your opinion of what's known as direct democracy? Should the people be allowed to have their say, or is it better if elected representatives make the big decisions?

RM: Grassroots democracy works in the villages. However, at a state level, it can prevent anything from getting done. Elected politicians should decide, we should trust our representatives. We gave them our vote. We vote and it's our fault if we don't.

SWZ: Let's talk about Virgl hill. For years, nobody paid any attention to it. But when entrepreneur Peter Thun came up with a (no doubt self-serving) idea, the Virgl suddenly became a gem. And one that had to be protected from development at all costs.

RM: I'm not familiar with the Thun project, but in my opinion that would be a place for a kind of landmark there. Why shouldn't the Virgl be used?

SWZ: Do you think it's a shame that Peter Thun has given up?

RM: Yes, an entrepreneurial initiative to revitalize the neglected area near Bolzano was squashed.

SWZ: How much tourism can South Tyrol take? Have we reached the pain threshold, or do we have wiggle room?

RM: To attract guests in the off-peak season, South Tyrol needs to make better use of existing tourism facilities. Cultural tourism would be a new approach. In the high season, South Tyrol has reached its limits and traffic is a problem.

SWZ: So what's your view on designating new tourism zones in areas of South Tyrolean communities with good tourism infrastructure? This political route is controversial even in tourism circles.

RM: I think you need to look at it on a case-by-case basis. Let's take Villnöss/Funes for instance. Even with the beautiful Eisack Valley as its backdrop, Villnöss doesn't have adequate accommodations for tourists. Thousands of people come to Zans by car and head for the mountain pastures from there. Basically, this is a case of picnic tourism. These guests stay, eat, and drink their own provisions. They don't sleep in Villnöss, so contribute nothing to the local economy. Villnöss needs more accommodations and should be able to offer its guests special benefits in the Puez-Odle Nature Park.

SWZ: Do regional politics lack a vision for South Tyrol?

RM: Yes, definitely. South Tyrol has made impressive progress—not least thanks to Silvius Magnago and Luis Durnwalder. But over the past few years, it's true that a vision has been lacking. The way forward is unclear.

SWZ: Perhaps shift the responsibility to entrepreneurs?

RM: Yes, entrepreneurs should collaborate on our key technologies—forestry and woodworking, cable cars, alpine technology, energy. We should spread tourism, industry, and subsidies more evenly across the region.

42
BONDS

He who knows people is a wise man;
he who knows himself is an enlightened man.

—Laozi, founder of Taoism

People disapprove of politicians favoring those they share a bond with, and they're ambivalent about the same approach in the business world. But in the mountains, bonds in the literal and figurative sense are welcomed. And what about one of life's most important bonds—marriage?

I have been ostracized, slandered, and harmed by people I have shared personal bonds with. The worst thing for me was when I was kicked out of my family home at the age of seventy-five, by my wife. I was given no warning or reason. Despite being often apart from my wife and children while on my many expeditions, I am a family man. We also traveled to places together and I was often at home for months at a time.

I had planned to grow old with my family and had already ensured that my wife and children had financial stability.

I had already given members of my family their inheritance. But when I was asked to leave the family home, I was suddenly completely on my own, uprooted and with nowhere to live. I wondered how I would cope.

People who thought they knew me imagined I'd be able to handle it. My family bonds no longer needed repair—they were rendered obsolete. So, I tried to navigate life on my own—as I always had in the face of disappointment and emergency. But was I living an illusion now that I had "escaped"? In the past I had always managed in an emergency. But how would I cope all alone this time?

In an interview with Gebi Bendler and Dominik Prantl for *bergundsteigen* magazine in autumn 2021, entitled "Messners Seilschaften" (Messner's Climbing Partnerships), the "author, museum curator and erstwhile alpinist Reinhold Messner discussed wives, fathers, and friends as mountain partners, the improper use of the word *Kameradschaft* (camaraderie)—and envy as a companion":

berg: Reinhold, who do you most like to climb with in the mountains right now?

RM: My wife Diane.

berg: Do life partners make a good team on the mountain too?

RM: Why not? There are plenty of examples in early alpinism and later on with Rudi and Helga Lindner. Paul Preuss, who I feel a close affinity to, whimsically observed in an article: "I had close ties to something like twenty-seven women—just via a rope."

berg: Unfortunately, experience has shown that combining these sorts of bonds and a love life is often difficult.

RM: I've never had a life partner I would climb difficult routes with. It just never materialized. My wife and I don't climb as a couple either. As part of our studies of mountain peoples, we do climb mountains. For instance, we tackled the highest mountain in Ethiopia shortly before the pandemic. We hike and climb together via ferratas and easy climbing tours, nothing too stressful that could cause problems. I'm done with extreme tours.

berg: What makes someone a good climbing partner in the mountains?

RM: They must be more than able to handle the problems that are likely to arise.

berg: Even you were a beginner once. Who took you with them?

RM: My partners fell in my lap. First, my father. Then, even when we were still naïve climbers as children, we set out to climb the Odle Peaks on our doorstep. When we were thirteen or fourteen, Günther and I did relatively big tours together.

Later, I was lucky enough to find older, more experienced partners who literally showed me the ropes. They showed me how to set up proper belays and place protection. These sorts of experiences at a young age were important, the instincts I evolved, and the tutelage of someone like Sepp Mayerl shaped me.

Later it became a problem because Peter Habeler and I, both of us Mayerl's former students, became more famous than him. Interestingly, teachers often can't bear to be outdone.

berg: Who outclimbed you?

RM: I never had that problem.

berg: Which one? Being outclimbed or jealous?

RM: After 1970, my amputated toes stopped me from climbing as I had done before. It was no longer possible. After giving up my passion for climbing, I took up mountaineering. But I never felt any rivalry toward the young climbing generation.

berg: You've now got married for the third time. How many people have you had a long-term climbing bond, akin to a marriage, with?

RM: During my alpine tours, I had half a dozen people I went climbing with often. I made ten first ascents with some of them. And I climbed dozens of first ascents with my brother Günther. On the eight-thousanders, I eventually cut the expeditions down to just a few people. And they were almost always the same: Oswald "Bulle" Oelz, Wolfgang "Wolfi" Nairz, Gottfried "Friedl" Mutschlechner, Hans Kammerlander. And Peter Habeler, of course.

berg: Am I wrong, or do you not talk much in your books about the partners you rope up with in the mountains—apart from your brother?

RM: I write in detail about my climbing partners. They were important to me when I was out and about. And in the stories I told afterward. I would ask you to go back and read these chapters. Why are my climbing partners Kammerlander and Habeler still the best-known mountaineers in the German-speaking world today?

berg: Because they're good?

RM: Because they were outstanding, and I pointed this out. They featured in my books and talks. But stories of evil friends who forget their pals sell well. I know journalists who play the "Messner-grabs-it-all" card, without even reading the book about the story.

berg: OK, let's talk about your bonds in a real and figurative sense. I'm thinking the first one was with your father. You once said that he raised you and your brothers like cattle. Was the bond to your father more important on the mountain than in real life?

RM: Yes, but there were reasons for that. We lived in a narrow-minded valley. The rules were made by the priest and the mayor, and it was normal for children to work for their families. My father was strict, he was a teacher in the valley. Yet in summer, from the age of five, we were allowed to go to the Gschnagenhardt Alm, the most beautiful alpine pasture in the Dolomites. From where we went climbing.

Up there, the world was a different place. It was like being part of a clan. It seemed like priests, mayors, and teachers all ceased to exist. Up there, the cliché that the mountain meant freedom was true. After all, mountaineering means being responsible and swapping all freedom for responsibility.

berg: What do you remember of tours with your father?

RM: They were good. In fact, very good, because he encouraged me. When I was ten or twelve years old, he took me up the Grosse Fermeda, on grade III and grade IV tours, to the Villnösser Turm. We had a hemp rope and mountain boots of the type worn back then. Later, we added a hammer and a few pitons. At fourteen, he let me lead. That made me confident. My climbing instincts evolved as a result. When I was thirteen or fourteen, he watched my solo ascent on the Kleine Fermeda south face, which was a grade IV route.

berg: You made your peace with your father?

RM: Definitely. I've made my peace with everyone. I don't hold grudges. I expect the same solidarity from the people I partner with.

berg: You described your brother Günther, who died in an accident on Nanga Parbat, as the best person imaginable to be roped up with on a mountain. What made him so special compared to others?

RM: Peter Habeler was clearly a better climber, better than both of us. Peter was two years older than me and four years older than Günther, which was a big advantage at that age. Günther had started working and had less time to climb than I did. I always led when it was just the two of us. But he had stamina and was a partner who gave his all. Also, because we were brothers, we knew each other inside out.

berg: You climbed the Gasherbrum peaks, Mount Everest, and other mountains without bottled oxygen with Peter Habeler. What sets him apart?

RM: When it comes to climbing and mountaineering, Peter Habeler is ingenious. Because he started early and often went off on his own, he has instincts that only people who have grown up in the mountains have.

berg: Let's talk about some other positive things. What was so special about your bond with Hans Kammerlander?

RM: Like Peter, he developed his instincts at a young age and learned to survive. And he was in peak fitness.

berg: Would you call your long-standing partnership with Kammerlander a friendship?

RM: I wouldn't describe my climbing partners as friends. They're akin to marriages of convenience. Sometimes, we got friendly, but that feeling dissipated over time. After climbing several eight-thousanders and hiking all around South Tyrol, I asked Hans if he wanted to go to Antarctica with me. I told him he would only have to learn how to navigate. He said: "No. Not interested." But we parted with a feeling of mutual respect. And not at odds with one another.

berg: Hans Kammerlander takes a slightly different view. He believes you can only entrust your life to a friend.

RM: If you want to know more about camaraderie and the bonds between climbers, then read my book about Willo Welzenbach [*Der Eispapst: Die Akte Welzenbach*, available in German only]. The between-the-wars version of camaraderie was a scandal.

berg: Historically, the notion of a *Seilschaft* (rope team) suggested a bond and camaraderie until death. Which clearly bothers you.

RM: Yes, that's true. Because it's a deception. Welzenbach was the most important mountaineer of the 1920s and 1930s. And we're talking worldwide. His companions tried to break him. Paul Bauer, who had done long tours with him, sought out the minister to say that Welzenbach wasn't "capable of camaraderie." Take the story of Erwin Schneider on Nanga Parbat or Heinrich Harrer at the "50 Years of the Eiger North Face" celebrations in Grindelwald, where he just kept repeating how important the "rope team" was—these are lessons on the cliché of camaraderie.

berg: Do you enter into these sorts of climbing partnerships just as a means to an end?

RM: No, I've stayed friends with a few mountaineers, such as with Oswald "Bulle" Oelz, for over fifty years now.

berg: The Nepalese are now also very successful in the high mountains. Does Nirmal Purja's first winter ascent of K2 still count as alpinism?

RM: Definitely. First of all, he climbed all eight-thousanders in seven months—

berg: But with oxygen. And some mountaineers don't believe that he did K2 in winter without oxygen.

RM: Supplemental oxygen is a trifle compared to preparing the route. Preparing the route makes the ascent so much easier whether oxygen is used or not. Today, oxygen masks are a secondary consideration. Oxygen has been part of these undertakings since 1922. One of the reasons why "conquering" the big eight-thousanders was possible in the first place was that people learned how to use oxygen equipment. If someone does it without—okay. However if someone climbs a mountain, but then says, look at me, no oxygen! I have to laugh. Climbing a prepared route is much easier both mentally and physically, and because you can just follow the other climbers in front of you in single file.

berg: Nirmal Purja only started mountaineering four years ago.

RM: He's not a traditional mountaineer either. He has realized a goal on the eight-thousanders that no European has attempted. Then he successfully climbed K2 in winter, something that twenty previous expeditions, some of which had a lot of resources behind them, had not achieved.

berg: You don't exactly shy away from the media. Is your relationship with the media a bit like a climbing partnership? After all, they helped you to become famous and ultimately reach the fourteen eight-thousanders.

RM: Oh, definitely. In the beginning, magazines even paid for our stories. That's now passé.

berg: With hindsight, would you describe yourself as a good partner in the mountains?

RM: Sepp Mayerl first taught me how to build anchors and belay. Sometimes I've been lucky, true, but I've never lost a partner because I wasn't belaying properly.

43

AMBIVALENT TESTIMONIAL

Art must give what nature does not have.

—painter Joseph Anton Koch

The Covid-19 pandemic threw something of a wrench in the works. I was stuck in Munich with my wife, Diane, who is from Luxembourg. As a South Tyrolean and Italian citizen, I wasn't allowed to return to my home and could no longer visit friends. The museums, now run by my daughter Magdalena, had to stay closed for a long time (perhaps too long). I don't want to talk about what were deemed to be sensible rules in Europe in this respect. Shops, malls, restaurants, bars, and gyms—anything commercial—were allowed to stay open. But anything associated with arts and culture, such as museums, galleries, cinemas, theaters, and concert halls, had to close.

During the pandemic, people got more selfish and less empathetic. My attempt to find a solution to the dispute with the DAV (German Alpine Club) had failed. And my willingness to act as an unpaid ambassador for South Tyrolean wine during this critical time was torpedoed by the IDM (Innovation, Development, and Marketing), of all organizations, which was tasked with promoting South Tyrol as a brand.

Founded in 2007, the South Tyrol Wine consortium is a platform for marketing and promoting the image of South Tyrolean viticulture. It's an association of regional winery cooperatives, South Tyrolean wineries, and independent winegrowers.

During the pandemic, wine sales collapsed due to the lockdown and the crisis in the hospitality industry. Still, our IDM commissioned an advertising agency to check whether I was a suitable ambassador for South Tyrolean wine.

The conclusion, on the German- and Italian-language South Tyrolean *salto* news portal in October 2020, was that:

> Reinhold Messner is ambivalent testimonial material. Some of his seemingly attractive features also harbor risks. The all-encompassing focus on his persona as an extreme mountain athlete is in danger of overshadowing everything else.

And it continued:

> Reinhold Messner is a household name on the German market with an extremely high profile in a target group relevant to South Tyrolean wine.
>
> His fame and media presence, which appear positive initially, do entail a risk that he is already too easily available to the German media. The trick with brand ambassadors is to strike just the right balance between making yourself known and making yourself scarce. The more sought-after

> a personality and the less frequently they are available to the media, the greater the chance that the media will report on the person in an advertising context. However, the more often the person is available without any link to the advertising message, the less willing the media are to report on the brand.

Apart from the fact that these types of analyses usually reflect the client's wishes and can be interpreted ambivalently, I wonder who was pulling the strings in South Tyrol. However, by then, I was old enough to come to terms with my image. And, despite the resistance, I ended up taking part in the advertising campaign. I was delighted to receive a few crates of wine in return, which I enjoyed with Diane.

Back then, I was also thinking foremost about how to preserve traditional alpinism with our Messner Mountain Heritage start-up.

UNESCO in 2019 listed alpinism as an intangible cultural heritage, responding to alpine associations from France, Switzerland, and Italy who had submitted the application. I wondered what type of alpinism they meant.

On International Mountain Day, December 11, 2019, UNESCO declared alpinism a tradition worthy of protection. It defines alpinism as follows: ". . . the art of climbing up summits and walls in high mountains, in all seasons, in rocky or icy terrain." In addition to the requisite technical and intellectual skills, it emphasizes the ethical and aesthetic aspects of this mountaineering tradition that originated in the Alps. This includes the sense of team spirit, as symbolized by the rope connecting the alpinists, the mutual assistance they provide each other, and the ability to take responsibility for their own actions. But it also embraces the ecological approach of leaving no trace of your presence on the mountains. This explains traditional alpinism. It draws on the narrative of 250 years of mountaineering and the notion of heading out into the wild.

Sport climbing was included for the first time at the 2021 Summer Olympic Games. The arena was the Aomi Urban Sports Park on an artificial island in the Aomi district, Kōtō ward, in Tokyo Bay.

The men and women's competitions included speed climbing, bouldering, and lead climbing. Some twenty athletes were allowed to take part in each event, with a maximum of two from each nation. After qualifying, six athletes reached the final round. Adam Ondra, probably the best sport climber in the world at the time, was the favorite in the men's category. This was quite an achievement since he was older than most of the other climbers, which put him at a disadvantage in sport climbing—a monkey-like race up an artificial structure.

This type of climbing—in an air-conditioned space, on artificial structures—is a fabulous sport. But it is not traditional mountaineering. Neither is climbing Mount Everest on a prepared route.

Some influencers like to claim that anything's possible if you believe in it. That's what it says in the coaching manual too, but this doesn't apply to alpinism. Because what alpinism definitely is *not* is: "The triumph of human will over the forces of nature." It is about surviving in places not meant for human beings.

After his Everest expedition in 2018, the Nepalese Nirmal Purja (known as Nims), a Gurka, or elite soldier in the British Army, decided to climb all fourteen eight-thousanders within a year. He left the army and renounced his pension entitlements to take a big risk on what he called his Project Possible. So, he must have been pretty sure of what he was doing. He then proceeded to climb Everest and Lhotse in one day, Makalu two days later, and the four Karakoram eight-thousanders as well as Nanga Parbat within three weeks. He sometimes used bottled oxygen and where available followed prepared routes of commercial expeditions. He always had support from a handful of Sherpa crews accompanying him. He did everything as announced. He made no secret of the helicopter flights he took between the base camps either. His followers watched as Nirmal pulled off the venture with determination, perseverance, and, ultimately, diplomatic skill. Many people from the West had talked about the idea of managing all fourteen 8,000-meter mountains within a year. But nobody had ever tackled them. And this Gurka from Nepal did it in seven months.

It's true that mountaineering is again changing. Climbing is now an Olympic discipline; indoor climbing on artificial holds is a fantastic, booming sport measurable in terms of difficulty grades, elapsed time in seconds, and height in meters. Trad alpinism is what Alex Honnold does—as well as free soloing the walls of El Capitan in Yosemite Valley. Free soloing is an art that, currently, only he has mastered to this degree. It's a fascinating discipline of alpinism, but with few imitators—fortunately.

Today, the many tourists who climb the world's most famous mountain peaks—Mount Everest, Aconcagua, Kilimanjaro, Mont Blanc—on commercial expeditions and organized routes are at least prepared to attempt the ascent.

Whereas Jost Kobusch, who not only forgoes supplementary oxygen, rope partners, and Sherpa help, in the end doesn't attempt the summit either.

His "classic form of mountaineering by fair means, with its close-up, deep-flow experiences, and rebirth at the end" is skillful PR. And there's nothing wrong with that. He's more of an influencer than an alpinist. Traditional mountaineering, however, is not about big announcements and click rates. It is about attitude and action.

44

MY LAST EXPEDITION

My attitude is to love life, to accept adversity, and not to fear death.

—Reinhold Messner

At the age of seventy-five, I found myself facing a void once again. I had been driven out of the family. I had already realized most of my dreams. And now I had only old age to look forward to. Looking back on a successful life does not carry you forward. On the contrary, it's our daydreams that motivate us in the here and now that make a successful life possible.

I accepted my new situation—it had nothing to do with fate—and spent a year living as a bachelor and a hermit in the attic of Juval Castle.

In my hermitage was Elton John's album *A Single Man* and Kris Kristofferson's book *The Pilgrim*, the first biography I'd ever read. And Milarepa, the Tibetan siddha, with his wisdom, was there too—"my religion is to live and die without regrets."

Ultimately, it was my attitude to life that saw me through. I did not respond with defiance, or anger, but with calm. Salvation came in the person of a young woman. We met, hesitant at first, established a common language, and then fell in love and became a couple.

With Diane at my side—she can do everything I'm bad at—I started going back to the mountains. Our shared dreams took us to Nepal, Bhutan, and Ethiopia. Shortly before the pandemic, we climbed the highest mountain in the region, and founded a fledgling business enterprise, MMH (Messner Mountain Heritage). We set up home, and built a nest in Sulden, a mountain village in South Tyrol at the foot of the Ortler. It lies directly below the north face I had climbed sixty years previously.

Diane walked quickly, fleet of foot, and soon became confident—her movements emphasized her beauty. I had found the right partner. And she wanted to stay with me. How lucky I was!

Living alone as you get older just accentuates the ageing process. How grateful I am to be able to share my ideas, and to join in Diane's innate curiosity.

We soon found that we both had more opportunities than we could have wished for. There were requests for lectures, film productions, and book contracts. We quickly realized that less is more.

With her youthful enthusiasm, Diane took me with her—on trips, to international debates, to projects beyond my horizons. At last, someone to motivate *me*, after all these decades where I was the motivator of others.

Approachability and sociability have never been my strong points. Diane was good with people, and she knew how to involve them, to bring them into our world.

Back in South Tyrol, this also created more closeness, more than I had experienced for decades. I could finally start to forget all the criticism and headwinds I had faced. I was able to make suggestions for a future where I would not face opposition and resistance. South Tyrol, my *Heimat*, could become my responsibility, not an opponent to constantly fight.

The following extract is from an interview I gave to *ff* in 2020:

ff: You're an ambassador for South Tyrol now more than ever, according to IDM, the agency for economic and business development. What does that mean?

RM: I'm an ambassador for and a defender of South Tyrol's autonomy. I enjoy the role, though it would seem that our work is still ignored locally and hushed up by our monopolized media.

ff: What visions are there for South Tyrol when it comes to tourism?

RM: I would like to see parking spaces built into the mountains in the valleys heavily frequented by tourists. People could then continue their onward journeys by train or shuttle bus. This works really well in winter. Bike tourism has great potential, we should be doing more to support this logistically. Sustainability has become the big issue. Talking of sustainability, there's a few other things I could tell you about. . . .

ff: Please do.

RM: I'm not happy with my Museum in the Clouds on Monte Rite in the province of Belluno, because it's outside of South Tyrol's borders.

ff: Since when have borders posed a problem for such a cosmopolitan as Reinhold Messner?

RM: I'm not talking parochial nationalism here—I'm talking about practical details. From a PR point of view, it's not easy to communicate that we have five museums in South Tyrol, but one outside. People think, what does he mean outside? I've been looking for a new location for some time now. Now there's an opportunity in Sexten, where the Helm cable car is being dismantled. Tourism entrepreneur Franz Senfter and I believe that the mountain station could be left intact and upcycled—to make something useful out of something currently useless. It wouldn't take much to transform the building into a cultural center or museum. Demolishing it would be a waste. Instead it could become a building with an incredible view, where you would see that it once was a cable car station. The proposal, however, to reclassify the area as a cultural zone was turned down by the authorities. For not being sustainable enough! We feel that this project would offer a long-term, sustainable solution with considerable cultural added value.

ff: Seriously?

RM: If this project is not sustainable, then I don't understand the meaning of the word.

ff: Your museum plans always seem to encounter resistance.

RM: Yes, it all started with Juval Castle and the glass roof. It took ten years for people to recognize that it was more sustainable to install a glass roof than to be continuously repairing the castle walls. I fought for five years to start a museum at Sigmundskron Castle—until I was able to start it with the support of the provincial governor Luis Durnwalder. Otherwise, it would have been left to run to ruin.

ff: You've spent your whole life working for South Tyrol. . . .

RM: Perhaps you understand now why I ask for solidarity.

ff: Let's look a bit further afield—over the parapet, as it were. The coronavirus pandemic has had a positive effect in at least one respect, it has helped to broaden our views. How should we be promoting South Tyrol from now on?

RM: We need to learn how to tell our story better. Storytelling is just as important as nice hotel rooms. There are many South Tyroleans who don't possess a narrative. They fail to tell the story of this place: their village, their local region, their house. I provide structure and context when it comes to the mountains. It's not enough just to put a viewing platform on top of a mountain and assume that's all there is to it, like we did in Schnalstal/ Val Senales.

ff: What do you mean when you talk about your "final expedition"?

RM: The concept involves a journey around the world. The idea is to organize a festival over several days in selected cities. With press conferences, public discussions, in a similar way to what I do here at the Messner Mountain Museum Firmian (Sigmundskron Castle) with our "discussions around the fire." There will be films and a talk about preserving traditional alpinism with which I mean to pass on my mountain heritage.

ff: Do you mean your personal mountaineering heritage?

RM: I'm talking about the heritage of traditional alpinism that is in danger of being lost. Because pure sport climbing, particularly at the climbing wall or gym, has become more and more important. Climbing has become an Olympic sport—and that's a good thing—but sport climbing has nothing to do with alpinism. What is happening on Everest or on the Matterhorn is tourism, not mountaineering in the classic sense. To organize these festivals, I've founded a new company—Messner Mountain Heritage. There are already enquiries from St. Petersburg, Moscow, and Japan, and America will follow. It's going to be my last "expedition."

ff: What exactly is this heritage?

RM: Alpinism started in the Alps 250 years ago. Since then, it has grown into a tradition and an attitude. My topic is the story of how this happened—its history, philosophy, narrative, and vision.

Mountains are more than piles of stones. They are more than rock, ice, storm, and wind. Mountains are symbols of the sublime—and they deserve our respect.

45

MISSED THE SUMMIT?

Reinhold Messner, the first person to climb all fourteen eight-thousanders without oxygen, is to be stripped of his world record because he stopped five meters below the true summit of Annapurna, but thought that he had reached his goal.

—*Schweizer Bund* newspaper

What can I say? I think it's completely wrong. He did it! He was first! Without him, we wouldn't be where we are today. When he climbed all fourteen summits forty, fifty years ago, no one would have been able to or dared to do this, perhaps not for another hundred years. These days we get flown in by helicopter, they bring us up quite high, and then we start climbing. Back then, he didn't even have a proper weather report.

—Mingma David Sherpa, December 2, 2023

For some years now, a chronicler from the small southern German city of Lörrach has been saying that numerous attempts made on the eight-thousanders did not actually reach the summit. According to Eberhard Jurgalski, I was five meters short of the summit of Annapurna. On a flat, corniced summit ridge. If he was hoping that his claims would trigger an avalanche among famous mountaineers, this was not the case. So, from that point on, he sold his story by using only my name and finally received some attention. When Jurgalski's evidence was presented in the *Spiegel*, it became immediately clear how the "serious" chronicler was launching his "research" in the media. A corniced summit ridge changes over time—the point I reached at the summit was different to the one marked on the photos. I had described it in sketches to the chronicler.

It was pretty stupid that the photos in the *Spiegel* also mixed up the main summit with the east summit, which is not just a few meters but a kilometer away from the west, or main, summit.

If they made such serious mistakes, how would I be able to trust chroniclers in future? Perhaps the mistakes were made by the magazine? After two months

On the corniced summit ridge

there was still no correction—neither from the "renowned alpine historians" cited nor from the *Spiegel*. As they say, there's no cure for malice, so I decided to keep quiet about it.

In the summer of 2022, I gave an interview to the Swiss-German *Tages-Anzeiger* newspaper where I discussed the whole issue:

T-A: Mr. Messner, the team of chroniclers says that you stopped a few meters short of the summit on Annapurna. This means that you were not the first man to reach the summits of all the eight-thousanders. What happened on Annapurna?

RM: Hans Kammerlander and I exited the northwest face and reached the summit ridge—in high winds and fog. I therefore am really unable to say whether I reached the highest point. I admitted to the team of researchers that I maybe was a few meters west of the highest point. But this is irrelevant.

T-A: Why?

RM: Kammerlander and I had just made an alpine-style first ascent of the hardest face on Annapurna. On the last day of the climb, we got caught in a bad storm but made it up despite the considerable risk. On the summit ridge the wind whipped up by the gale was so strong that we had to fight not to fall off. I won't let anyone tell me that the ascent in 1985 of a nearly 4,000-meter face with what was pretty basic equipment is not valid. Especially as the highest point was not marked. For me, I was at the top—and nobody can take that away from me. These people don't understand that mountaineering has changed enormously.

T-A: You'll have to explain what you mean by that.

RM: The first phase of alpinism was all about conquering. It was all about being the first to reach the highest point of a mountain. In the Alps this phase finished over a hundred years ago. In the Himalaya, it ended in the 1970s.

T-A: Before you had climbed any of the eight-thousanders.

RM: Alpine conquest was never my thing. For me, Annapurna was not about the summit. The summit is just the final bit at the top. I was more interested in climbing big, difficult faces in a particular style.

T-A: Alpine style with minimal equipment, no oxygen, and no fixed ropes. This meant that you could move faster and spend less time in the death zone.

RM: This is why I feel happy with my ascent of Annapurna, totally happy.

T-A: But you wanted to be the first man to have climbed all eight-thousanders. And that was not about the route, but reaching the highest point.

RM: I had never had this idea of a record attempt. If I wanted to be the first to climb all eight-thousanders, why was I selecting hard routes that I might fail on?

T-A: Are you saying that there was no race to complete all these summits, especially with Polish climber Jerzy Kukuczka, who was putting pressure on you and getting closer and closer?

RM: There was this competition whipped up by the media. Two years before Annapurna, I climbed two eight-thousanders for the second time—Gasherbrum I and II. This was my most creative act—an alpine-style double eight-thousander traverse. If I was supposed to be in a race to complete them all, why would I do this?

T-A: You're claiming not to have been a deliberate part of this unofficial competition?

RM: I went along with it, after all I could have decided to do something else. To that extent, I was part of it. But I never started this competition to climb all eight-thousanders. For me, it was mainly about creativity and climbing in a particular style. The competition idea only really became established in the final phase.

T-A: Where does the idea come from of defining everything by the highest point and wanting to create a "number one" in the world in high-altitude mountaineering?

RM: Sport climbing is a competitive sport, and now it's an Olympic sport. For me though, climbing has always been about adventure. You have to know the history of mountaineering to be able to understand my attitude and what we did.

T-A: Tell us more.

RM: For fifty-five years, the best mountaineers tried to climb the eight-thousanders. And they failed. Every single one of them. Then all the eight-thousanders were climbed—within a period of fifteen years. That was the end of it, because there were only fourteen of them. They're countable because there is a finite number. If you take the seven-thousanders, no one could ever climb them all. There are just too many of them. It was always all about the eight-thousanders. However, in the second phase, where I was active, it had less to do with the summit itself and more to do with the route up the mountain. The summit was just one part of it. This approach had established itself to such an extent in the Alps that we were climbing the hardest faces, and were not even bothered about the summits. When we reached the end of the route, we would just abseil back down.

T-A: So it was all about the style of the ascent?

RM: Exactly. The summit became secondary.

T-A: Why were you angry then?

RM: Angry is the wrong word. This controversy has no relation to what we achieved back then. The chroniclers are denying my creativity and trivializing the whole aspect of mountaineering. Mountaineering is an adventure. Adventures are not measurable!

T-A: But these chroniclers are not trying to deny you that. They're just saying that Messner stopped short of the highest point by a few meters, therefore he never stood on the true summit of Annapurna.

RM: So the message is this: Messner may have stood a few meters from the actual peak and about five altitude meters lower, although he thought he was standing at the highest point after the first ascent of a huge face. Five meters compared to 4,000 meters. I think that the comparison is clear. It's laughable.

T-A: That might well be. But you're famous for being first to climb all eight-thousanders. You didn't get all this public recognition for tackling extraordinary routes on the eight-thousanders, the aspect that you say is central to you. Does this perception annoy you?

RM: No, because the climbing scene does give me that recognition. They recognized what I achieved. Yet to this day, the general public does not really understand that new direction in alpinism. It was not then and is not now about conquering; it is about the adventure.

T-A: You've written dozens of books and given many talks on these topics. Did your message fail to get through?

RM: Some people only count up to fourteen, theirs is a narrow vision. Many of my detractors have never even stood on a high mountain. It's important to understand the essence of my books, to empathize with the emotions, to be out in the mountains yourself or to engage intensively with mountaineering.

T-A: So, you would have no problem if the list of mountaineers who climbed all eight-thousanders was to be deleted?

RM: I'm not prepared to play this game. One more thing. Other chroniclers wanted proof from me that I didn't abandon my brother at the summit of Nanga Parbat. It's all so long ago, I can't even remember some of it. But I'm sure that—the same as my colleagues at the time, the other climbers who also reached all the eight-thousand-meter peaks—I never deliberately stopped before the highest point.

T-A: As a comparison, if someone starts a hundred-meter race, but stops at 99.9 meters, then they do not get a hundred-meter time. If you didn't stand at the summit, then you've not been to the top.

RM: We were adventurers, climbing in a natural wilderness where the conditions are different every day, new, and unpredictable. There is no exact measurability in this world of mine. From a historical point of view, it would also be careless to call into question all the first eight-thousander ascents of the 1950s. What is considered the true summit has often changed over the years. I have a question. Where is the summit on Cerro Torre?

T-A: You tell us?

RM: Is it there where the rock face ends? Or is it above this, where the snow ends? On K2 the highest point is buried under ice. It's easiest to know on Mount Everest, the highest point is now marked. In our generation, the most successful mountaineers are the ones who have survived the most difficult ascents. So, I can only laugh about the summit issue.

46

ACCOLADES

Writers whose work criticizes the place they come from have been attacked as traitors. They are accused of anger and rage toward their locality. But a critical stance is a special form of Heimatliebe *(loving where you come from).*

—folklorist Elsbeth Wallnöfer

Accolades are a tribute to age. The kudos that would have been welcome when you're young and facing difficult projects is often only presented to you when you're old. Maybe sometimes accolades are even a form of apology—for previous misconduct or shame?

By now, I've made my peace with South Tyrol and was delighted to receive an honor, which North Tyrol had primarily suggested.

I talked to the *Neue Südtiroler Tageszeitung Online* newspaper about the award in February 2022:

TO: Reinhold, you're going to receive an accolade from the state of Tyrol. What's your response?

RM: I'm quite happy about it because three liberal, relatively social democratic people have also received this offer.

TO: You say "offer"?

RM: Yes, because you're asked if you want to accept the award beforehand. In the past, I often declined. But considering the way things are currently in South Tyrol, this award is a statement. . . .

TO: What do you mean by "the way things are currently"?

RM: I don't feel happy in South Tyrol at the moment. I can see that the region is falling apart. As a minority, we have it tougher than other democracies. I'm an old man living in seclusion—due to the pandemic—watching the world go by.

TO: You didn't think for a moment about not accepting the award?

RM: No, because the accolade is also a statement in favor of the state governor—

TO: Arno Kompatscher is currently under huge pressure—

RM: Because the *Dolomiten* newspaper is giving him hell? No, I don't think he's under pressure, as Kompatscher's excellent ratings in the polls show. In the past, someone who was penalized by Athesia media was finished.

TO: Do you think so?

RM: Nobody has been treated as badly as Kompatscher and his followers by the *Dolomiten* for a long time. People grasp that the provincial governor has integrity. I have nothing against Athesia. . . .

TO: But what then?

RM: I'm against the quasi-media monopoly and the way it has been utilized for fifty years.

TO: Are the awards for the journalist and politician Lilli Gruber, the writer Joseph Zoderer, and you a tribute to a different kind of South Tyrol?

RM: In the 1980s, the three of us and Alexander Langer took a different view. I went to Innsbruck without any desire to settle old scores during the awards ceremony. Although the vice-chairman of the South Tyrolean heritage association and an Athesia author brought up old prejudices that were fueled by the *Tageszeitung* newspaper.

Meinrad Berger's and Günther Rauch's comments were published in the *Dolomiten* readers' letters in February 2022:

> Accolades should not be employed for exchanging blows. If the virtually hourly incendiary statements by Reinhold Messner (a former sympathizer of the radical left-wing Lotta Continua organization) against the "monopoly press in South Tyrol" aired on February 18, 2022, by public broadcaster RAI South Tyrol are anything to go by, it's obvious that the ceremony in Innsbruck is going to be hijacked to do battle. There's no other explanation for Governor Arno Kompatscher's own decision (according to yesterday's *Dolomiten*, ". . . personally and not, as is usually the case, at the suggestion of the Tyrolean Provincial Institute") to present the Tyrolean award to three quite uncontroversial personalities from the far left. Which has

nothing to do with the actual purpose of presenting Tyrolean accolades. In this case, the focus is on falsified historical misrepresentation and provocation. We can't help but be left with the impression that all too familiar, nostalgic, left-wing-influenced circles are trying to exploit the ceremony to get back at publishing house Athesia in an unprecedentedly treacherous manner. Which is not the intention behind the Tyrolean awards. This is nonsense.

47

"WHINY WIMPS"

Set the bird's wings in gold and it will never soar again in the sky.

—polymath Rabindranath Tagore

I'm part of the Boomer generation. Born at the end of the war and having grown up in modest circumstances, I witnessed how European prosperity has grown, right up until today. When we Boomers became the enemy of young people, who call us "irresponsible, wasteful, self-satisfied"—I tried to put things into perspective.

We Boomers created much of the prosperity that Generation Z is now using to accuse us of being collectively guilty for global warming and climate change. Values such as creativity, peaceful coexistence, and hard work are ridiculed as cases of risk minimization.

We were prepared to take responsibility, contribute to society, be innovative and inventive, pay a lot of taxes, and to fill up social security coffers. Was this generational justice or foresight? All that, and now we have to talk to robots in our dotage?

When asked whether nature was now taking revenge for what we have done, I told the *Neue Südtiroler Tageszeitung* newspaper in October 2022:

> No, nature's not taking revenge. Nature is just there and has no goals. We human beings have objectives, so only we can make mistakes. Of course, global warming can be traced back to the Age of Enlightenment and industrialization, which enabled mankind to produce and design in a completely different way than in the past.
>
> We had the chance to use cheap fossil fuels, which led to widespread prosperity over the last 200 years, including here in South Tyrol.
>
> Of course, way earlier, we should have started mitigating the damage done. The Club of Rome predicted early on that it would be hard to fix the damage. But there was still cheap energy, conveyor belts were running, and the industrial revolution worked, which is how today's wealth was created.

> And now young people who have grown up in this prosperity are saying that the previous generation was a criminal one! And yet it's *this* generation that's allowed young people to skip school on Fridays to protest!

In an open letter, the director of the heritage association, Florian Trojer, and three other authors responded with harsh criticism. The gist of their message was that I had reproached the Fridays for Future activists for being "whiny wimps." My comments were not to be left unchallenged. Here's their open letter:

> Old white men like Reinhold Messner (and us, even if not quite so old) tend to reshape reality to fit their own world view. And they tend to throw a tantrum if someone says as much.
>
> Just like a young child throwing its toys out of the pram, or old white men lashing out to avoid taking any responsibility. Which is exactly what happened in an interview with Reinhold Messner and his wife in the *Dolomiten* on September 26. During the interview, Messner calls all young people, including those from Fridays for Future, whiny wimps. He goes on to say that they come from a position of privilege and yet are trying to make the older generation, to which Reinhold Messner and we belong, take the blame for climate change without taking any responsibility themselves.
>
> However, this view has a tiny flaw. It's not today's young people who benefitted most from the economic upturn of previous decades and the efforts of past generations, but we, white old men in Western countries. We're the privileged ones who have only experienced booming economies our whole lives. And we have another advantage, which we're still exploiting to the full right up until today. We dumped our waste on future generations without further ado or taking responsibility. As a result, we've consumed more land than the whole of the human race before us, destroyed more biodiversity than ever before, and caused climate change, for example by flying around the world to climb mountains.
>
> Which is why we should follow the examples of the young activists from Fridays for Future. We need to step up via activism, raising awareness, and taking action, instead of just claiming that we're being patronized.

> Signed by,
> Georg Kaser, climate researcher
> Thomas Egger, Climate Club South Tyrol
> Josef Oberhofer, Nature and Environmental Protection Organization
> Florian Trojer, director South Tyrol Heritage Association

This is my response in an interview, again with the *Neue Südtiroler Tageszeitung* newspaper, which I have revised and updated:

> South Tyrol also has its share of frustrated thinkers who turn my interviews into the opposite of what I said. This has been going on for thirty years, but is now becoming virulent again. It's also about envy among intellectuals. . . .
>
> They call me a "jealous god" and my museum nothing but a tourist attraction.
>
> I'm interested in content. In the case of the heritage association, I wonder just what they've achieved? What have they done for South Tyrol? And the language they use—I would never say "whiny wimps."
>
> When Juval Castle was to be given a glass roof, local conservationists accused me of destroying Juval. However, Juval had already been left to deteriorate. The heritage office approved a permit to fit a new glass roof. This was followed by a campaign against the roof. But, in the end, who saved Juval? Neither the state, nor the heritage association, but me.
>
> Peter Ortner, then chairman of the local heritage organization, also went public dozens of times to torpedo my idea. I wanted to turn Sigmundskron into something of value. The governor, Luis Durnwalder, picked up on this. In response to a Europe-wide call for proposal bids, nobody else had the courage to submit a project.
>
> The aim was to fill Sigmundskron with meaning, to run it with my own resources and without public subsidies. The local heritage association didn't submit any project. Perhaps they lacked the courage to refurbish the ruins, which had been left to fall apart for five hundred years?
>
> I have nothing to criticize the Fridays for Future movement for. I'd like to talk to their representatives who ventured into the public eye and sought debate. I share many of their views and they are right about many things. But I don't think it's enough to skip school on Fridays. Just protesting is of

little use. It would be better for young people to go to university, conduct research, learn, and develop technologies to counteract environmental problems. If anyone can save the world, it's the researchers, the smartest minds. And then we all have to cut back and curb what's taken the upper hand—consumption.

My wife, Diane, and I developed some approaches to the problem in a book called *Sinnbilder—Verzicht als Inspiration für ein Gelingendes Leben* (Renunciation as Inspiration for a Successful Life), which shows how doing without can improve the world.

48

UP AND AWAY

Every cultural initiative should be welcomed, even if it only serves to promote tourism. Like the Hadid-Messner museum on the Kronplatz.

—Klaus Gasperi, South Tyrolean theater director, stage designer, and polemicist

I don't think there can be any other place where different landscapes intertwine so closely as on the Gschnagenhardt Alm in the upper Villnöss/Funes valley, where my small alpine hut rests. The pastures, paths, and woods are shaped by man, while the pale towers of the Dolomites rise above them, at the mercy of the forces of nature for millions of years. Today I know that it is these contrasts—between natural landscapes and cultivated landscapes—that have shaped me and my view of the world, since my earliest childhood. There would be no meadows, mountain pastures, or forest edges in front of my hut if they had not been mowed, grazed, and managed for centuries. There would be none either if man had neglected landscape conservation or lost respect for the primeval landscape.

I have lived my dreams, and now they have become memories. The images are often superimposed and shared with a young love. What more could I ask for? So, I cannot be disappointed anymore, I think.

Sure, I've been lucky a few times. Lucky in the sense of fortunate. But I've also grown in the face of resistance by learning to overcome obstacles—whether high rock faces or my being misunderstood. I've grown because I dared to get better and better, in my own way.

The things I did were rarely exceptional, but sharing them with others today creates meaning and brings happiness. Especially when love is involved. Losing love is like falling into the void; finding it again is being lifted up.

My semi-nomadic existence caught up with me late in life and left me asking—what now? Losing your family in your mid-seventies is a bitter thing and the suffering it has caused is real.

We each of us retell our lives and reinvent our pasts, usually without even realizing it. This is the story of my life, and that story contains both truth and fiction. Sometimes the reshaping and reinterpreting is the product of wishful thinking motivated by ideals: as if our lives ought to make sense, at least in retrospect. We always look for reasons for our behavior. We seek a narrative over the course of our lives. But if you want to be able to look back on a successful life, it's too late to wait to do it only when you get older.

What keeps me young and active is living a successful life in the here and now, not analyzing how I became what I am. The way I see myself has little to do with fate. Contradictions and coincidences have played a role, but so has having the courage to dare.

In June 2022, I answered a series of questions on this for the *Berliner Zeitung*:

BZ: Would you rather have lived in a different era?

RM: No. My generation had some real adventures! Unfortunately, these are disappearing, because everything is being made safe these days. There is hardly any wilderness left. Every point of this planet has been recorded by satellites, seen, and made accessible.

BZ: Instead, we now experience adventures through high-risk sports.

RM: But this has less to do with adventure and more to do with the adrenaline kick. The way I see it, adventures mean heading into the wilderness. It's not about breaking records, or speed ascents, it's solely about surviving.

BZ: On your first eight-thousander tour, you had heavy, 5-kilo radio telephones. Don't you wish you'd had today's modern technology with you, for example when you were fighting to get your brother Günther down alive?

RM: We would have used modern technology, no question. However, I had a set of basic principles. I would not use bottled oxygen and masks, drilled bolts for protection, strong drugs, or modern communication tools. This is what I call simplified, fast, and light alpinism.

BZ: How do you feel about the use of stimulants, such as methamphetamines, in alpinism?

RM: In my time, these products were frowned upon, they could be dangerous on the mountain. If you don't make it down in time, you're dead. If my brother and I had taken these substances on Nanga Parbat, we both would have died.

BZ: You also call for alpinism without bottled oxygen.

RM: These days the routes are prepared with fixed ropes. That's an even bigger help, and it also means that you can climb at night. You just hold on to the ropes. With a headtorch, even if you can only see ten meters in front of you, that's enough.

BZ: How have your own courage and fears changed over the decades?

RM: These days I don't climb difficult routes anymore. I always needed good reserves of courage, to overcome my fears. I knew that I could die in the mountains. With self-assuredness, experience, control, and courage, you overcome a lot of your fears even with minimal equipment. But there is always a certain amount of fear that remains. And there are always unpredictable elements, such as the weather or rockfall from an earthquake. These days, virtually no one climbs a mountain without having the option to be able to call a helicopter in an emergency.

BZ: You also have responsibility not just as an alpinist, but also as a father. How has your attitude changed in this regard?

RM: The things I have done were irresponsible toward my parents. I couldn't justify the risks associated with high-altitude mountaineering in terms of my own family either. But it was the way I lived my life, and I stand by it. In addition to shouldering our responsibilities, we have the right to lead our own lives.

BZ: And what does your life look like now?

RM: I've founded a project together with Diane, my third wife, to tell the story of traditional mountaineering around the world. This is to leave something behind that goes beyond what I have experienced and learned. I want to pass on a *Haltung* (a frame of mind, a view of life) that could shape the relationship between people and mountains.

BZ: Have you ever been in a climbing gym?

RM: Climbing gyms have turned climbing into a popular sport. But they are not a new form of mountaineering. Mountaineering involves engaging with nature, not with plastic holds on an artificial wall. I say, we need to head out into nature!

BZ: Have you ever thought about retiring? It's hard to imagine you no longer doing anything in public.

RM: I've owned a tiny wooden cabin on an alpine pasture in the Dolomites for fifty-two years. It's the most beautiful place in the world. I'm currently in the process of making the energy supply self-sufficient. One

> day I will sit up there with my wife and watch the stars. There's a big age difference between Diane and myself. This means that we have a big responsibility toward each other in more ways than one.

I've often sat on the wooden bench on the balcony outside my cabin on the Gschnagenhardt Alm, listening to the wilderness stored deep inside me. The Geisler Peaks stand in the slanting light of the afternoon sun, and I know that the world of my childhood will never return. The stone pines, the light-colored cirque above, the silhouettes of the Dolomite towers each look different than they used to. They are no longer the same. I have stood on those summits so many times. I overcame so many difficulties and dangers up there, as I did in the Himalaya later on too. But my longing for the future has given way to a desire to start to take leave.

I've had enough. Enough of resisting, enough of overcoming resistance and fighting the headwinds, enough of dealing with the countless attempts by society to keep me from realizing my dreams. For the rest of my life, I never want to have to stand up to critics or defend myself again. Not anymore. No.

When the setting sun colors the mountains and the sky, I feel safe and protected. It's not my connection to this place that makes it my *Heimat*, it is not the people here; it is nature.

Years of being marginalized and excluded forced me into isolation. As a result, I became "*der Andere*" (the different one). I am a different person now than the one I was before I set out into the world. I have learned to read nature up in the *Arena der Einsamkeit* (Arena of Loneliness) and nature protected me. Right to the end. As does the young woman who now stands at my side, after my second wife got rid of me.

When I was little, they used to call us valley kids the *Pitzacker Räuber* (Pitzacker Robbers) after the village where we lived. We made our own rules for the games we played. Sometimes I heard farmers refer to us as *Gesindel* (scum) even though they lived and worked under the same skies, in the same woods, and on the same meadows as we did. We weren't used to praise, so it didn't hurt. Later, I was to face far worse accusations and repeated attempts to stop my plans and discredit me. Yes, I found myself on my own from an early age with my projects and later with my dreams.

We were a big, extended family, and the children were mainly left to their own devices. The older children looked after the younger ones. It was only a stone's throw from the village to the stream, and beyond the stream was the forest where we could hide. The higher we went up, the wider the valley became and the farther the horizon receded. As kids we were almost always together, so being completely alone for a moment was a strange feeling, where every step seemed to echo across the forest floor, crying out for justice.

Today I can see that the many obstacles I faced made me pull up stakes and move away. Away from the envy, resentment, and hatred. I only ever learned to take off in a headwind—and in my dreams.

49
AGAINST THE WIND

All museums, especially the world-famous ones in big cities, also serve to promote tourism. Our Messner Mountain Museums and Messner Mountain Heritage employ nature outside and art inside to tell the story of the relationship between human nature and mountain nature.

—Reinhold Messner

My documentary *Mount Everest: The Last Step* received an Austrian film and television Romy award in 2019. During his presentation speech, my friend and climbing partner Christoph Ransmayr portrayed my life as steps "against the wind":

> For a traveler, the very first steps and the very last steps mark the beginning and the end of a journey, whether they lead to a longed-for destination or to death. Given that even a line as the crow flies is a line and not a path and that we are all pedestrians even when we fly by plane, this journey image applies to most of our endeavors. It then appears to us as a path to happiness or the way of the cross.
>
> But how often can we say whether we have actually reached the end of a journey? If we have actually done everything and overcome all the associated hardships to reach one of our goals? Perhaps it might require further attempts and even more willpower to finally reach a place where a moment of peace, or even bliss, awaits us.
>
> One of the few journeys that leaves no room for such doubts, is the journey to the high places, the journey into the mountains.
>
> It is a journey that leads us through time, away from the populated or devastated plains of the present to bare rock and empty ice landscapes, which lie before us just as they did before the Stone Age traveler. Down below, the valley, and with it civilization and progress, disappear beyond the steep rock walls and ravines—as if by disappearing, they had never really existed, and the world had always only consisted of gasping for breath, exhaustion, rock, and ice.

But only routes like these allow us to say, even in a state of deadly fatigue, that we have arrived. At the summit, when the next step would be a step into the void. It's only then and from there that all our thoughts and all our longings lead us back to our loved ones, to a sheltered life or to the fears and threats that await us.

I don't know anyone who knows more about journeys, about precipices, about reading the landscape—and about turning back—than my friend Reinhold Messner. As if anyone who uses *all* his strength to travel into the distance or to a summit, and who is incapable of recognizing the unattainable, would waste his life on mere coordinates. Or end up too exhausted to return home and remain forever in the region of his projected longing.

Reinhold Messner led the way on many of the trips and hikes we shared together in the deserts and mountains of India, Nepal, and Tibet. Through the pack ice of the High Arctic, on the Arabian Peninsula, in South America, Central Africa, and Indochina, and even on the volcanic cones of the South Seas. However, one of the most-unforgettable memories for me is from the route to the summit of the Ortler in South Tyrol. I was still pretty inexperienced with ice axes and crampons at the time, and had hacked my way up a glacier wall tied to the end of his rope more like a woodpecker than a climber.

Messner in a storm

After overcoming the ice wall, Reinhold offered me the lead. I hadn't gone more than thirty paces over the untouched firn when I felt a sudden tug on the rope. All that lay before us was a glistening expanse of white snow under a deep blue sky. "I wouldn't take that next step," Reinhold said, and gently pulled me back toward him.

Standing next to me, he struck the glistening ground with his ice axe. Suddenly, I saw a black flash shooting across the blinding white surface toward me. The firn had camouflaged the glacier. It began to collapse ten or twelve meters in front of us, revealing a fracture line headed right toward us and a bottomless void. It was only one step away.

Anyone who is able to sense, even under immaculate snow, what would be the end of all journeys, and who understands so much about the steps we take, about pausing for thought, and about the laws of knowing when to turn back; who is able to describe all of this to us, in books, talks, and films; that person has already contributed hugely to our experience of reality. And they deserve not just a golden statuette of a film goddess, but also our respect, our admiration, and—from the more emotionally gifted among us—our affection.

Dear Reinhold, the fact that your most recent steps, after so many journeys through the wilderness, have brought you safely to a land governed—or rather, ruled—by barbarians proves that you have lost neither your seventh, eighth, or ninth sense for hidden voids. Nor have you lost your intrepid fearlessness.

On this occasion of your legally binding affinity with a goddess, I wish you what the Tibetans wish each other when they depart and return: *Tashi Delek*. Which, as you know, means "may all good things come to you," both in an inner *and* outer sense.

50

DISCARDED

A woman can love more deeply, but also be crueler than a man.

—Laozi, founder of Taoism

At the end of 2017, my world changed—not the wilderness, but the home to which I had always returned.

It was a few days before Christmas. I was sitting in the kitchen of our family flat in Meran, which I had given to my wife several decades ago, drinking my morning coffee. My wife, Sabine, came in and demanded that I leave our shared home. It sounded like a request, but it was tantamount to an expulsion.

I had little time to object. I was just about to leave to go to Germany for work—to give a talk. I felt the full destructive force of her words, but did not understand them.

The mood in the house before I left—I don't cancel fixed appointments—was like being in a court when the judgement is read out. I neither wanted to hear it nor did I understand it. How would I live on my own? I did not feel desperate or afraid, but my emotions were paralyzed. I pushed the causes and the consequences of being abandoned far away. Thank god the children were all grown up. I had already put the family fortune in their hands.

When I said goodbye and got into the car, it felt like I was being discarded. As I drove northward on the motorway over the Brenner Pass the rawness resonated deep inside me.

After traveling from South Tyrol to Munich, I phoned the eldest of our three children. She reassured me that everything would be fine.

I was seventy-three years old. I had made provisions, especially for my family, and for the most part I had already shared out my inheritance. Anna, my youngest daughter, was to have Juval Castle, although I still had a right of residence there.

Back in Meran, there was not much more to discuss. I was to leave the family flat by the beginning of April. I had to leave my art collection there and head off to take care of myself.

It was winter. I drove to Juval in heavy snowfall to make the small flat in the attic ready to live in, before traveling to Nepal with my teammates from the 1978 Everest Expedition. When I returned, I moved into a little-used section of the castle. Access to it involved a slight risk of falling.

I'm sure that the people who knew me well thought that I would be fine alone. That I would cope with isolation and solitude as I've always done. The kids thought, Dad has survived far worse situations. But they forgot that I was also feeling the effects of ageing. My senses were duller, I was less vigorous, and my strength—both physical and mental—was starting to fade.

Initially, as a single man, I carried on as I had before. I traveled, gave talks, and climbed mountains here and there. With my family soon dispersed, only memories remained. Harmony has always been important to me—I suffered most from the loss of the children.

My sister and my brothers stood by me. They refused to let themselves be used. We had always stood together and supported each other, as our parents and grandparents had done.

Yes, Sabine had been against my museum project right from the start; it had consumed all my focus for decades. And yes, I was often away on expeditions for months on end: no easy thing for any partner to deal with—all the loneliness, fear, and insecurities brought on by that.

I took to the mountains and in their solitude looked for a new purpose in life. The tragedy on Nanga Parbat had taught me to cope with life and death without regrets. Through the few near-death experiences I've faced over the years, I had learned not to dwell on the past, and instead to accept the here and now as the only possible way forward. And so, we got divorced.

Eight months after the final farewell, I met Diane. During our first date, I asked her if she could cook. It didn't put her off and we started dating. It took some time before we became lovers. But we have remained a couple to this day, although Diane was increasingly ostracized by some in my family.

51

IN LOVE

Together, just the two of us.

—Diane Messner

Diane is from Luxembourg. She has a grown-up son, comes from a modest background, like me, and can do everything that I can't. Where would I be without her? Me, the internet refusenik, the invalid with zero fashion sense. I'm not exaggerating. She's turned our home into a warm nest with candles and incense. Our walks together are romantic outings.

Diane loves her dog Flint, whom I now call Flintolino. And she loves me, looks after me, cooks for me, and accompanies me. She's thirty-six years younger than me and takes care of our household and business ventures.

Some people might assume that she lives a life of luxury. Not so; she met me as an impoverished adventurer. I was "Reinhold with the empty pockets"—who had already handed over his goods and possessions to the next generation, and done it before he had to give up his habits. I was never that interested in owning things. I was more interested in doing things, of putting ideas into practice. Diane helps me with this.

And she has this gift too. Developing projects together, spending half the night discussing forms and colors, is one of our shared passions. She is never against things; she's *for* things, for things together with me.

Our love grows in the firelight in the evening, watching the starry skies, with a secret kiss at the reading desk. We do as much as we can together, but withdraw separately to focus on the task at hand if it demands our undivided attention.

If we're apart for a few days, my longing for her grows, my longing for a home. The nightmares of the past have disappeared; my health has improved and with Diane I feel a new zest for life. I often ask myself, what did I do to deserve such attentiveness, devotion, and love?

Diane can lose her temper, but even in anger she is always understanding of my quirks and weaknesses. If I had not been abandoned, I would never

have experienced the happiness that has now come to me in my later years. It is Diane who lifts me up. It's our love that inspires us. To the end of the world.

Will we ever change our ways, stop and slow down? Who knows. There is powerful longing for closeness. And the curiosity remains. We're planning trips that we want to take together, and books that we feel are worth writing. Most of all, we're planning to be together as much as possible. I know what it's like to experience the happiness you feel upon returning to a place of safety after your life has been in danger. To fall into Diane's arms and dance with her through the storm is the very height of happiness. With the wind behind me, in the tornado of love.

52

CENSORSHIP

We alpinists do something that we assume is impossible.

—alpinist Alan Rousseau

In April 2022, the *Neue Südtiroler Tageszeitung Online* ran an article under the headline "Protest against RAI Censorship":

> On Tuesday, March 28, the film *Heimat–die andere Erzählung* (Heimat–the other narrative) was shown at the Mairania cultural center by the Ost West Club Meran. The film directed by Karl Prossliner documents the life of the outstanding South Tyrolean historian Leopold Steurer. However, RAI (Radiotelevisione Italiana) South Tyrol refused the rights to broadcast certain television clips. And sixty-five prominent South Tyrolean cultural representatives protested.

I only played a small role in this debate. But what's interesting is that it shows how censorship is still possible in South Tyrol, even today. The article continues:

> A central part of the film is dedicated to a debate that started in the 1980s, due to Steurer's research into the Option period and deserters during the Second World War, who had since been forgotten. This debate is illustrated in the film when it shows a clip from the television programme *Am runden Tisch* (At the Round Table) by RAI Bolzano from 1982, where Josef Rampold, Reinhold Messner, and Friedl Volgger were guests.
>
> On Tuesday evening, visitors to the film showing in Meran witnessed an extraordinary scene. The film was stopped before the clips in question were shown and the three guests' statements were instead spoken by actors. The film was then resumed.
>
> The reason for this was that RAI South Tyrol has refused to release the rights to the television clips in question. Despite the fact that the film is

> financed by taxpayers' money and remains a subject of considerable public interest, *Heimat–die andere Erzählung* was not shown in its full length.
>
> Since the refusal to release the short debate between Rampold, Messner, and Volgger was not given any justification, it should certainly be regarded as a form of censorship.
>
> Without wishing to go into the fact that this is already a very delicate time for media reporting and its consequences for society, given that RAI South Tyrol considers itself a public service and should certainly see itself as such, we find this intervention extremely serious.

People repeatedly asked me why these television clips could not be shown. I don't know the answer. I also found myself wondering why an agency in Berlin had to be called in to check my suitability as an ambassador for South Tyrol's wine producers. I had offered to appear in an advertising campaign free of charge. Who was the suitability review initiated by? Erwin Hinteregger took responsibility as CEO of IDM (South Tyrol's economic development and tourism agency). But exactly who tried to prevent my involvement at the time, and why they did it, remains a mystery to this day. The same applies to key statements from the press conference at the German Alpine Club museum on Munich's Praterinsel regarding the Nanga Parbat tragedy in 2003. Those statements are still being kept secret.

Erwin Hinteregger, head of IDM, wrote to me:

> Regarding the regrettable incident in connection with your name as ambassador for South Tyrolean wine, IDM made a serious error, for which I take full responsibility.
>
> I would like to sincerely apologize for this mistake. As a public body, IDM is required to investigate and document certain processes. The employee responsible here commissioned what was a completely superfluous market analysis.
>
> South Tyrol is lucky to have Reinhold Messner. South Tyrol could not have a better ambassador to represent South Tyrolean values. He has been communicating the authenticity, quality, essence, and uniqueness of our region all over the world with his high international profile for decades, in a manner that is priceless and apparent for all to see.

> The fact that you agreed to promote the South Tyrolean wine sector free of charge, a sector which has been hit particularly hard by the current crisis, once again demonstrates your magnanimity and humanity. And, especially in these difficult times, our five thousand winegrowers and the whole of South Tyrol is particularly grateful for your support.

I acknowledged his response, but I was not satisfied with his answer.

The German Alpine Club also continues to have a problem with releasing film clips concerning my person. Why is that? Its almost one and a half million members (what an amazing increase) have a right to know. They also have a right to know why I was stopped from using any of the DAV platforms in the past. Lifting this decision did not set the record straight; it just avoided the issue.

In certain societies, you could argue that it is a sign of distinction to fall under censorship. In a democracy, it is tantamount to disenfranchisement.

53

GROUP TOURS IN THE DEATH ZONE

We wake and we sleep. Sometimes our waking hours feel more like a dream. It's hard to understand what we felt up high on Jannu. The three of us relied on the help of so many people to get there and back.

—Alan Rousseau, on the first alpine-style ascent of Jannu's north face, i.e., without bottled oxygen, prior fixed ropes, or porters above base camp

There's only one way to deal with all the conspiracy theories about high-alpine climbing—ignore them. Because insiders use them as a weapon, and outsiders are unable to comprehend what is involved.

Take, for example, the Tyrolean mountain guide Lukas Furtenbach, one of the most successful organizers of group trips to the eight-thousanders. He completely disagrees with me when I try to explain the difference between adventure and tourism in the mountains. He's well aware that it's the infrastructure at Mount Everest—routes prepared in advance, pre-stocked camps, bottled oxygen depots, medical support, Sherpa guides—that makes it possible for paying guests to join the queue to reach this prestigious summit. This has nothing to do with the pioneering achievement of Hillary and Tensing. Of course, this kind of expedition is faster and safer than climbing independently and taking full personal responsibility, as we did.

I wrote about this at the time in the German press, including the *Frankfurter Allgemeiner Zeitung*, the *Sächsische Zeitung*, and the *Nürnberger Nachrichten.* Today it's not the summit, but the journey that's the goal. It's no longer about being the first to reach the summit. The colonial mentality has given way to climbing harder routes rated according to their difficulty. This is what I tried to do, using the simplest means possible—without bottled oxygen or radios. On our ascents, the summit was just the turnaround point.

Others have promoted themselves and their businesses by using my name while at the same time discrediting or even doubting my style of high-altitude mountaineering. This is just something I have to live with. My opinions, too, have often polarized the debate, and have been easy to manipulate and misuse. In Solu-Khumbu in Nepal I helped build a Sherpa Culture Museum—out of respect for the Sherpa climbers, not to exploit them.

At these extreme heights, climbing is a matter of life and death. There is no measurability, as conditions can be completely different from one day to the next. It's complete tumult and total anarchy. Yes, mountaineering is a product of the decadence of the last two hundred years of civilization. We assign it subjective importance; we climb it "because it's there," although it is completely useless.

In the mountains, we see the consequences of global warming and climate change earlier than they are seen at lower altitudes. And in the same way, we also see human behavior patterns exposed and revealed in the danger zone.

When there are hundreds of people at the base camps, expeditions keep to themselves—there is no team spirit. On K2 in 2023, dozens of climbers clambered over the body of a dying Pakistani porter. We see examples of similar behavior in our cities. When millions of people live together, many neither know nor respect each other. The world we live in has become a sterile place—and the Covid crisis just made things worse.

Selfishness is growing; empathy is shrinking. This applies to the mountains and to our society. The events on K2 clearly show how little solidarity there is left in the world.

The Sherpa Culture Museum in Namche Bazaar

In the past, it's not as if there was no competition on the mountain. In the 1960s and 1970s, it was exciting to see who would manage to climb the hardest route. But when there was an accident, everyone on the mountain would stop their own ascent and work to retrieve and carry a weakened or injured climber down. They worked together, using every means possible. This was an unwritten law.

There are thousands of examples of rescue stories that can be told. Nearly every extreme mountaineer responded to emergencies in this way, even if it was dangerous and difficult. Since then, though, mountaineering has lost its innocence. Group tours to the death zone might well have high safety standards, but solidarity and willingness to help has dwindled.

How about my attitude to fear? I've seen many terrible situations, and I've had near-death experiences. Fear is a constant companion. As explorers of limits, if we had no fear, we would all die. It's our fear that tells us, "up to this point, but no further." I've built up a wealth of experience to draw upon. When planning a tour or objective you must first evaluate things correctly. It's about choosing a mountain, and a route that matches your or your team's abilities. We mountaineers climb up to the limits of what is possible for us. We should not let our doubts and fears paralyze us. I failed three times on an eight-thousander. Each time I had to go back and start again. I had to put in the training and raise the finances. These failures helped me to learn. We learn so much more through our failures than through our successes.

Despite the residual risks, I would always set out with a good feeling—that I would get back safely. Otherwise, I would not have left in the first place. I never thought that I would get so old. Eighty!

I feel grateful, but I also accept that the ageing process is unstoppable, and that life will get harder. It makes me extremely happy to be able to continue to create and to not be alone, even though some in my family have turned their backs on me.

Of course, I've made mistakes. I lost my brother, I lost seven toes, I shattered my right heel, I've neglected and forgotten friends—but I have always found new challenges. Today, I feel responsible for passing on the values of traditional alpinism and a love and respect for the high mountains to the next generation.

The attitudes and values of traditional alpinists must not be allowed to die. And the Sherpas, the Hunzas, and the Baltis should finally be recognized as true, full mountaineers—not just porters. I dedicated a museum to them in Namche Bazaar, Solu-Khumbu—the Sherpa Himal, to honor this recognition.

54

REACHING MY DESTINATION

You can't conquer eight-thousanders. You can't compete on the mountain. Not against others, and definitely not against the mountain itself. You'll never win. Nature is always bigger. There is also a big difference between being strong at low altitude and being strong in the high mountains. These are very different types of strength. I have seen big men crumble.

—mountaineer Mingma David Sherpa

Even the worst headwinds calm down at some point. If you let them push you along too long, you could find yourself back at square one. However, if you shoulder them head on, then you might make it through to reach your goal. Maybe I should have resigned as a climber, an author, and a speaker, but I stuck to my guns and am still standing. I might have lost the Bolt War, but by fighting it, I gained a better understanding of the history of mountaineering. My explanation of the Yeti legend earned me a lot of ridicule; in the end, though, my story has not been repudiated. I don't just want to be proved right. Yet in many cases my findings have prevailed. It was often said that I would go bankrupt. And there were plenty of extreme attention seekers who sought to steal the show and successes I had worked for. But, you know, so what? Maybe I could have saved myself a whole lot of trouble while fighting all this headwind, if I had been able to turn myself into a *Luftgänger* (air walker) in time, as someone who is not fearful and follows their heart.

In the meantime, I've had heart surgery twice, allowed myself to get annoyed about those DAV blockheads yet again, and am still the only witness for Nanga Parbat. I still don't know how to turn red rockets into blue rockets or how to reach the summit of the holy mountain Kailash riding on a sunbeam.

How do I feel? Not "hooray, I'm still alive." More a sense of respect for all those who have not been as lucky as me.

55

LEBENSFREUDE

I became successful because climbers who were better than me died, not because I was particularly good. There were definitely better climbers than me.

—Reinhold Messner

Free Spirit: A Climber's Life is the title of my first autobiography. Was the price I paid for living the life I have as a free spirit perhaps too high? I'm now eighty years old. I know what it means to experience complete isolation. I've stumbled from one death zone to the next. Up there, it's the oxygen that is lacking; down here it's meaningfulness. I survived at the top of the world's highest mountains without reaching for a bottle, so hitting the bottle here at the bottom would just be avoiding matters. And how long could I keep that up? I've withstood the downward spiral of despair, and seen the absurdity of life dissolve to turn into possibilities, into visions to be nourished. Was this not how I have led a successful life for so many years?

Each time I asked: Should I risk it? Turning a cable car mountain station into a cultural meeting space. Incorporating a house into a mountain, invisible from the outside and harmonious with the rock. Upcyling unusable structures and useless land. Now that's sustainability. Reusing stone, concrete, and steel, not throwing them away.

Sense grows out of sensuality. Understanding grows out of feeling and experience. It's only in death that we lose all of our senses. Which is why we do not need to fear it.

Everyone should have the freedom to seek happiness. This search underpins all the values that shape how we live together. And this freedom to seek happiness is something that we should be able to renegotiate.

The pursuit of happiness will not carry us to the summit. Nor will honor, fame, wealth, or power. The only thing that makes our dreams come true is enthusiasm.

With Diane at the Geisler Group

And by being in touch with yourself, you can share your electric enthusiasm and your *Lebensfreude*, your spirit, with others.

I don't want to modify the world just so that it fits with my *Weltanschauung*. Yes, I have benefited from the economic booms that my generation has lived through and from the hard work and commitment of previous generations. I was able to travel the world to pursue my passion for experiencing adventures. I've been privileged. In my lifetime, I've only really experienced economic upturns.

And now as things are going downhill in Europe, I'm signing off. I've reached my destination.

The many times people have tried to put me down, their techniques were always the same, twisting my own words and then turning them against me. Or putting words into my mouth.

I was made a target, and various organizations turned against me many times during the different phases of my life.

I have no desire to criticize the youth of today. The Sherpas have my total respect. Today, they understand the role that they have played in Himalayan mountaineering. I helped to set up the Sherpa Himal museum in Namche to underline this. Their achievements are remarkable.

I plan to continue to contribute to the discussion.

Where I come from, people have written that I've always "had lots to say and an extremely critical mind." Michael Fink on the news website *Südtirol Online* (stol.it), on February 19, 2022, went on to say:

> [Messner] still has lots of plans and ideas for a good future for South Tyrol and its inhabitants—especially for the narrow-minded ones. Sometimes his suggestions are green, the next day they stink of petrol. It's all one and the same. The "other" South Tyrol is also flexible—the good, open-minded, cosmopolitan, intelligent, far-sighted, even visionary South Tyrol. The opposite, as it were, from the clumsy, backward, stupid, and small-minded South Tyrol. The mob seems to live in the latter, somehow. Those who look after their front gardens, water their geraniums, plant their potatoes, but apart from that have no other interests or hobbies.

People who would like to be involved in public debates, but who are not formally invited to contribute or participate, often express themselves in letters to the editor, at regulars' tables in inns and cafés, and on the internet. Social media exchanges have become increasingly problematic, because people are less accountable: nobody knows who's behind them or which interests they represent.

I'm glad to have led an active life, to have grown up in an age without the internet, and to remain off the grid to this day. Genuine discussion and debate are important; they encourage the cultivation of language and taking responsibility.

Ten years earlier, Dr. Michl Ebner deservedly received the same award that I received, the Medal of Honor of the province of Tyrol. Nevertheless, for over fifty years the Athesia publishing house, which Dr. Ebner heads up, has never missed an opportunity to oppose my actions. He finally praised me, after all this time, in his position as president of the Chamber of Commerce of Bolzano:

The Reinhold Messner Haus in the Tre Cime region of the Dolomites

"The award of this high honor is an expression of recognition and thanks for your commitment as a mountaineer, museum founder, and museum operator. I am very grateful for everything that you have done over all these years."

Even in gale-force winds, I learned to keep moving forward and not to look back when the mob—incited by the media—was coming up close behind me.

I would look to the wide, open world and wait until the rabble-rousing and mockery subsided. Just as a mountaineer does on Mount Everest, when the monsoon meets the jet stream.

Only then would it be time to set off again—to find peace as an air walker. I learned to take off against the wind—and to soar when the wind dies down.

TRANSLATOR'S NOTES

Chapter 3: Lessons from My Mother

p. 26 **Josef Messner has been one of the Optants:** In 1939, the Nazi regime in Germany and the fascist regime in Italy signed the Option Agreement. Afterwards, the German-speaking population of South Tyrol had to choose between emigrating to the German Reich as *Optanten* (Optants) or staying in South Tyrol as *Dableiber* (stayers), but giving up their culture and language. The majority voted to leave, but only a small part was resettled due to the outbreak of the Second World War. However, the Option split the population of South Tyrol.

Chapter 4: Boiled Dumplings

p. 30 **The direttissima (super direct) style of aid climbing was introduced to the Dolomites in 1958:** In July 1958, Dietrich Hasse and Lothar Brandler, with the help of Jörg Lehne and Siegfried Löw, made the first ascent of a new direct route up the north face of Cima Grande. For more information, see "Hasse-Brandler," by Ivo Rabanser, translated from Italian by Alexandra Ercolani in UP, published in 2006. www.up-climbing.com/en/bouldering/news-bouldering/via-hasse-brandler.

Chapter 5: A Hut at the Edge of the Woods

p. 35 **After going to Switzerland for a winter attempt on the Bonatti Route:** To learn more about this route on the Matterhorn, see "Climbing in History: Bonatti Route on the North Face of the Matterhorn," by Damien Tomasi, published by Grivel in December 2021. grivel.com/blogs/grivel-stories/climbing-in-history-bonatti-route-on-the-north-face-of-matterhorn-by-damien-tomasi.

p. 37 **But it is precisely this uncertainty that fuels our sense of adventure:** To understand Messner's perspective, read "Between Safety and Boldness," by Derek Franz, published in *The Alpinist* in 2023. alpinist.com/features/between-safety-and-boldness.

Chapter 6: The Red Rocket

p. 49 **Felix and I didn't call to each other on a spur on the South Summit:** In Messner's account, Kuen and Scholz were on the ramp to the South Shoulder, while the Messner brothers were at the Merkl Gap, a notch in the southwest ridge above the Merkl Gully about 80 to 100 meters away. See Messner's account in "Nanga Parbat 70," published in *Alpinismus* magazine, and "Es Ist Mein Bruder," by Greg Child, published in *Outside* magazine, January 1, 2006. www.outsideonline.com/outdoor-adventure/climbing/es-ist-mein-bruder.

Chapter 7: Not a Good Writer

p. 54 **Further public debate by the expedition members could only lead to an embarrassing repeat of the affair of 1953:** In his letter, Walter Pause is referring to the 1953 German-Austrian Nanga Parbat expedition, marred by recriminations, in which Hermann Buhl reached the summit in a solo attempt.

p. 64 **Today, any doubts have long since been cleared up:** In 2003, a number of 1970 Nanga Parbat expedition members were so confident that Günther Messner's body lay on the south face of Nanga Parbat that they should all be considered *Schafsköpfe* (blockheads) if Günther's body was ever found on the western side. See the *Süuddeutsche Zeitung* article "Messner versus Röhle:Leithammel und Schafsköpfe." www.sueddeutsche.de/leben/messner-versus-roehle-leithammel-und-schafskoepfe-1.463169.

Chapter 9: The Bolt War

p. 70 **a vehement critic of my stand on "climbing safely, without bolts":** Refer to Messner's well-known essay "The Murder of the Impossible," published in *Mountain* magazine in 1971.

p. 71 **I was interested to follow . . . *ÖAZ*:** To learn more about the history of the Austrian Alpine Club, visit www.alpenklub.info/geschichte-des-oeak/history-of-the-austrian-alpine-club.

Chapter 12: Intrigue for Intrigue's Sake

p. 80 **I describe both climbs in my book *The Challenge*:** Messner's book *The Challenge* was translated by Noel Bowman and Audrey Salkeld and published by Oxford University Press.

p. 82 **Ten years later, Toni Hiebeler came to see me at Juval Castle:** BERGE Verlag: Nürnberg, Olympia Verlag, Zeitschrift, *"Berge"—Das internationale Magazin der Bergwelt* (Mountains—The International Magazine of the Mountain World)

Chapter 15: "Called a Fool"

p. 91 **Alpinism is only just over two hundred years old:** The birth of modern alpinism can be traced to the 1700s when Genevan naturalist Horace Bénédict de Saussure offered a large reward to anyone who could find the way up Mont Blanc.

p. 95 **Mr. Messner, do you view May 8, 1978:** On May 8, 1978, Reinhold Messner and Peter Habeler became the first to climb Mount Everest without supplemental oxygen.

Chapter 21: End of a Legend

p. 124 **Trenker, who was popular in both Berlin and Rome, couldn't decide whether to "opt for the Reich":** Hitler and Goebbels were fans of Trenker's earlier works, but then distanced themselves from him. Goebbels noted in his diary that "This pig (Trenker) did not opt for us in South Tyrol." Trenker did not oppose national socialism, but was seen as less opportunistic than other film directors, such as Leni Riefenstahl. The South Tyrolean population was deeply divided. Those who wanted to stay (*Dableiber*) were condemned as traitors; those who wanted to leave (*Optanten*), the majority, were defamed as Nazis.

p. 125 **In reply to your comments in *Alto Adige*:** *Alto Adige* is an Italian daily newspaper, based in Bolzano and sold across South Tyrol.

Chapter 22: The Suffering Game

p. 130 **only Messner's breathing was unusual:** For more information, see "Physiological and Neuropsychological Characteristics of World-Class Extreme-Altitude Climbers," by Oswald Oelz and Marianne Regard of University Hospital of Zurich, published by American Alpine Club in 1988. publications.americanalpineclub.org/articles/12198808300/Physiological-and-Neuropsychological-Characteristics-of-World-Class-Extreme-Altitude-Climbers.

p. 132 **In the same year, 1987, Ludger Lütkehaus published a rather different opinion:** See his article "Aufstieg für den Abstieg" in Germany's ZEIT newspaper, edition no. 27/1987, published 26 June 1987. www.zeit.de/1987/27/aufstieg-fuer-den-abstieg.

Chapter 24: No End to the Madness

p. 140 **As Scott wrote in his diary:** Refer to the diary entries online at the Polar Museum of the Scott Polar Research Institute at the University of Cambridge. www.spri.cam.ac.uk/museum/diaries/scottslastexpedition.

Chapter 26: Ötzi the Iceman

p. 152 **Slightly further away in the same direction:** For a photo of the objects, refer to the article "Ötzi the Iceman: What We Know 3 Decades After His Discovery," by Jennifer Pinkowski in *National Geographic*, published September 15, 2021. www.nationalgeographic.com/premium/article/otzi-the-iceman-what-we-know-3-decades-after-his-discovery.

p. 152 **Messner couldn't see any remains of the backpack:** Learn more about Ötzi and his equipment at the South Tyrol's Museum of Archaeology. www.iceman.it/en/equipment.

Chapter 28: Expo Hannover and Member of the European Parliament

p. 163 **Given that the upper platform of Leitner's Skyliner middle station:** To learn more about this station, refer to "Freier Blick auf Gelbes Wellblech" (Clear View of Yellow Corrugated Iron), published in *Spiegel* in May 2000. www.spiegel.de/reise/aktuell/expo-seilbahn-freier-blick-auf-gelbes-wellblech-a-77800.html.

Chapter 29: Brussels Backbencher

p. 165 **We had to fight for our lives to reach solid ground:** Refer to the article by William D. Montalbano, "Ice and Trekkers' Dreams Shattered at Top of World," featured in the *LA Times* on March 11, 1995.

p. 165 **I slipped and fell down in the courtyard:** Refer to *My Life at the Limit*, by Reinhold Messner, English translation by Tim Carruthers published by Mountaineers Books in 2014.

Chapter 30: White Wilderness

p. 175 **There is no point in being a "conquistador of the useless":** This passing reference to Terray is in relation to his book *The Conquistadors of the Useless*, by Lionel Terray, English translation by Geoffrey Sutton published by Mountaineers Books in 2008.

Chapter 31: The Battle for Sigmundskron Castle

p. 181 **without the approval of Mr. Ebner:** Michl Ebner is an influential media proprietor, European Member of Parliament, and millionaire. See, for instance, "Krankhaftes Nicken" in *Spiegel*. www.spiegel.de/politik/krankhaftes-nicken-a-1a151b2d-0002-0001-0000-000017596480.

p. 181 **This is a campaign orchestrated by the "Christian brothers":** Messner is referring to Michl Ebner, influential media proprietor, European Member of Parliament, and millionaire, and Toni Ebner, editor-in-chief of *Dolomiten* newspaper.

Chapter 36: Excluded

p. 209 **By remaining silent on the issue, the DAV (which represents a membership of more than a million):** The DAV now has approximately 1.5 million members. www.alpenverein.de/verband/ueber-den-dav/der-dav-in-zahlen.

Chapter 39: Interjections

p. 209 **Namely, our limitations:** In the original German edition of this book, Messner mentions that this chapter is based partly on an article he wrote in 2006 for *CI–Das Magazin der Creativen Inneneinrichter* (CI–The Magazine of Creative Interior Designers).

p. 218 **which explains my experiment with the "house in the rock":** To see what the house looks like, refer to www.metallritten.com/de/felsenhaus--4-23.html.

Chapter 42: Bonds

p. 230 **If you want to know more about camaraderie and the bonds between climbers:** *Der Eispapst: Die Akte Welzenbach*, by Reinhold Messner, available only in German, was published by Fischer Taschenbuch in 2021.

Chapter 52: Censorship

p. 265 **"Protest against RAI Censorship":** RAI stands for Radiotelevisione Italiana, the national public broadcasting company of Italy.

Chapter 53: Group Tours in the Death Zone

p. 268 **Alan Rousseau epigraph at beginning of chapter:** See the full interview with Alan Rousseau in *Alpinist* magazine, published on May 29, 2024. https://alpinist.com/features/three-years-for-seven-days-on-jannu.

p. 269 **On K2 in 2023, dozens of climbers:** See, for instance, a 2023 article in *The Guardian* by Nadeem Badshah. https://amp.theguardian.com/world/2023/aug/10/record-speed-mountaineer-denies-climbing-over-dying-sherpa-on-k2.

Chapter 55: Lebensfreude

p. 273 **Turning a cable car mountain station into a cultural meeting space:** Messner is referring to the Reinhold Messner Haus on the Helm, a mountain in the Puster Valley in the heart of the Dolomites.

SELECT SOURCES

The following interviews and articles are excerpted and quoted in this book.

Abendzeitung München, 1981.

Alpinismus, no. 10, 1970.

Bendler, Gebi, and Dominik Prantl. Interview with Reinhold Messner, "Messners Seilschaften" (Messner's Climbing Partnerships). *bergundsteigen*, Herbst 2021.

Berger, Meinrad, and Günther Rauch. Statement "Zur Vergabe der Ehrenzeichen" (On the Awarding of the Medals of Honor). Reader's letter. *Dolomiten*, February 19/20, 2022.

Berghold, Dr. Franz. "Reader's letter to the editor." *Der Spiegel*, September 5, 1979.

Bild newspaper, August 18, 1992.

Commentary piece. *Süddeutsche Zeitung*, January 18, 2019.

de Gregorio, Walter. Interview with Reinhold Messner. *Weltwoche*, no. 51/52, 2005.

"Die Sache mit den Raketen" (The Thing about the Rockets). *Alpinismus* no. 10, 1970.

"Die Wildnis verändert die Sicht der Dinge" (The Wilderness Changes Our Perspective on Things). Interview with Reinhold Messner. *Focus*, 40, 1998.

"Etappensieg im Streitfall Messner–Gericht erlässt Einstweilige Verfügungen" (Preliminary Victory in Messner Dispute–Court Issues Interim Injunctions). *Süddeutsche Zeitung*, 2003.

ff–Das Südtiroler Wochenmagazin, 1981.

Fink, Michael. On www.stol.it.

Franceschini, Christoph. "Besoffene IDM?" (Was the IDM Drunk?). *SALTO: Das zweisprachige Südtiroler Onlinemagazin* (salto.bz), October 20, 2020.

——. Interview with Reinhold Messner. "Lehrstück in Mediendiktatur" (A Lesson in Media Dictatorship). *Neue Südtiroler Tageszeitung*, 2001.

Gasser, Hans. *Tiroler Tageszeitung*, November 24, 1971.

——. *Kurier*, 1972.

"Gipfelsieg" (Summit Victory). *ff–Das Südtiroler Wochenmagazin*, South Tyrol, 2001.

Herrligkoffer, Karl Maria. "Reader's letter to the *Süddeutsche Zeitung*." July 9/10, 1977.

Huber, Thomas, Sr. "Nanga Parbat Ist Authentisch" (Nanga Parbat Is Authentic). Reader's letter. *Berchtesgadener Anzeiger*, 2010.

Ihlau, Olaf. "Ein Gipfelstürmer steigt hinab ins Elend. Edmund Hillary's Rettungsaktion für die Sherpas" (A Mountaineer Descends into Misery: Edmund Hillary's Rescue Operation for the Sherpas). *Süddeutsche Zeitung*, June 21/22, 1980.

Interview with Reinhold Messner. *Alpinismus*, no. 12, 1981.

Interview with Reinhold Messner. *Bergsteiger* magazine, no. 9, 1976.

Interview with Reinhold Messner. *ff–Das Südtiroler Wochenmagazin*, no. 33, 2012.

Interview with Reinhold Messner. *ff–Das Südtiroler Wochenmagazin*, no. 30, 2020.

Interview with Reinhold Messner. *Neue Südtiroler Tageszeitung, October 8, 2022.*

Jakobs, Hans-Jürgen, and Achim Zons. Interview with Reinhold Messner. *Süddeutsche Zeitung*, July 2, 2003.

Kaser, Georg, Thomas Egger, Josef Oberhofer, and Florian Trojer. Open letter to Reinhold Messner. *salto*, October 4, 2022.

Klemmer, Axel. *ALPIN–Das Bergmagazin*, 1998.

Kratzer, Clemens. *ALPIN–Das Bergmagazin*, 1998.

Kronbichler, Florian. Essay about Maria Messner. *ff–Das Südtiroler Wochenmagazin*, August 1993.

——. Interview with Reinhold Messner. *ff–Das Südtiroler Wochenmagazin*, August 17, 2000.

Kurier, September 24, 1991, and September 27, 1991.

Langer, Freddy. "Der Yeddybär." *Frankfurter Allgemeine Zeitung*, September 28, 1998. Made available by the Frankfurter Allgemeine archive.

Larcher, Markus, and Georg Mair. "Leadership Gefragt" (Leadership Required). In "Sommergespräch mit Reinhold Messner" (Summer interview with Reinhold Messner). *ff–Das Südtiroler Wochenmagazin*, no. 28, 2007.

Lerch, Monika. *CliniCum*, 11/2005.

Lütkehaus, Ludger. *Die Zeit*, no. 27, June 26, 1987.

"Man Ist da Oben wie ein Zombie Unterwegs" (You Move Like a Zombie Up There). Interview with Reinhold Messner. *Schwäbische Zeitung*, May 5, 2018.

Margreiter, Prof. Dr. R. *Medizin und Sport*, no. XVIII, Book 1, 1978.

Messner, Reinhold. *Baumeister*, no. 6, 1998.

——. "Committment: Die Freiheit, die Ich Meine" (Committment: What I Mean by Freedom). *CI–Das Magazin der Creativen Inneneinrichter*, no. 1, 2006.

——. "Irrläufer am Pol" (Madness at the Pole). *Frankfurter General Zeitung*, no. 291, 1989.

——. "Unbesiegter Dhaulagiri" (Dhaulagiri Unconquered). *Bergsteiger* magazine, 06/1977.

——. "White Wilderness." *Berg*, 02/2000.

——. "Zurück in den Aufbruch" (Back to the Beginning). *Tiroler Tageszeitung*, October 14/15, 2000.

Oberhofer, Artur. Interview with Reinhold Messner: "Wir zerbröseln" (We're Falling Apart). *Neue Südtiroler Tageszeitung Online*, February 15, 2023.

Peterlini, Hans Karl. "Meinungsterror gegen Messner" (Terror of Opinions against Messner). *ff–Das Südtiroler Wochenmagazin*, March 21, 2002.

Pfeifer, Christian. Interview with Reinhold Messner: "Südtirol fehlt die Vision" (South Tyrol Lacks Vision). *South Tyrolean Wirtschaftszeitung*, no. 32, August 27, 2010.

Reader's letter from Dieter Lehner. *Alto Adige* newspaper, September 19, 1994.

Reader's letter in response to various articles by Achim Zons. *Süddeutsche Zeitung*, January 1, 2005.

"Reinhold Messner on Luis Trenker." *Bunte* newspaper, April 2, 1987.

Reinhold Messner in interview with Swiss newspaper *Tagesanzeiger*, July 25, 2022.

Reinhold Messner in interview with the *Berliner Zeitung*, no. 133, June 11/12, 2022.

Reinhold Messner in *Frankfurter Allgemeine Zeitung*, September 27, 2023, *Sächsische Zeitung*, September 26, 2023, and *Nürnberger Nachrichten*, October 31, 2023.

Report on the Siegi Löw Memorial Expedition to the Rupal Face of Nanga Parbat 1970. www.herrligkoffer-stiftung.de/index.php/14-stifter/expeditionen/8-siegi-loew-gedaechtnis-expedition-zur-rupalflanke-des-nanga-parbat-1970. Retrieved April 15, 2024.

Rühle, Alex. "Das Streiflicht." *Süddeutsche Zeitung*, January 18, 2019.

Seitz, Josef. Interview with Reinhold Messner: "Es ist eine lebenslange Last" (It's a Lifelong Burden). *Focus*, no. 24, 2003.

Sittner, Gernot, and Tanja Rest. "Von Herden und Hammeln. Nach dem Eklat: ein Streitgespräch zwischen Heinz Röhle, dem neuen Präsidenten des Deutschen Alpenvereins, und Reinhold Messner" (Herds and Lead Sheep. After the

Scandal: A Discussion Between Heinz Röhle, the New President of the German Alpine Club, and Reinhold Messner). *Süddeutsche Zeitung*, June 13/14, 2009.

Stephan, Rainer. "Ein Bär zum Aufbinden: Reinhold Messner und der Yeti" (Pulling Our Leg: Reinhold Messner and the Yeti). *Süddeutsche Zeitung*, September 24, 1998.

Tesson, Sylvain. Interview with Reinhold Messner. *Philosophie Magazin*, 04/2016.

Vanis, Erich. "Hasse, Messner und der Siebente Grad" (Hasse, Messner, and the Seventh Grade). *Österreichische Alpenzeitung*, 1450, July-August, 1983.

Vonmetz, Luis. "Am Seil mit Reinhold Messner–Erlebnisse und Gedanken" (Climbing with Reinhold Messner–Experiences and Memories). In *Bergerleben*, magazine of the AVS (Alpenverein Südtirol–South Tyrolean Alpine Club), 05/2019.

ABOUT THE AUTHOR AND TRANSLATOR

RONNY KIAULEHN

Born in South Tyrol in 1944, Reinhold Messner is the most famous mountaineer and adventurer of our time. He has accomplished some one hundred first ascents, climbed all fourteen eight-thousand-meter peaks, and crossed the Antarctic, Greenland, Tibet, and the Gobi and Takla Makan deserts on foot.

After serving as a member of the European Parliament, he founded the Messner Mountain Museums and Messner Mountain Foundation, which supports mountain people around the world. To learn more about Messner, visit www.reinhold-messner.de.

CHRISTOPH NIEMANN

James Heath is a copywriter, climber, and translator specializing in mountain sports and mountain literature. Born in 1972, he grew up in Bristol and learned to climb on the gritstone edges of the Peak District and in the mountains of North Wales. James is based in Hamburg, Germany, and works for a portfolio of international brands in the mountain sports industry. For more information, visit www.jamesheath.de.

recreation • lifestyle • conservation

MOUNTAINEERS BOOKS, including its two imprints, Skipstone and Braided River, is a leading publisher of quality outdoor recreation, sustainability, and conservation titles. As a 501(c)(3) nonprofit, we are committed to supporting the environmental and educational goals of our organization by providing expert information on human-powered adventure, sustainable practices at home and on the trail, and preservation of wilderness.

Our publications are made possible through the generosity of donors, and through sales of more than 700 titles on outdoor recreation, sustainable lifestyle, and conservation. To donate, purchase books, or learn more, visit us online:

MOUNTAINEERS BOOKS

1001 SW Klickitat Way, Suite 201 • Seattle, WA 98134

800-553-4453 • mbooks@mountaineersbooks.org • www.mountaineersbooks.org

An independent nonprofit publisher since 1960

YOU MAY ALSO LIKE:

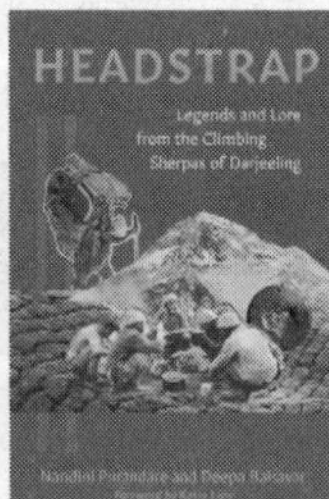